AF531512

WOMEN, CRIME AND PRISON LIFE

WOMEN, CRIME AND PRISON LIFE

Dr. MADHURIMA
Reader in Sociology
University School of Open Learning
Panjab University
Chandigarh

Foreword by

Dr. (MRS.) RAJESH GILL
Professor in Sociology
Chairperson, Department and Centre for Women Studies
Panjab University
Chandigarh

DEEP & DEEP PUBLICATIONS PVT. LTD.
F-159, Rajouri Garden, New Delhi - 110 027

WOMEN, CRIME AND PRISON LIFE

ISBN 978-81-8450-251-0

Printed in India at MAYUR ENTERPRISES
WZ Plot No. 3, Gujjar Market, Tihar Village, New Delhi - 110 018

Published by DEEP & DEEP PUBLICATIONS PVT. LTD.,
F-159, Rajouri Garden, New Delhi - 110 027 • Phone : 25435369, 25440916
E-mail : ddpubs@gmail.com • ddpbooks@yahoo.co.in
Showroom :
2/13, Ansari Road, Daryaganj, New Delhi - 110 002 • Telefax : 23245122

Contents

Foreword

It gives me immense pleasure in writing this foreword for an extremely pertinent and timely study undertaken by Dr. Madhurima in an area, which has so long escaped the kind of academic gaze it deserved, more because of the difficult terrain it entails than for any other reason. Given the unenviable patriarchal system that we survive in, where a woman cannot afford to make a mistake, particularly of the kind that lands her as a criminal, women under trials/convicts constitute a category, asking for a hermeneutic understanding, empathetic enough to present 'her' point of view (other than the 'official'). The present work is welcome in this backdrop more so since it unveils the huge discrepancy that characterizes the more recent correctional approach to criminal justice, marked by reformatory zeal on the one hand, and the extremely apathetic and insensitive system that actually exists at grassroots, on the other. The author has done a commendable job in compiling the most recent and highly diverse theoretical and empirical literature on criminality, especially female criminality, over the years. The book very effectively brings out the need to evolve gender sensitive conceptualizations and theorizing in the field of criminal justice, which rests in fact upon purely masculine idioms and interpretations.

The analysis made on the basis of personal interviews under very challenging conditions brings out the interface between class and gender, in the sense that a sizeable majority of the women studied are poor, illiterate and lower/backward castes. It raises some very interesting questions, viz. is female delinquency/crime only peculiar to women in poverty? Is it that the women criminals from more affluent sections never find their way towards these prisons, filled with pathetic conditions and indifferent officials? What does this journey through the conviction/trial transform them into and finally, do we need to evolve different conceptualizations to understand these 'underclass' women delinquents and the rich and educated women criminals? Very significantly, the analysis indicates that quite a few women convicts/under trials had committed the crime in connivance with their male accomplices, underlining the need to use the feminist interpretation with a little caution.

The pathetic conditions under which these women prisoners survive point out to the issue of human rights, which as per the present ideology holds equally true for criminals. If handcuffing has been constitutionally prohibited in our country except in some very special circumstances, how can we justify poor women caught on the wrong foot with a complete denial of a basic hygiene, palatable food, physical well-being and enough space, both physical and social? Madhurima has made a very bold attempt at problematizing an area which had almost been taken for granted. The work questions not only the criminal justice system that is completely gender-blind, it also underlines the patriarchal ethos that persists in the system of criminal justice irrespective of whether the functionaries happen to be male or female. The prison set-up which is based upon a specific conception of crime is constituted of officials who operate along the same gendered stereotypes, treating an inmate as only a criminal and not a human being. It won't matter whether these functionaries are men or women in as long as their typifications remain alike.

The work calls for very basic changes not merely at the level of constitutional and legislative reforms, which have already been sufficiently undertaken, but more importantly, at the level of the mind sets of both men and women, towards a gender sensitive understanding of crime and the criminal, who has to be helped revert back to her femininity, within the folds of family and motherhood, that have evaded her for an act of hers, she would never like to repeat.

DR. (MRS.) RAJESH GILL
Professor in Sociology
Chairperson
Department and Centre for Women Studies
Panjab University
Chandigarh

Preface

The literature on prisons in general and women prisoners in particular has largely remained a part of fiction writings. Lack of interest by social scientists in this area was mainly due to its apparent triviality or for smaller percentage of women prisoners. The contemporary experiences of women in prison at the beginning of 21st century must be understood in the light of increase in their incarceration. Women are criminalized for the same types of crimes as in the past with the critical addition of drug and violent crimes. Many research studies have found that women's crime tend to reflect the role that 'economic disadvantage' plays in their criminal careers. Gender likewise plays a role in shaping the women's response to poverty. It would be therefore inadequate to discuss crimes committed by women without focusing on their prison life.

Prisons housing men have been studied in detail. Comparatively, little is known about the inmates in women prisons. The needs and requirements of the female prisoners have been treated with a large measure of indifference. When most women first enter prison, they find themselves in harsh and rigid institutional routine which deprive them of privacy and liberty, and subject to a stigmatize status with extremely scarce material conditions. With the passage of time they adapt to the new environment. But their incarceration leaves a permanent imprint not only on their lives but also on the lives of their children since most of them are the prime caretakers of their children. As the number of prisoners is increasing, it is important for the policy-makers to develop an understanding of the specific issues and concerns related to women prisoners. A major objective of this research is to peep into the lives of these imprisoned women behind forbidden walls.

The book has been organized into seven chapters. The First Chapter provides an overview of the problem of women prisoners. To start with worldwide women prison population including India has been discussed. Subsequently through review of literature various research studies highlighting incidence, profile, causes, consequences of incarceration, etc. has been discussed. Thereafter, the major theoretical frameworks have been presented with relevant critique of each. Finally, I have presented my perspective to enable the reader to understand the present approach for this study.

The Second Chapter focuses on methodology where different prisons undertaken for this study have been explained. Objectives, sampling and technique of data collection have been explained. The Third Chapter addresses the prison administration in India, starting from the ancient through current times. Government of India has formulated various welfare committees to reform the conditions of the prisons and the prisoners. A brief discussion of these committees has also been provided in this chapter. Data on current number of jails has been provided. In the Fourth Chapter, the profile of the inmates starting with state-wise and prison-wise status of prisoners along with demographic, social and economic variables has been presented. The Fifth Chapter titled 'Types of Crime' highlights the legalistic, individualistic, social behavioral and legal classifications. Further, types of crime, namely property, violence, sex, drugs and miscellaneous committed by women have been presented in the light of various social, demographic and economic factors. The reasons for crime and consequences of confinement also form a part of this chapter. Chapter Six, 'Life of Inmates in the Prison', introduces the readers to the inmate's life after incarceration, their relations with their family members, jail staff and other inmates. Living conditions especially health-related issues are the highlights of this chapter. The Seventh Chapter on 'Summary and Conclusion' focuses on the main findings of the study. I have managed to distil from literature, the essential features, which are related to the present findings. Some of the results are predictable but others are unexpected.

In conclusion, it can be stated that study such as this can be used not only as a window to see inside but as a mirror to reflect upon prison life, and its shortcomings and inadequacies.

DR. MADHURIMA

Acknowledgements

I owe special thanks and gratitude to a number of people who helped me in carrying out the research reported in this book. To begin with, I wish to thank my host University and employer who provided me an opportunity and full support to carry out this work. I wish to thank the Offices of the Inspector General of Police of Punjab, Haryana and UT of Chandigarh who provided me permission to visit the prisons in their states. Throughout the period of field work I have been generously accommodated.

My thanks are also due to prison staff that helped me to carry out interviews without interruption. I am highly indebted to the inmates of the prison under study, who participated in this study and helped me in providing all the sought information from which the present study grew.

I am extremely grateful to Prof. Mrs. Rajesh Gill who gave valuable suggestions and took out time to write the Foreword.

I owe a great debt to my dear mother Mrs. Santosh Mahajan who took care of my family in my absence during field work. I would also like to appreciate the understanding behavior of my son Abhrr during the entire process.

I would also like to thank Mr. Shailendra Jain, Advocate, Punjab and Haryana High Court, for his help.

I sincerely thank Mr. G.S. Bhatia of Deep and Deep Publications (P) Ltd. for publishing this book.

Finally, but not the least my thanks are due to my husband Harish Verma for his understanding and helpful suggestions throughout the completion of this book. He assumed the additional responsibilities of editing the entire manuscript and typing most of it.

DR. MADHURIMA

Abbreviations

IPC	Indian Penal Code
NCRB	National Crime Records Bureau
SLL	Special and Local Laws
UNODC	United Nations Office on Drugs and Crime
UT	Union Territory

Introduction

Prisons are environments that are likely to contain a high number of socially excluded people. However, the prisoners do not exist in a vacuum as they have lives before imprisonment, and return to these lives on release. The way in which they choose to learn and participate in society before prison, during their sentences and upon release, are important. The basic reason for the existence of prisons is that society, which expresses its wishes through the means of courts, finds it necessary to separate and isolate some people who have broken the law. The concept of this segregation is as old as the society itself. Conventionally, prisons have been used for punitive purposes only. It is only in the recent past that public opinion has been generated to accept the notion of using imprisonment to reform and rehabilitate the inmates. In spite of the fact that prison system has, during the past some decades, undergone a massive change both in its objective and in its physical structure, the basic character of prisons as closed institutions with little public scrutiny continues to this day.

Prison, prison life and the condition of prisoners have acquired a crucial importance during recent years in India. However, literature reveals that work in the field has been confined, except in rare instances, exclusively to the study of male prisoners. The female prison community has been overlooked. It is anticipated that research findings of this study would provide effective stimulus and database for policy-makers in the future.

In the layman's language, prisons are thought of as crime fighting devices. It was believed that exposing offenders to prisons reduces crime but the size of prison population has increased manifold worldwide. Critical social theorists such as Michael Foucault (1977) have argued that prison invented delinquency in the sense that the individual criminal was one of the products of the formation of the prison. Foucault went on to explain that prison needs to fail in its task of controlling criminality if it is to survive as a prominent social function. One need not adopt Foucault's perspective to confront the paradox of the prison.

A growing interest among Sociologists in reflexive analysis (Bourdieu, 1992) provides a platform for thinking about the social location of the prison and its growth. This analytical viewpoint situates prison within human experience and also within social life. One therefore expects prison to have various effects on its inmates inside the walls and that these effects change the way people on the outside understand the social significance of the prison. Prisons and it's inmates are no longer seen as isolated from other aspects of society. Therefore, increase in the number of female prisoners can be interpreted both as a product of shifting social forces as well as a provocation of social change.

Until recently females were seldom studied as offenders or as victims in the system of criminal justice. Various explanations have been given for this neglect. As offenders, women have constituted a much smaller percentage than their proportion in the population. The types of offences for which women are imprisoned and the lengths of sentence they receive, suggest that they present little risk to the society. Most arrested females are usually first time offenders. They do not recidivate as often as do males. It is a common perception that prisons are for men. The last decade has, however, seen a surge in both the number and the proportion of incarcerated women. Although they still make up a small percentage of the total prison population, yet they are the fastest growing population. Further, their involvement in more violent crimes has awakened the researchers from their slumbers to take a serious look at the females in criminal justice system.

Feminist thinkers continue to propagate the idea that any crime committed by women is not independently done as one male partner definitely accompanies her. In case she is alone, she is the victim of male atrocity. Such prejudiced views have further hampered the research in this area. Naffine (1996) has pointed that there is a tendency to reduce explanations about the motives underlying female behaviour to a single issue, i.e. to see women as victims of circumstances. The current trend of seeing women as victims, economically exploited by society, and as individuals physically and sexually exploited is the problem of oversimplification. It also denies any element of choice on the part of individual woman. At some point of time in their lives, some women have chosen to use violence to pursue a criminal career. These women make conscious decisions. Therefore, there is a need to focus on women's ability to reason and reflect on their circumstances rather than viewing them as conditioned and unselfconscious objects. This study is of great interest since the issue of women in prisons as victims appears to be less strongly pursued in India than in other parts of the world because it assigns passive and helpless role to women.

Gender is thus fundamental but largely ignored issue in criminal justice system because women offenders are different from men with different pathways to crime, different life circumstances and different habilitative or rehabilitative needs. This study focuses on the need for the management of criminal justice system including prisons, as applied to the women offenders.

In order to have an insight of the lives of women prisoners, it is essential to understand and appreciate the prison world, including prison population. It is for this reason that a brief prolific image of the prison population worldwide and in India in general, and women prisoners in particular, has been presented below.

PRISON POPULATION—WORLDWIDE

More than 9.25 million people are held in penal institutions throughout the world, mostly as pre-trial detainees (remand prisoners) or as sentenced prisoners. Almost half of these are in the United States (2.19 million), China (1.55 million plus pretrial detainees and prisoners in administrative detention) and Russia (0.87 million).

The United States has the highest prison population rate in the world, some 738 per 100000 of the national population, followed by Russia (611), St Kitts & Nevis (547), U.S. Virgin Islands (521), Turkmenistan (489), Belize (487), Cuba (487), Palau (478), British Virgin Islands (464), Bermuda (463), Bahamas (462), Cayman Islands (453), American Samoa (446), Belarus (426) and Dominica (419).

However, more than three fifths of countries (61 percent) have rates below 150 per 100000. The rate in England and Wales at 148 per 100000 of the national population is above the mid-point in the World Prison Population List (Walmsley, 2007).

Prison population rates vary considerably between different regions of the world, and between different parts of the same continent. For example:

- In Africa the median rate for western African countries is 37 whereas for southern African countries it is 267;
- In the Americas the median rate for south American countries is 165.5 whereas for Caribbean countries it is 324;
- In Asia the median rate for south central Asian countries (mainly the Indian sub-continent) is 57 whereas for (ex-Soviet) central Asian countries it is 292;
- In Europe the median rate for southern European countries is 90 whereas for central and eastern European countries it is 185; and
- In Oceania (including Australia and New Zealand) the median rate is 124.5.

Prison populations are growing in many parts of the world. Updated information on countries included in previous editions of the World Prison Population List shows that prison populations have risen in 73 percent of these countries (in 64 percent of countries in Africa, 84 percent in the Americas, 81 percent in Asia, 66 percent in Europe and 75 percent in Oceania).

WORLDWIDE WOMEN PRISON POPULATION EXCERPTS

According to World Population Briefs, Monaco has the highest female prisoners' population, i.e. 29.7 percent followed by Liechtenstein i.e. 28.6 percent and Maldives, i.e. 21.6 percent. Countries having female prisoners' population between 15 to 20 percent are Hong Kong, Bahrain, Thailand and Myanmar. Kuwait, Vietnam, UAE, Ecuador, Laos, Taiwan and Singapore have female prisoners' population of 10 to 15 percent. Countries that fall in the bracket of 8 to 9 percent of female prisoners' population are Malaysia, Macau (China), USA, Netherlands, Nepal and Spain. Chile, Philippines, Russia, Belarus, Syria, Australia, Nicaragua and Finland fall in the bracket of 7 to 8 percent. The countries with 6 to 7 percent of female prisoners' population are Peru, Costa Rica, Hungary, Norway, Japan, Columbia, Panama and Ukraine. Portugal, Austria, Saudi Arabia, Cambodia, Argentine, New Zealand, Switzerland, Greece, Venezuela, Germany, Czech Republic, South Korea, UK, Mexico and Oman have female prisoners' population of 5 to 6 percent. The countries having female prisoners' population of 4 to 5 percent are India (4.8 percent), China, Scotland, Indonesia, Romania, Belgium, Italy, Denmark, Egypt, Iceland, Kenya and Sweden. There are some countries where female prisoners' population is in the 3 to 4 percent range. These are Lebanon, Croatia, Bangladesh, France, Iran, Ireland, Mongolia, Turkey, Tanzania, Angola, Swaziland, Poland, Uganda, Bulgaria. The countries with female prisoners' population in the bracket of 2 to 3 percent include Afghanistan, Libya, Morocco, Namibia, Rwanda, South Africa, Mali, Iraq, and Israel. There are a few countries where female prisoners' population is between 1 to 2 percent. These are Bahamas, Ghana, Sudan, Tajikistan, Nigeria, Pakistan, Sri Lanka, Bosnia, Algeria and Qatar. A few countries have less than 1 percent of female prisoners' population, i.e. Solomon Islands, East Timor, St. Kitts and Nevis, and Granada.

Countries like Yemen, Gibraltar, Nauru do not have any female prisoners' population.

TOTAL PRISONER POPULATION—INDIAN SCENARIO AT THE END OF 2006

According to National Crime Records Bureau (NCRB) data of 2006, prison inmates lodged in various jails in India are categorized as convicts, under-trials and detenues. In India out of the total 373271 prisoners, 116675 were convicts, 245244 were under-trials, 2275 were detenues, and 9077 were other prisoners. The state of Uttar Pradesh accounted for the highest number of convicted prisoners (16289) and under-trial prisoners (50163) in various jails at the end of 2006. The Central Jails accommodated higher number of female convicts in the State of Maharashtra (385). The state of Tamil Nadu has reported the highest number of Detenues (651) kept in various prisons. Gujarat has reported 49 female detenues in their jails which was the highest among all the States and UTs.

The highest number of convicts, i.e. 48.9 percent were in the age group of 30-50 years followed by 37.7 percent in the age group of 18-30 years. Most of the under-trial prisoners were in the age group of 30-50 years.

Out of the total convict population of 116675, 36337 were illiterate, 52932 had education up to high school, 19368 had education above high school but below graduation, 5680 were graduates, 1639 were post-graduates and 719 held some technical degree.

Out of the total under-trial population of 245244, 93313 were illiterate, 103548 had education up to high school, 35313 had education above high school but below graduation, 9559 were graduates, 2479 were post-graduates and 1032 held some technical degree.

POPULATION OF WOMEN PRISONERS IN INDIA

According to NCRB data of 2007, women lodged in prisons are still a minority. They comprise only 4.8 percent of the total prison population in India. Their number has, however, increased in the last few years. NCRB figure reveals that number of females arrested for criminal activities in 2003 were 151675. This shot up to 154635 in 2006, an increase of 2 percent in three years. 339 women convicts with their 374 children and 1031 women under-trials with their 1197 children were reported in prisons in the country at the end of 2006.

Also, women prisoners in Tihar jail, the country's largest prison has increased from 490 in 2006 to 525 in 2007. Interestingly, the nature of crime committed by them too is gradually witnessing a sea change. Though, softer crimes like drug trafficking and prostitution are the favourites, women are now trying their hands at kidnapping and murder. So far 3439 women were arrested for murder in 2007.

REVIEW OF LITERATURE

Until recently, the pervasive problem was that women prisoners have largely been neglected by the researchers. Much of the initial research identified the incidence and profile of women prisoners. Due to an increase in the population of the female prisoners and changes in the types of crimes committed by them, the issue has gained popularity over the last few years.

For the purpose of analysis different research studies in the review of literature have been divided into sub-headings like incidence, why rates of women crime is increasing, profile, causes, types of crimes, differences in crime by women and men, consequences, family support, children of the imprisoned mothers, problems related to the prison systems, relations within prison, and problems of inmates after leaving the prison.

Incidence

Women represent the fastest growing segment of prison and jail population. Chernoff & Simon (2000) examined female crime rates in 27 countries over the past 35 years. The results showed that there has been an overall increase in total crime rates in all the countries and that the more economically advanced and industrialized countries have higher crime rates than the less developed nations. In 1970, there were 5600 women incarcerated in Federal and State prisons in the US. At the year end 2000, 91612 women were in State or Federal prison i.e. 6.6 percent of the total prison population (Bureau of Justice Statistics, Prisoners in 2000).

According to Australian Institute of Criminology (2001) the number of women incarcerated in Australian prisons has almost doubled since 1991 from 607 to 1124. While the rate of incarceration for men per 100000 has increased from 194 to 240 since 1991 (an increase of 24 percent), the rate of women per 100000 has increased from 9.2 to 15.3 (an increase of 66 percent).

In Iran rates of female imprisonment have nearly doubled between 1981 and 1991 (from 25 per 100000 to 45 per 100000). Women accorded for only 5 percent of the prison population in 1994 (Abdy, 1992, Fassaei & Kendall, 2001).

The proportion of female charged with criminal code offences increased from 1977, 14 percent to 19 percent in Canada (Trevethan, 2000).

Correctional data from South Korea indicated that 5.3 percent women constituted Korean prison populations in 2006 (International Center for Prison Studies, 2006).

Increase in Women Crime

Sociologists and Criminologists have proposed a number of potential explanations for the differences in crime rates observed across various sub-populations. Many researchers believed that social pressures such as unemployment, poverty, income inequality, substandard housing and inferior education, disproportionately afflicted minority populations lead to greater levels of frustration and aggression (Hawkins, 1986, Parker, 1989). Others emphasized the dissolution of the two parent family structure as a factor contributing to greater violence (Harvey, 1986, Sampson, 1987). Family dissolution reduces both formal and informal social controls at the community level, which in turn may increase propensities for violence. Still other highlighted cultural differences across demographic groups (Anderson, 1999, Wolfgang & Ferrracuti, 1967).

Adler (1975) reported that lifting of restrictions on women's behavior gave women the opportunity to act like men that is to be violent, greedy and crime prone. Simon (1975) explained an increase in property crimes by women (especially larceny, fraud and embezzlement) because of getting increased opportunities to work (public spheres).

Rocawich (1987) reported that deteriorating economic conditions were pushing women to the brink faster than men. As the primary caretakers of children, women may be driven by poverty to engage in more crimes for survival. Chapman (1980) studied the connection between labour force participation, and revealed an increase in female criminal activity during times of economic hardship. The smallest increase in arrests coincided with periods of the greatest increase in economic activity with the most common offence being that of shop lifting. Changes in laws and practices were commonly referred to as a main factor in rising imprisonment rates for women.

Profile of the Women Prisoners

A number of studies have been conducted to identify the characteristics of women prisoners. Some researchers have discussed their marital status, age, education, class and racial background. Others have focused on the abusive background of the inmates.

Marital Status

According to Boritch (1997); Johnson (1986), majority of women were unattached, i.e. single, divorced, separated or widowed. On the other hand, Kim *et. al..* (2007) reported that majority of women, i.e. 69.4 percent were legally married, 12 percent were re-married, while only 6.6 percent were single. Bilmoria (1981), Borbora *et. al..* (2008), Garg (2006), and Nagla (1982) also reported that majority of the women inmates were married. Number of researchers reported that majority of the incarcerated women were the mothers of children up to 18 years of age (Caddle and Crisp, 1997; Dressel and Barnhill, 1994; Gursanky *et. al.*, 1998). Further studies have revealed that women were the primary and sole caretakers of their children prior to incarceration.

Age of Inmates

Kim *et .al.* (2007) reported that incarcerated women ranged in 20 to 74 years of age group, with a mean age of 44 years. Travethan (2000) reported that the proportion of young females has increased from 13 to 23 percent, in contrast, the proportion of adult females increased from 14 to 18 percent. Garg (2006) on the other hand reported that very less numbers of young girls were involved in crimes. Bailey & Hayes (2006) reported that prison population is ageing with adults under age 25 representing a steadily declining share while the number of prisoners in older age groups continue to grow.

Educational Status of Inmates

Female criminality has been found to be associated with educational status of the inmates. Fassaei and Kendall (2001) reported that compared to general population, imprisoned women were more likely to be uneducated or illiterate. Abdy (1992) reported similar findings in his study of Iranian prisoners. The majority of respondents indicated that they did not complete high school because their parents either disapproved of furthering the education or needed them to work in order to financially support the family. Chesney-Lind (1997) also gave similar findings. Kim *et. al.* (2007) reported that of all the incarcerated South Korean women who killed their spouses, over half did not complete the school education. Nagla (1982), Moyer (1985), Parsad (1982) have also maintained that illiteracy was an important factor in women criminality. High school drop-out rates and lower educational attainment were strongly associated with women prisoners (Bailey and Hayes, 2006; Blumstein, 1993; Schreiber & Poggie, 1988).

Social Class

A number of studies highlight that women prisoners more commonly belonged to the lower economic background (Moyer, 1985; Nagla, 1982, and Schreiber & Poggie, 1988). Kim *et. al.* (2007) on the other hand found that more than half of the incarcerated women belonged to the middle class.

Race

Some studies have tried to find out an association between race and female criminality. It is argued that more black women were incarcerated in the US (Bailey and Hayes, 2006; Kurshan, 1996). Among African-American women 346 per 100000 in the population were incarcerated whereas fewer than 80 per 100000 among Whites, Latinos and other groups were incarcerated. Contextual factors such as unemployment, poverty and lower educational attainment were associated with the race (Blumstein, 1993; Bailey & Hayes, 2006). Some researchers suggested that the American history of slavery (Wacquant, 2002) and racial bias in various stages of criminal justice system, including policing, prosecution and sentencing (Free, 2002; Beckett *et. al.* 2006; Taxman *et. al.* 2005) also partially explained higher rates of incarceration of African-American.

History of abuse among Inmates

Researchers suggest that most of the women prisoners were themselves the victims of various kinds of abuses. Morash *et. al.* (1998) reported that more than 43 percent of women inmates had been physically or sexually abused before their admission to prison. Willis & Rushforth (2003) reported that women incarcerated had experienced higher levels of abuse, economic hardships and other adversity in their lives. Browne *et. al.* (1999) reviewed six national and local studies of incarcerated women and concluded that the prevalence of physical and sexual assault was high in imprisoned women as compared to women in the general population. Results indicated that majority of the women experienced at least either of childhood violence, childhood molestation, intimate partner violence and adult physical or sexual assault. Trauma experienced as early as childhood increased the likelihood of criminal involvement. For example, child abuse was consistently related to the likelihood of delinquent and criminal behaviour. Greenfeld & Snell (1999) reported that nearly 6 in 10 women in state prisons had experienced physical or sexual abuse in the past; just over a third of imprisoned women had been abused by an intimate partner in the past, and under a quarter reported prior abuses by a family member.

Researchers on the basis of extensive study in Australia concluded that 64 per cent of women in a Victorian prison had a history of physical or sexual abuse, and the prevalence of physical abuse was twice as high for women with drug or alcohol abuse problems (74 per cent compared to 36 per cent of others) (Denton, 1994); 42 per cent of women in Queensland prisons in 2002 were victims of sexual abuse before the age of 16 (Hockings, *et. al.* 2002); in 2001, 77 per cent of women in West Australian prisons had a history of abuse, 74 per cent as an adult and 57 per cent in childhood (WA Department of Justice, 2002).

In 1997, over half of women in prison in the United States reported a prior history of physical or sexual abuse (Ekstrand, 1999); 57 per cent of women in a prison study in Texas experienced abuse in childhood and 75 per cent were victimized as adults, the majority by male partners (McClellan, *et. al.* 1997); and 68 per cent of women in Canadian prisons reported a history of physical abuse and 53 per cent reported sexual abuse (Shaw, *et al.* 1991).

Causes of Female Offending Behaviour

A number of studies have been conducted to identify the causes of female offensive behaviour. Some of the researchers have attributed criminality to biological reasons. Sociologists, on the other hand, have tried to identify different social variables for criminality. For the purpose of analysis, different studies have been divided into sub-parts.

Female criminality was earlier explained in biological terms rather than by social and economic forces.

Social and Environmental Factors

Adler (1975) and Simon (1975) argued that it is the social circumstances, and not biology that explains the causes of crimes by females. Daniel & Kashani (1983) discussed sociological and environmental factors that might have contributed individually or collectively to the causation of crime. They noted that a majority of female violent crimes were intra familial and related to life experiences. Bilmoria (1983) reported that domestic factors played an important role in compelling many women to adopt criminal behavior. Ghosh (1993) reported that broken homes, conflicts and unhappy intra-familial relations, widening of the spheres of occupational and social activities, mass media, wide circulation of pornographic literature have in advertently contributed to criminality among women. Ahuja (1969), Bilmoria (1981) and Kuchreja (1986) stated that stressful family situation and marital maladjustment, conflict prone relationship with husband, and other members of the family compelled women to commit serious crimes like murder. Mishra & Gautam (1982) have pointed that female criminality was largely due to broken homes and crisis of changing social values. Browne, *et. al.* (1999) reviewed six national and local studies of incarcerated women and concluded that the prevalence of physical and sexual assault was high in this population relative to women in the general population. Paramaguru (1984) mentioned that illiteracy, poverty, suspicion, marital maladjustment, emotional tensions, broken families, imbalances in sex matters, and social disorganization commonly led women to criminal tendency. Davies (1999) mentioned that the main reason for involvement of women in criminal activity was economic. Prostitution, shop-lifting, thefts, frauds and drug-related offences were mainly done for economic reasons. When women did not have resources or were unable to obtain sufficient money from traditional and legitimate sources, they indulged in illegal and criminal activities.

Drug and Alcohol Abuse

A few researchers have used drug and alcohol abuse as an important reason for criminality. Carlen (1985) noted that the use of drugs for excitement was an important factor related to women's criminality. Phillips and Harm (1998) and Covington (1998) have noted a high correlation between drugs and incarceration. They stated that the 'war on drugs' is becoming a 'war on women', with policy shifts linked to drug enforcement impacting heavily on women. Drug and alcohol use were considered as important factors in criminal offending (White & Gorman, 2000; Fagan, 1990, Chaikin & Chaikin, 1990). The main reason for committing crime as cited by 30 percent women was drug use and 7 percent said that it was related to alcohol abuse. Additional analysis showed that as drug problems increased the frequency of criminal behavior also increased, including crimes such as drug possession and sale (McClellan *et. al.*, 1997).

Types of Crime

There are many studies which suggested that females were less aggressive than males and thus engaged in soft crimes. Shakur (1978) reported that women offences were rarely vicious, dangerous or profitable. Their crimes arose from difficult circumstances within society. Most women were in prison due to relatively minor offences, property crimes, sometimes referred to as poverty crimes. In another study it was reported that 43 percent of women were in jail for larceny, fraud or forgery as compared with 15 percent men. Additionally, women were less likely to be imprisoned for violent offences. 35 percent of the men were in for violent crimes as compared to 24 percent of women. In general, women were less likely to be involved in homicide than the men (Brown & Kirk, 1987).

Most women committed crimes of a lesser violent nature, like shop lifting (Lloyd, 1995). Willis & Rushforth (2003) reported that female offenders were more likely to be incarcerated for drug offences, assault and robbery. Greenfeld & Snell (1999) indicated that most of the women were involved in larceny and drug offences.

Heidensohn (1991) reported that women committed all types of crime, although to a much lesser extent than men, particularly with regard to violent crime.

Chernoff & Simon (2000) reported that in those countries in which the women occupied higher status measured by formal years of schooling and representation in the labour force, positive and significant correlations was found with the arrest rates for thefts and fraud. There was also a strong negative relationship between female arrest rates for homicide and their status in society. Fassaei & Kendall (2001) indicated that women with higher social class status (greater income and higher education) were more often imprisoned for forgery and fraud as well as violent offences. On the other hand, those of lower class status were more likely to be involved in sexual and drug offences.

Only a small percentage of women were arrested for violent crimes (Greenfeld & Snell, 1999; Steffensmeier & Schwartz, 2003). When women were incarcerated for violent offences, the offences were of a much less serious nature than those by men, and often too the behaviors have only recently been defined as "offences".

Even when women commit violent offences, gender and abuse play an important role in their crime. Women convicted for murder or manslaughter, many had killed their husbands or boy friends who repeatedly and violently abused them (Sokoloff, 2005; Johnson, 2003). Singh (1981) also reported that majority of the violent crimes committed by women were related to husbands or close relatives. The murder was committed after a prolonged or repeated provocation. Due to frustration in intimate familial relationship, women took to an extreme step to stop aggression.

Women are much more likely to kill in self-defense in response to their male partners' physical aggression and threats, and the recidivism rates for such crimes are extraordinarily low, i.e. it is unlikely for women to repeat homicide. This female use of lethal counterforce was documented in numerous studies (Brown & Kirk, 1987, Bannister, 1989). Other researchers pointed out that besides the provocation that immediately triggered the female homicide and was recognized by the court of law, female homicide was often a response to preceding years of male abuse (Rubin, 1987). Feminists viewed the killing of an abusive partner as a women's last attempt to protect herself or her children from further physical and mental harm (Ogle, *et. al.* 1995, O' Keefe, 1997). In Leonard's study (2002) the results showed that the battered women killed their abusers because they found no legal way to stop life threatening violence. The research findings indicated that battered women often having a history of criminal or violent behavior supported these assertions (Browne, 1987; O' Keefe, 1997). Compared to 40 percent of other female inmates, fewer than 20 percent of the battered women had killed their partners. O' Keefe's (1997) revealed that of the battered women who killed their partners, 80 percent had no previous criminal record. Bilmoria (1983) observed that all the murders involved a single victim and there was no evidence of multiple murder or mass murder by a woman.

Mann (1988), on the other hand, reported that women who were involved in homicide had records of previous arrests for violent crimes, such as assault, battery and weapons charges.

Differences in Crime by Women and Men

Different researchers have tried to find out differences between men and women offenders in terms of their crimes and treatment in the prison. The types of crimes for which male and female offenders were sentenced to prison differ significantly. Several types of violent crimes committed by males were rare among the population of female inmates. Most prominent among these were sex related offences such as sexual assaults and incest (Legislative Council Staff, 2001).

In various research studies it was found that the men committed more crime in comparison to women. Even in cases of men and women belonging to the same class and one of the same groups, it was observed that males were more prone to commit crime. Further, it was reported that males committed more offences of serious nature than those committed by females. Males accounted for the use of vast majority of those arrested for crimes involving force or fraud. Regarding the types of crime or age, male's involvement was substantially higher than females. Men's violence against partners was much more frequent, extensive and serious than women's violence against their partners (Dobash, *et. al.*. 1992; Reiss & Roth, 1993).

Pollak (1950) reported that female criminality is masked since crimes by women remained under-reported to a greater extent than do the crimes by men. He concluded that men and women committed about the same number of crimes, but the crimes of women such as, illegal abortion, prostitution and shoplifting were infrequently reported.

A debate in the recent criminology literature has focused on the handling of female offenders as they are processed though the criminal justice system. There are two competing perspectives. The first perspective, i.e. the chivalry or paternalism hypothesis which echoes the perception of female inmates as victims, argues that women are treated more leniently than men at various stages (Crew, 1991). The second perspective, i.e. the "evil women" hypothesis which parallels the female inmate as sub-human perspective holds that women often receive harsher treatment than men in the criminal justice system and suggests that this different treatment results from the notion that criminal women have violated not only legal boundaries but also gender role expectation (Chesney-Lind, 1984).

Farrington and Morris (1983) found through empirical evidence that women did receive less severe punishments. Majority of females were the first-time offenders, and had committed a less serious form of the relevant offence, stole smaller or fewer items, used less violence, and so on. Prior history of offending, and seriousness of offence are fundamental factors in determining the severity of sentence, for any offender.

Women in prisons have some needs that are quite different from men's, especially with regard to pre and post-natal care of pregnant women and mental illnesses. Many needs that were non-criminogenic in male offenders might be criminogenic in female offenders (Hart, 2000). Women offenders were also more likely to become addicted to drugs (Leclair, 1990; Huling, 1991).

Family Support

According to Healy, *et. al.* (1999) families played a vital role in reintegrating prisoners into meaningful social life. Positive ties between an inmate and their families, either family of origin or their current family were strongly associated with reduced recidivism. Similarly, a study by Harrison (1997) found that those inmates who were assisted to maintain family relationships while in prison, returned to prison at the low rate of 2 to 4 percent. In addition to post-release success and decreased recidivism, prisoners who maintained family relationships have indicated reduced disciplinary problems while serving their prison sentence, improved mental health during incarceration and/or release (Fuller, 1993, Klein & Bahr, 1996).

Consequences of Incarceration

Research suggests that incarceration is a time of immense stress for inmates and that the personal consequences of imprisonment can be devastating. Imprisonment meant the loss of a job, of significant relationships, and of the legal custody of children (Bowker, 1980; Pollock, 1990; Trevethan, 2000).

An incarcerated mother would experience considerable difficulty and distress concerning her child's welfare and changes in their relationship (Fuller, 1993; Kingi, 1996; Sheridan, 1996; Caddle & Crisp, 1997). Gursansky, *et. al.* (1998) found that women incarcerated in a South Australian prison commonly expressed concerns about the effects that their sudden and traumatic separation had on their children, and on the mother and child relationship. The incarcerated mothers felt that rearing and caring was the maternal responsibility. Mothers in prison reported feelings of anger, anxiety, sadness, depression, shame, guilt, decreased self-esteem and a sense of loss when separated from their children (Keaveny & Zauszniewski, 1999; Pennix, 1999; Young & Smith, 2000). Women prisoners themselves frequently cited concern for their children as their biggest problem or worry in the prison.

Women often had no one else to turn to and were in a danger of permanently loosing the custody of their children. For all imprisoned mothers, the separation from their children was one of the greatest punishments of incarceration, and engendered despondency and feeling of guilt and anxiety in them (Church, 1990).

Bhadauria and Mathur (1981) referred to marital dissolution as one of the main consequence of imprisonment. Morris and Wilkinson (1995) found that having an adequate housing was the most cited problem faced by women after their release from the prison. In addition, multiple debts were common with financial circumstances.

Children of the Imprisoned Mothers

Since a large number of women incarcerated in prison are mothers, a lot of research has recently implied a considerable amount of distress amongst incarcerated women as a consequence of separation from family and children.

Philips and Harm (1998) noted that whilst many male prisoners were fathers, 89 percent left their children in the care of the biological mother, whilst for women inmates only 22 percent had children cared for by their biological fathers. The children of female prisoners frequently ended up in the care of immediate or extended family (Gabel,1992; Dressel & Barnhill, 1994; Sheridan 1996; Gursansky, *et. al.*, 1998; Healy, *et. al.*. 1999). Gable & Schindledecker (1993) found that approximately 75 percent children of the incarcerated mothers were cared for by the women's parents or other relatives with less than 10 percent cared for by the husband's and 15 percent by friends or in foster homes.

Hiedensohn (1997) outlined the problems in housing young children in prisons as the 'least suitable place for rearing', being isolated from the real world, severely restrictive and institutional in nature. Either way, whether offspring were retained or removed, children effectively bore the punishment.

Chatto Raj (2000) reported that the miserable conditions of children who were staying in prisons along with their mothers suffered due to seclusion from the normal familial environment. Pandey (2004) reported that young children living with their mothers in prison mostly belonged to lower castes and poor economic background. The prisons lacked basic facilities for education, recreation, health, nutrition, rehabilitation for younger children. Although imprisonment of either parent is traumatic for the children, the adverse effects are aggravated when it is their mother who is imprisoned. When fathers are imprisoned, typically the mother cares (or continues to care) for the children. In contrast, when a mother is imprisoned there is a high likelihood of family breakup and the children are likely to be placed in the care of relatives or left to fend for themselves.

Woodrow (1992) pointed the level of 'damage' for 'prison orphans' (children whose mothers were in prison) through specific processes associated with the separation, which she found occurred in detrimental ways. For example, there was often no opportunity to explain to the children as to what was happening, to reassure them, or even to ensure that they would be well cared for.

Researchers, looking at the impact of a father's imprisonment on children, have found a range of social, behavioural and psychological difficulties (Gabel, 1992; Dressel & Barnhill, 1994). Given the effects of paternal incarceration on children, one would surmise the incarceration of the child's mother, who is commonly the primary caregiver, would have even further detrimental effects to the child's overall well-being (LeFlore & Holston, 1989).

A few researches have highlighted the problems of children who suffered multiple problems associated with their loss. Disruption of the attachment bond between mother and child is particularly deleterious between the ages of 6 months and 4 years (Fuller, 1993). Other problem areas and behavior inhibited by children of incarcerated parents included physical health problems, hostile and aggressive behavior, use of drugs or alcohol, truancy, running away from home, disciplinary problems, withdrawal, fearfulness, bed-wetting, poor school performance, excessive crying, nightmares, problems in relationship with others, anxiety and depression, and attention problems (Lowenstein, 1986; Korbin, 1989; Gabel, 1992; Fuller,1993; Dressel & Barnhill, 1994; McClellan, *et. al.* 1997).

Children of released parents often become confused, unhappy and socially stigmatized. The frequent outcomes were in school-related difficulties, low self-esteem, aggressive behavior, and general emotional dysfunctions. If their parents were negative role models, children failed to develop positive altitudes toward work and responsibility. They were five times more likely to serve time in prison when they became adults than children whose parents were not incarcerated (Beck, *et. al.* 1993).

Problems Related to the Prison Systems

Many researchers have focused on the problems faced by women in prison. Stoller (2000) on the basis of complaints filed by women prisoners reported two types of health care problems faced by women prisoners, viz. access to medication, and access to the type of care needed.

The fact that "missed medications" was the most common complaint suggests that lack of availability of medicines, when needed, is a serious problem. Nearly 22 percent of the women had missed important medications at least once while many had missed them repeatedly. This was a common complaint from women with HIV/AIDS. Women with diabetes, asthma, heart disease, hypertension, cancer and a host of other ailments are also put to grave risk when prescribed medications are missed. Based on reports by prisoners, the health care that is available can actually be detrimental.

According to Amnesty International (1999), adequate provision of medical care is one of the most pressing problems facing women prisoners. Women in custody have an increased incidence of chronic health problems. Barriers to care include the use of non-medical personnel to provide health care, a co-payment system that requires prisoners to pay for medical services, frequent delays in medication refills, diagnostic testing and follow up treatment, failure to provide preventive care and a shortage of qualified medical professionals. Medical treatment was often unavailable, inappropriate and inconsistent (Schreiber & Poggie, 1988).

Lack of space and constant movement of high number of women in and out of institutions were also cited as problem by many women prisoners. It was stated that crowding led to double bunking, restrictions on the availability of employment and a tense threatening climate (Morash, *et. al.* 1998).

Many prisons were notoriously over crowded and inadequate in facilities (Church, 1990). Overcrowding sometimes means that women who had been held for trivial offences were incarcerated in maximum security institutions for lack of other facilities. Women prisons were often particularly ill-equipped and poorly financed. They had fewer medical, educational and vocational facilities than men's prisons (Dobash, *et. al.* 1986). Job training was also largely unavailable. When opportunities existed, they were usually trained for traditional female occupations (Church, 1990).

Farrell (1998) noted the generally inadequate visiting policies and environments in most institutions, and reported that many staff held the opinion that family visits were a privilege rather than a right.

Reproductive rights were non-existent for pregnant women in prison. Few states in the US provided medical aid funds for poor women to get abortion (Church, 1990). All the essentials for a healthy pregnancy were missing in prison, i.e. nutritious food, fresh air, exercise, sanitary conditions, extra vitamins and pre-natal care. Women in prison were watched throughout their delivery (Dobash, *et. al.* 1986). In 1985, California Department of Health study indicted that a third of all prison pregnancies ended in late term miscarriages (Church, 1990).

44 percent of women under correctional authority, including 57 percent of the women in US State prisons, reported that they were physically or sexually abused at some point in their lives. Many women in prisons in the United States were victims of sexual abuse by staff, including male guards touching their private parts while conducting searches (Bureau of Justice and Statistics, 2000). In most prisons, guards had total authority and the women could never take care of their basic intimate needs in a secure atmosphere free from intrusion. In the ostensible name of security, male guards could take down or

look over a curtain, walk into a bathroom or observe a women showering or changing their clothes.

In the closed environment of prisons, women are especially vulnerable to sexual abuse, including rape, by both male staff and other male prisoners. There are countries where women prisoners are held in small facilities adjacent to or within prisons for men. In some prison facilities, there were no separate quarters for women and they may be supervised by male prison staff. They were also susceptible to sexual exploitation and engaged in sex for exchange of goods such as food, drugs, cigarettes and toiletries (Plugge, *et. al.* 2006).

Relations within Prison

Prisons were also sometimes places of violence and danger (Bartollas, 1990). Violence was often recorded not only between inmates but also between inmates and prison staff. Prison was an unnatural social environment, and it can take some time to adjust to it (Toch, 1979). Inmates can experience chronic boredom and loss of control over daily routine, and must learn the social norms governing relations among inmates and between inmates and prison staff (Hawkins, 1976).

Mackenzie, *et. al.* (1989) compared the characteristics, adjustment and coping of female offenders serving three types of prison sentences which are, newly entered inmates with short sentences, newly entered inmates with long sentences, and inmates with long sentences who had been incarcerated for a long-term. There were few differences among these groups in demographic experiences and the criminal justice system. The inmates did not appear to experience different problems to cope with their experiences in different manners. The newly entered inmates were more apt to be members of "play" families and they were more concerned about safety. The newly entered short timers reported less control of events in the environment. Those who had served long-terms in prison reported more situational problems such as boredom, missing luxuries, and lack of opportunities.

Problems of Inmates after Leaving the Prison

People released from prison remain largely uneducated and usually have little in the way of a solid family support system. A survey in five major U.S. cities revealed that 65 percent of all employers said that they would not knowingly hire an ex-offender (regardless of the offence), and 30 to 40 percent said that they had checked the criminal records of their secant hires (Holzer, 1996).

Women released from prison encountered difficulties like finding housing and employment (Petersellia, 2000). Mishra (1985) wrote about the lower status women prisoners in the family and society and lack of provisions for their rehabilitation in the society.

Gaps in the Literature

Our knowledge in this area is anecdotal. In contrast to the massive documentation on all aspects of male delinquency and criminality, the amount of research carried out in the area of women and crime in India is very limited. There are number of reasons for this neglect. One of the most important explanations is that women tend to commit fewer crimes than men. Women represent less than 5 percent of the total prison population in India. The absence or the inadequate empirical studies carried out on 'women in prison' in this region reflects the continuing obfuscation and erasure of the subject. From the review of literature, it is clear that quantitative and qualitative studies are necessary to elicit the data required to explain the lives of women prisoners and to redress their problems.

To fill up the gaps in the existing literature, a focused study on women lodged in prisons has been undertaken. It is strongly believed that women in prison need to be seen within the context of status of women in the Indian society. Another issue of concern is the treatment that women get while in the prison. Prisons provide excellent research sites for the study of the relations between macro and micro-social processes. There is much more than punishment in prison and society needs to know about it. Of course prison administrators and staff care as much, if not more, about offenders than many outsiders. All these questions need to be answered.

Another reason for taking up this study was to go in-depth to find out the motives behind female criminality.

THEORETICAL FRAMEWORK

Review of literature focuses on the fact that this problem requires attention, especially in the Indian context where the research is anecdotal. Scholars have used different theoretical frameworks to understand the nature and extent of criminal behaviour, to identify major causal factors associated with the problem and to suggest ways to control anti-social behaviour.

Theories of crime have varied greatly over time. These theories of crime are nearly as old as the phenomenon they try to explain. Various scholars have attempted to build different theories to explain crime systematically. Below is the discussion on each of the following theories of crime:

1. Biological theories
2. Psychological theories
3. Socio-Psychological theories
4. Sociological theories
5. Critical theories
6. Feminist theories

BIOLOGICAL THEORIES OF CRIME

Although the major theories of biological explanation of criminal behaviour were developed in the 19th century, biological explanations can be found much earlier. The relationship between criminal behaviour and body type can be traced back to 1500's; and the study of facial features and their relationships to crime to the 1700's. Traditional biological theories focus on anatomical and physiological abnormalities within an individual which separate law breakers from the law abiding individuals. An individual's physical trait index, a bodily constitution with an associated mental and psychological makeup, is the cause for violation of the rules of society. Rational decisions have nothing to do with it. Although environmental conditions and situations can provoke or restrain criminal behaviour, they do not cause the commission of a crime. While some normal persons may on occasions succumb to temptations and pressures to commit crime, the real criminal is born with criminal traits. The advocates of biological framework view the criminals as a distinct set of people who are biologically inferior to law abiding citizens. The belief that criminals are biologically or genetically inferior to the "general population" persists despite the paucity of data that favors such a conclusion. Biological theories mention that there are certain types of people who because of certain genetic deficiencies, physiological excess or constitutional deficits are disposed to criminals behavior. The biological theorists argue that criminal is born with criminals traits. They are distinct set of people who are biologically inferior to law abiding citizens.

Lombroso's Theory

The most important of the early biological theories, the one from which nearly all the biological theories stem, was first introduced in 1876 by Cesare Lombroso in his book, "The Criminal Mind". Lombroso observed the physical characteristics (head, body, arms and skin) of Italian prisoners and compared them to Italian soldiers. From these comparisons he concluded that criminals were physically different from law abiding citizens and that these differences demonstrated the biological causes of criminal behavior. He claimed that:

1. Criminals constitute a distinct 'born' type.
2. This type of criminal can be identified by certain physical abnormalities or stigma such as asymmetrical face, large ears, excessively long arms, flattened nose, retreating forehead, tufted and crispy hair, and insensibility to pain, eye defects and other physical peculiarities.
3. The stigmata are not the cause of crime but rather the symptoms of atavism or degeneracy. Thus, according to Lombroso, atavism and degeneracy are the basic causes of crime.
4. A person who is the criminal type cannot refrain from committing crime unless he lives under exceptionally favourite circumstances.
5. Not only criminals differ from non-criminals in physical characteristics but they can also be distinguished according to the type of crime they commit.

Initially, Lombroso came out with only one type of criminals, the born criminals but later he identified two other types of criminals viz. criminaloid or occasional criminals who differed from born criminals only in degree and who indulged in crime owing to precipitating factors in environment, i.e. when they got an opportunity to commit crime; and criminals by passion who were in complete contrast with the born criminals in terms of nervous and emotional sensitiveness, and in motives of crimes such as love or politics.

Lombroso while emphasizing the biological causes of crime, he did not entirely neglect the sociological causes. Lombroso originally viewed the great majority of criminals as born criminals, but later reduced the proportion to 35 percent of male and 14 percent of female criminals as he added more social, economic and political conditions as factors in crime. Nevertheless, the concept of born criminal remained the centre piece of Lombrosian theory.

Later in the late 19th century, Lombroso and Ferrero wrote a book called, "The Female Offender". They examined the skeletal remains of female offenders and the bodies of living female prisoners. They concluded that the number and types of physical abnormalities in female offenders indicated the extent to which women were predisposed to criminal acts. They even attempted to determine which particular acts women were more likely to commit. The born female criminals had criminal qualities of the males plus the worst characteristic of women. These included deceitfulness, cunning and spite. Criminal women were generally more male than female therefore biologically abnormal. However, this approach was strongly criticized.

Criticism

The main criticism against Lombroso's explanation is his collection of the facts that were confined to organic factors as he neglected psychic and social factors. His approach has no predictive value because many who have the characteristics they have attributed to criminals do not become criminals and many who do not have these characteristics do become criminals. Feminists have also leveled complaints at this angle of criminology which assumes that females are controlled by their biology and are incapable of thinking for themselves. This approach fails to account for the role of other reasons such as social and economic which are responsible for a female's criminal act.

Charles Goring and E.A. Hooten Theory

Charles Goring measured the characteristics of 3000 English convicts and a large number of non-criminals in 1913. He maintained that there was no such thing as a "Physical criminal type". However, he himself explained crime on the basis of hereditary factor. He compared brothers as well as fathers and sons, attempting to show that the correlations for general criminality, as measured by imprisonment, were as high as for two other categories he measured.

1. Ordinary physical traits and features.
2. Inherited defects, insanity and mental diseases.

He then attempted to show that correlations were the result of heredity, not environment.

Goring's study came to be viewed by many scholars as the definitive refutation of Lombrosian theory of the criminal as an evolutionary atavism since he accepted the Lombrosian notion that criminals are born with criminal traits. His own theory dismissed the effects of social factors on crime and proposed that criminals are inherently inferior to law-abiding citizens.

Of all the measurements he took, Goring found statistically significant differences between prisoners and civilians on two characteristics, i.e. body stature and weight. The prisoners, in his study, were shorter and thinner than the civilians. They were also judged to be of lower intelligence. Goring took these findings as evidence that criminals suffer innately from both a "defective physique" and "defective intelligence". He believed that since crime was basically the result of an inherited organic deficiency, the criminal could not be reformed.

E.A. Hooten in "Crime and the Man" attacked Goring's methods and conclusions. Hooten conducted an elaborate study of 17000 subjects in several states. The study included meticulous measurements of the physical characteristics of inmates of prisons, reformatories, county jails and other correctional facilities. These were compared with measurements of same characteristics in college students, hospital patients, mental patients, policemen and firemen. Although he included "Sociological Gleanings" concerning prisoners, Hooten concluded that sociological factors are not important, because criminals are basically "organically inferior".

Criticism

Just as Hooten found Goring's techniques deficient, Hooten's work was itself criticized on several grounds. The differences he discovered between prisoners and non-prisoners were actually quite small. Furthermore, he did not take into account the fact that his civilian sample included a large proportion of fireman and policemen who had been selected for their jobs based on their size and physical qualities. Hooten ignored the similarities between the two groups. Goring's findings have been criticized on several grounds. He did not adequately measure the environmental influences; indeed, it is questionable whether all environmental variables can be satisfactorily isolated. He did not consider criminality among sisters. He assumed that mental ability is inherited but offered no proof. He assumed that removing a boy from his criminal father's home and placing him in some other environment at an early age was automatically putting him in a non-criminal environment.

In all these theories social and non-biological factor were recognized but they were seen as incidental. Most of them lacked empirical evidence. Biological theories have been regarded as unfounded and inconsequential.

PSYCHOLOGICAL THEORIES

Psychological theories of crime begin with the view that individual differences in behavior may make some people more predisposed to committing criminal acts. Psychological theories are usually developmental, attempting to explain the development of offending from childhood to adulthood, and hence based on longitudinal studies that follow up individuals over time. The emphasis of such theories is on continuity rather than discontinuity from childhood to adulthood. A common assumption is that the ordering of individuals on an underlying construct such as criminal potential is relatively constant over time.

Psychoanalytical Theory

Sigmund Freud who is credited with having made the great contribution to the development of psychoanalytical theory, did not advance a theory of criminality *per se*. His theory attempted to explain all behaviour and, in doing so, have implications for criminology. Freud saw original human nature as assertive and aggressive. According to him, "It is not learnt but deeply rooted in early childhood experiences. We all have criminal tendencies; but during the socialization process, most of us learn to control them by developing strong and effective inner controls. The improperly socialized child does not develop an ability to control impulses and acts them out or projects them inward". Freud hypothesized that the most common element that contributed to criminal behavior was faulty identification by a child with his or him to direct anti-social impulses inward or outward. "The child who directs them outward becomes a criminal and the child that directs them inward becomes neurotic", stated Freud. Freud's analysis of female offenders assumed the existence of biological inferiority in women. He connected a woman's lack of male genitalia with her inability to resolve her Oedipal Complex. He argued that this unresolved conflict led to an inability of women to control their impulses, therefore, making women more likely to commit criminal acts. Under Freud's framework deviant acts, criminal or otherwise were a part of women's frustration with their gender.

Psychoanalytical theory emphasized the importance of loving relationship and attachment between children and their parents. These theories suggested that there were three major personality mechanisms: the id, ego and superego. According to psychoanalytic theories, offending resulted from a weak ego or a weak superego, both of which followed largely from low attachment between children and parents.

Franz Alexander was more prolific in applying a psychoanalytic interpretation to criminal behavior. He viewed the criminal as some one who was unable to postpone immediate gratification in order to obtain greater rewards in the future. The criminal could not orient his behavior in line with the "reality principle"—a basic lesson to be learned during the anal stage of development through the social demands of toilet training. Alexander regarded the antisocial activities of the adult as exaggerated anal characteristics acquired in childhood. In fact, the initial prototype of the criminal act was the child's defecation at an undesirable locations. He did not ignore the etiological significance of environmental and social factors. In additions to genetic and early acquired tendencies, he thought family and general social forces contributed to the emergence of criminality.

Other psychoanalysts have suggested that criminal behavior is a means of obtaining substitute or compensatory gratifications of basic needs such as love, nurturance and attention which should have been normally satisfied within nuclear family relationships. Maternal deprivation has received the most attention, although the effects of paternal inadequacies have not been completely neglected. Bowlby (1953) is the best known illustration of the maternal deprivation theory. Bowlby claimed that maternal separateness and parental rejection are believed together to account for a majority of the more intractable cases (of delinquency) including "the constitutional psychopath" and "the moral defectives".

Criticism

In the eyes of many beholders, psychoanalyst provide one of the most inadequate statements about the nature of human personality, suffering from numerous logics of scientific errors as well as the lack of empirical verification. Evaluations of psychoanalytic criminology have concentrated on several logical and empirical deficiencies.

Cognitive Development Theory

According this approach, criminal behavior results from the way in which people organize their thoughts about morality and the law. Kohlberg developed the theory of moral reasoning. He posited that there are three levels of moral reasoning, each consisting of two stages. During middle childhood, children are at the first level of moral development. At this level, i.e. the pre-conventional level, moral reasoning is based on obedience and avoiding punishment. The second level, i.e. the conventional level of moral development is reached at the end of middle childhood. The moral reasoning of individuals at this level is based on the expectations that their family and significant others have for them. Kohlberg found that the transition to the third level, i.e. post-conventional level of moral development usually occurs during early adulthood. At this level, individuals are able to go beyond social conventions. They value the laws of the social system, however, they are open to acting as agents of change to improve the existing law and order. People who do not progress through these three stages may get arrested in their moral development and consequently become delinquents.

Criticism

Kohlberg's analysis has enjoyed only limited empirical support. The reliability of the moral judgment scale has not been established.

Intelligence and Crime Theory

Another type of psychological theory links crime with intelligence. Low intelligence, it is argued, causes crime. This approach also has long historical roots; early studies of family histories that found many people of lower intelligence in a family line of criminals concluded that criminal behaviour was caused by low intelligence.

The relationship between crime and intelligence got a boost in 1985 with the publication of 'Crime and Human Nature' by James Q. Wilson and Richard J. Herrnstein, who took the position that there is a clear and consistent link between criminality and low intelligence.

James Q. Wilson's and Richard J. Herrnstein's constitutional learning theory integrates biology and social learning in order to explain the potential causes of criminality. They argue that criminal and non-criminal behavior have gains and losses. If the gains that result from committing the crime (e.g. money) outweigh (e.g. being punished) then the person will commit the criminal act. Additionally, they maintain that time discounting and equity are two other variables that play an important role in criminality. Time discounting refers to the immediate rewards that result from committing the crime *vis-à-vis* the punishment that may result from committing the crime or the time that it would take to earn the reward by non criminal means. Because people differ in their ability to delay gratification, some persons may be more prone to committing criminal acts than others. Moreover, judgments of equity may result in the commission of a criminal act. The gains associated with committing the crime may help to restore a person's feeling of being treated unjustly by society. Wilson & Herrnstein hypothesized that there are certain constitutional factors (such as intelligence and variations are physiological arousal) that determine how a person weighs the gains and losses associated with committing a criminal act. According to Wilson & Herrnstein, physiological arousal determines the ease in which people are classically conditioned. Therefore, people who are unable to associate negative feelings with committing crime will not be deterred from committing criminal acts. In addition, they argue that impulsive and poorly socialized children of low intelligence are at the greatest risk of becoming criminals.

Criticism

Wilson and Herrnstein have only demonstrated that low intelligence and crime occur together frequently. They did not demonstrate that low intelligence is the cause of crime.

Psychopathy Theory

One of the most captivating concepts of psychological criminology has been that of a psychopath. Psychopathy is not so much a theory of criminal behaviour as it is a description of an individual who is involved in frequent and repetitive criminal activity.

The most popular explanation for the antisocial personality involves some variety of familial disturbances. Parental. rejection and parental absence brought about by divorce or separation are frequently suspected causative factors. Some theorists emphasized on maternal rejection while others focused on rejection by the fathers. McCord and McCord (1964) concluded that emotional deprivation and rejection by parents were primary causes of later psychopathy. Inconsistent and erratic discipline was also considered to be a potential source of psychopathic conduct. It is important to recognize that the

McCord's did not exclusively advocate the familial theory of psychopathy. They thought that disturbed familial relations may interact in some cases with certain kinds of physiological damage to produce eventual anti-social tendencies.

Maher (1966) portrayed the psychopath as a person who learns how to avoid negative consequences of his behavior, rather than how to control or eliminate the misbehavior itself.

Yochelson & Samenow (1976) argued that psychopaths are not only irresponsible in the sense that they avoid obligations, they are inconsiderate to people, and they are irresponsible in terms of the law. They see no obligation to keep within the legal limits that the society has outlined.

Criticism

This theory has been criticized for not providing intellectually satisfying explanation of how criminal thinking is acquired in the first place. This is a task which a comprehensive formulation of crime should not avoid. In fact, one might wonder whether the description of the "criminal personality" offers very much beyond that provided by the older concept of the psychopath. A redefinition of the psychopath will yield few benefits unless the redefinition possesses some major heuristic view.

SOCIO-PSYCHOLOGICAL THEORIES OF CRIME

Socio-psychological theories are basically combination of social and psychological aspects. Some of these theories emphasize sociological influences and others emphasize the role of individuals. The socio-psychological emphasis on crime as a learned phenomenon was anticipated by earlier scholars. Munsterberg stated that crime was acquired through imitation of the many examples of illegal conduct in society. Many scholars have argued that crime like other kinds of behavior is learned through imitation.

Modern socio-psychological theories can be divided into two categories viz. control theory and socio-psychological theory. The control theory assumed that people would frequently behave in an antisocial manner unless they are trained not to. The socio-psychological theory included a number of formulations that focused on the learning mechanisms by which criminal behavior is directly acquired and maintained.

Both categories of socio-psychological theories have been briefly discussed below.

Control Theory

According to control theorists, people do not engage in crime because of the controls or restraints placed on them. Control theory focuses on the factors that restrain the individuals from engaging in crime. These controls may be viewed as barriers to crime. Control theory goes on to argue that the people differ in their levels of control.

The control theory of Travis Hirschi dominates the literature, but others like Gerald Patterson, Michael Gottfredson and Robert Sampson have extended Hirschi's theory in important ways. Rather than describing the different versions of control theory, an integrated control theory that draws on all of their insights is presented.

The integrated theory lists three major types of control viz. direct control, stake in conformity and internal control.

Direct Control

Such control may be exercised by the family members, school, neighborhood residents, police and others. Direct control has three components namely setting rules, monitoring behavior and sanctioning crime. Direct control is enhanced to the extent that family members and others provide the person with clearly defined rules that prohibit criminal behavior, and that limit the opportunities and temptations for crime. Direct control also involves monitoring the person's behavior to ensure that they comply with these rules and do not engage in crime. Finally, direct control involves effectively sanctioning crime when it occurs.

Stake in Conformity

The efforts to directly control behavior are a major restraint to crime. These efforts, however, are more effective with some people than with others. For some people family members are very important and they are not ready to loose them by engaging in crime, as it will disrupt their relationship with them. Individuals who report that they love and respect their parents usually commit fewer crimes.

Internal Control

People sometimes find themselves in situations where they are tempted to engage in crime and the probability of external sanction is low. Yet many people still refrain from crime. The reason is that they are high in internal control. They are able to restrain themselves from engaging in crime. Most people believe that crime is wrong and this belief acts as a major restrain to crime.

According to Gottfredson and Hirschi "people who lack self-control will tend to be impulsive, insensitive, physical, risk-taking, short-sighted and non-verbal". One's level of self-control is determined early in life and is then quite resistant to change. Certain theorists also claim that some of the traits characterizing low self-control have biological as well as social causes.

Criticism

Most Control theories have a simplistic view of social control, they see it as a preventer of deviance only. They fail to see control as a possible cause of deviance.

Differential Association Theory

Edwin H. Sutherland first published the theory of differential association in 1939. Differential association has been categorized in number of ways. Nettler (1984) describes it as a Social Psychological theory; Cohen (1966) classifies it as a Cultural theory; Homans (1969) calls it a Socialization theory of crime; Hirschi (1969) classifies it as a Group Conformity theory; and Sutherland and Cressey refer to it as a Genetic theory. Sutherland intended his theory to be a sociological explanation of crime. However, this theory uses the individual as its unit of analysis rather than a group, community or society. It is for this reason that this theory has been included under Socio-psychological theories.

For Sutherland crime was a normal learning process; we learn crime in much the same way as we learn everything else and learning takes place in groups. Sutherland developed his theory to explain two forms of criminality. First, he wanted to explain why crime rates vary with different groups of people. He wanted to explain, for example, why city people are more likely to commit crimes than rural people; why males are more delinquent than females; why blacks are more prone to criminality than whites; and why there are more crimes in poverty stricken areas of cities than in other areas. To make sense of these different crime rates, Sutherland suggested what he called 'Differential social organization' or 'Differential group organization'. By differential group organization, he referred to the fact that a society consists of different groups of people some having a criminalistic tradition and others having an anti-criminalistic tradition. Groups with criminalistic tradition are thought to have a higher crime rate than those with an anti-criminalistic tradition. Differential Association theory suggests that crime is learned in ordinary everyday situations through a process of cultural transmission.

Sutherland outlined his theory in the following nine postulates:

1. Criminal behavior is learned.
2. Criminal behavior is learned in interaction with other persons in a process of communication.
3. The principal part of the learning of criminal behavior occurs within intimate personal groups.
4. When criminal behavior is learned, the learning includes :
   (a) techniques of committing the crime which are sometimes very complicated and sometimes very simple; and
   (b) the specific direction of motives, drives, rationalizations and attitudes.
5. The specific direction of motives and drives is learned from definitions of the legal code as favorable or unfavorable.
6. A person becomes delinquent because of an excess of definitions favorable to violation of law over definitions unfavorable to violation of law.
7. Differential associations may vary in frequency, duration, intensity and priority.

8. The process of learning criminal behavior by association with criminal and anti criminal patterns involves all of the mechanisms that are involved in any other learning.
9. While criminal behavior is an expression of general means and values, it is not explained by those general needs and values since non criminal behavior is an expression of the same needs and values.

Criticism

A multitude of criticisms have been aimed at various levels of differential association theory. Since Sutherland never elaborated upon his nine proportions, some authors have misinterpreted the meanings which he intended. One of these misinterpretations is whether mere associations with criminals are a sufficient cause of criminal behavior. If this were true, then obviously all correctional personnel should be criminals.

The theory does not address itself to the question of why some people who live in the same culture or even the same family, learn criminal behaviors and others do not. The theory assumes that within the social fabric there are opportunities to associates with criminal and non-criminal types of behavior, it did not venture to say why certain individuals seem to align with one or the other. The theory has been criticized since it overlooks the general goal of personality traits in determining criminality. The abstract nature of theory makes it difficult to test it empirically. Differential association theory has been criticized for its abstract nature which makes it difficult to test it. Another criticism of differential association theory is that it deals with its simplified treatment of the learning process.

Social Learning Theory

Social learning theory concentrates on the behavior of individuals. It recognizes that people actively construe the world around them in different ways, and that our expectations about the results of behaviour may be as influential as the actual contingencies we experience. Why do people engage in crime according to social learning theory? They learn to engage in crime primarily through their association with others. Primary groups have an especially large impact on what we learn. According to social learning theory, juveniles learn to engage in crime in the same way they learn to engage in conforming behavior through association with or exposure to others. In fact, association with delinquent friends is the best predictor of delinquency other than prior delinquency. However, one does not have to be in direct contact with others to learn from them, for example, one may learn to engage in violence from observation of others in the media. Social learning theory regards higher mental processes as necessary causal agents of complex human behavior (Bandura, 1969).

The most important learning mechanism in social learning theory is observational learning. Bandura (1973) points out a number of reasons for the major importance of observational learning, including avoiding costly mistakes, of obvious relevance to criminal behaviour and speeding up the rate of learning. The effects of observational learning include the acquisition of new patterns of behavior, the strengthening or weakening of previously learned inhibitions and the facilitation (in performance) of previously learned responses.

Most of social learning theory involves a description of three mechanisms by which individuals learn to engage in crime from others viz. differential reinforcement, beliefs and modeling.

Differential Reinforcement of Crime

Individuals may teach others to engage in crime through the reinforcement and punishment they provide for behavior. Crime is more likely to occur when it :

(a) is frequently reinforced and infrequently punished;
(b) results in large amounts of reinforcement (e.g. a lot of money, social approval or pleasure) and little punishment; and
(c) is more likely to be reinforced than alternative behaviors.

According to social learning theory some individuals are in environments where crime is more likely to be reinforced (and less likely to be punished). Individuals who are reinforced for crime are more likely to engage in subsequent crime, especially when they are in situation similar to those where they were previously reinforced.

Beliefs Favourable to Crime

Some people generally approve of certain minor forms of crime, like gambling, soft drug use, truancy, etc. Some people conditionally approve of or justify certain forms of crime, including some serious crimes. These people believe that crime is generally wrong, but that some criminal acts are justifiable or even desirable in certain conditions. Some individuals are taught that crime is not bad and they reinforce this idea. Criminals generally approve of criminal behavior. They hold general values that are conducive to crime. Such values can be realized through legitimate as well as illegitimate channels, but individuals with such values are likely to view crime in a more favorable light than others.

Modeling

Behaviour is learned through modeling. Modeling means imitating the behaviour of others. Individuals are more likely to imitate other's behaviour if they observe them getting reinforcement for their acts. Further, whether or not the behaviour modeled by others will be imitated is affected by the characteristics of the models, the behaviour observed and the observed consequences of the behaviour (Bandura, 1973).

Criticism

The learning framework cannot explain why certain people fall prey to learning influences while others are able to resist them. Learning may be a necessary ingredient in the development of crime, but it is probably not a sufficient one. We all are quite aware of the potentially rewarding consequences of property offences; however, few of us steal.

SOCIOLOGICAL THEORIES

The leading sociological theories focus on the immediate social environment, like the family, peer group, and school. They are most concerned with explaining why some individuals are more likely to engage in crime than others. Much recent theoretical work, however, has also focused on the larger social environment, especially the community and the total society. This work usually attempts to explain why some groups like communities and societies have higher crime rates than other groups. Sociologists argue that criminal behavior is learnt and is conditioned by social environment. Sociologists have used different approaches in studying the causation of crime. One approach explains crime in terms of pathological living conditions and breakdown of harmonious relations while another approach studies the relationship between crime and the social structure of society, and another approach relates crime to cultural conflict. We will briefly discuss all these theories.

Social Disorganization Theory

Social disorganization theorists were not primarily concerned with the study of crime itself but with the sociological problems of urban living. Criminals and deviants were seen by these theorists as a small minority occupying the margins of society principally because of their defective socialization and were depicted as existing in a state of social disorganization within these marginal areas or culture transmission.

Crime is said to be more likely in communities that are economically deprived, large in size, high in multi-unit housing like apartments, high in residential mobility (people frequently move into and out of the community), and high in family disruption (high rates of divorce, single-parent families). These factors are said to reduce the ability or willingness of community residents to exercise effective social control, that is, to exercise direct control, provide young people with a stake in conformity, and socialize these young people so that they condemn delinquency and develop self-control.

The residents of high crime communities often lack the skills and resources to effectively assist others. They are poor and many are single parents struggling with family responsibilities. As such, they often face problems in socializing their children against crime and providing them with a stake in conformity, like the skills to do well in school or the connections to secure a good job.

Social disorganization theorists like John Hagan points out that the number of communities with characteristics conducive to crime has increased for several reasons. First, there has been a dramatic decline in manufacturing jobs in central city areas, partly due to the relocation of factories to sub-urban areas and overseas. Also the wages in manufacturing jobs have become less competitive, due to factors like foreign competition, the increase in the size of the work force and the decline in unions. Second, the increase in very poor communities is due to the migration of working class to more affluent communities. Third, certain Government policies have contributed to the increased concentration of poverty.

Criticism

The main criticism against this theory is that it does not give adequate recognition to the selective migration. Low rents, social obscurity and reduced social controls attract the poor, the unsuccessful, the inefficient, the handicapped, and the defective. These are the people who may have already developed delinquent tendencies elsewhere. It is also criticized as based on unreliable statistical comparison. It neglects the psychological and biological factors in criminality.

Anomie Theory

Several sociological approaches trace their descent from the concept of anomie, originally described by Durkheim in the nineteenth century. Merton conceives of anomie as a disjuncture between the cultural goal of success and the opportunity structure by which this goal might be achieved. Anomie theories provide an explanation of the concentration of crime not only in the lower class urban areas but also in lower class and minority groups in general.

Anomie is the form that societal mal-integration takes when there is dissociation between valued cultural ends and legitimate societal means to those ends. The more disorganized or anomie the group, community or society, the higher is the rate of crime and deviance. Merton proposed that anomie characterizes American society in general and is especially high in the lower classes because they are more blocked-off from legitimate opportunities. High levels of anomie and social disorganization in lower class and disadvantaged ethnic groups, therefore, are hypothesized to be the cause of the high rates of crime and delinquency in these groups. Merton has identified five modes of adaptation available to those who react to the goals and means of society, conformity, innovation, ritualism, retreatism and rebellion. While Merton considers the last four modes of adaptation as deviance, he offers his category of "innovation" in support of the link between anomie and crime. He uses innovation to explain the high crime rates among the lower class or the poor segments of population.

Criticism

Merton has raised some criticism of his own theory. The theory does not take into account the social psychological variables that might explain the adoption of one adaptation over the other. It only briefly examines the rebellious behaviour and does not consider the social structural elements that might predispose an individual towards one adaptation over another. Merton acknowledging that it might not be possible to explain all types of behaviour defined his theory as a prelude to a full explanation of deviant behaviour. Merton's theory has been criticized by Albert Cohen, Clinard, Lemert and a few others. Their main arguments are:

1. Merton's theory is incomplete because he has not explained who will reject the goals and who will reject the means.
2. Merton's assumption that deviant behavior is disproportionately more common in lower classes is not correct. He has failed to account for "non-utilitarian" crime and juvenile delinquency in which people engage only for fun and not to meet specific goals of society.

Sub-culture Theory

The theory of anomie, as developed by Durkheim and Merton, established a framework for the development of sub-culture theories of delinquent and criminal behaviour. Albert K.

Cohen modified and developed Merton's work. In 1955, Albert Cohen's publication titled 'Delinquent Boys' set the stage for a new look at delinquency and the development of sub-culture theories to explain it. According to Cohen, the delinquent sub-culture not only rejects the mainstream culture, it reverses it. Thus, a high value is placed on activities such as stealing, vandalism and truancy which are condemned in the wider society. Cohen described the delinquent sub-culture in the following way: "Throughout there is a kind of malice apparent, an enjoyment of the discomfiture of others, a delight in the defiance of taboos."

The subculture or cultural diversity approach asserts that members of a subculture in which offending is highly frequent will typically be offenders simply by conforming to the prevailing social norms. Sub-cultural theories assume more socially determined variations in people's attitudes, beliefs and aspirations. The sub-cultural perspective holds that the conflict of norms, which engenders criminal behavior, is due to the fact that various class or ethnic groupings of people adhere to cultural patterns of behavior which are inconsistent with the dominant injunctions against certain types of crime. These illegal patterns of behavior are supported by the particular sub-cultural norms that actually exert pressure toward deviation from the consensual norms underlying the criminal law.

But the delinquent sub-culture is more than an act of defiance—a negative reaction to a society that has denied opportunity to some of its members. It also offers positive rewards to those who perform successfully in terms of the values of the sub-culture gain recognition and prestige in the eyes of their peers. Thus stealing becomes not so much a means of achieving success in terms of mainstream goals, but a valued activity to which it attaches glory, prowess and profound satisfaction. In this way lower working class boys solve the problem of status frustration. They reject mainstream values, which offer them little chance of success, and substitute deviant values, in terms of which they can be successful.

Criticism

Cohen has been criticized for his concept of class sub-culture. His description of delinquent sub-culture as no utilitarian, malicious and negativistic, is inaccurate. In fact, most of the activities of the lower class gangs are much more serious than what Cohen indicated. His theory has been criticized as ambiguous as concerning the relation between the emergence of sub-culture and its maintenance. A few scholars have even questioned the methodology of Cohen's theory.

Labeling Theory

Howard Becker propounded his labeling theory in 1963. According to him, deviance is not a quality of the act a person commits but rather a consequence of the application by others of rules and sanctions to an offender. The deviant is one to whom that label has successfully been applied; deviant behavior is behavior that people so label.

According to Becker, whether or not labeling occurs depends upon:

1. The time when the act is committed,
2. Who commits the act and who the victim is, and
3. The consequences of the act.

Thus, whether a given act is deviant or not, depends, in part on the nature of the act and in part on what other people do about it. Becker suggests that a distinction be made between rule-breaking behavior and deviance. Deviance is not a quality that lies in the behavior itself, but in the interaction between the person who commits an act and those who respond to it. Becker illustrated his views with the example of a brawl involving young people. In a low income neighborhood it may be defined by the police as evidence of delinquency and in a wealthy neighborhood as an evidence of youthful high spirits. The acts are the same but the meanings given to them by the audience differ. In the same way, those who commit the act may view it in one way and those who observe it may define it in another. In Becker's words, they are only doing what they consider necessary and right, but teachers, social workers and police see it differently.

Becker then examined the possible effects upon an individual of being publicly labelled as a deviant. A label defines an individual as a particular kind of person. A label is not neutral. It contains an evaluation of the person to whom it is applied. It is a master status in the sense that it colors all the other statuses possessed by an individual. Others see them and respond to them in terms of the label, and tend to assume that they have negative characteristics, normally associated with such labels.

Since individuals' self-concepts are largely derived from the responses of others that they will tend to see themselves in terms of the label. This may produce a self-fulfilling prophecy whereby the deviant identification becomes the controlling one.

Becker outlined a number of possible stages in this process:

1. Initially the individual is publicly labeled as deviant. This may lead to rejection from many social groups.
2. This may encourage further defiance.
3. The official treatment of deviance may have similar effects. Ex-convicts may have difficulty finding employment and be forced to return to crime for their livelihood.
4. The deviant career is completed where individuals join an organized deviant group. In this context they confirm and accept their deviant identity. They are surrounded by others in a similar solution that provides them with support and understanding.
5. Within the group a deviant sub-culture develops. The sub-culture often includes beliefs and values which rationalize, justify and support deviant identities and activities.

The sub-culture also provides ways of avoiding getting into trouble with conventional society. The young thief, socialized into a criminal sub-culture, can learn various ways of avoiding arrest from older and more experienced members of the group. Becker argued that once individuals join an organized deviant group they are more likely than before to see themselves as deviants and to act in terms of this self concept. In this context the deviant identification tends to become the controlling one. John Braithwaite extends labeling theory by arguing that labeling increases crime in some circumstances and reduces it in others. Labeling increases subsequent crime when no effort is made to reintegrate the offender back into conventional society, that is, when offenders are rejected or informally labeled on a long-term basis. But labeling reduces subsequent crime when efforts are made to reintegrate punished offenders back into conventional society. In particular, labeling reduces crime when offenders are made to feel a sense of shame or guilt for what they have done, but are eventually forgiven and reintegrated into conventional groups like family and conventional peer groups. Such reintegration may occur "through words or gestures of forgiveness or ceremonies to decertify the offender as deviant".

Criticism

Criticism against the labeling theory is that it employs good logic but does not explain the cause of crime. It entirely avoids the question of causation. It does not adequately explain the commission of the rule-breaking behavior itself. Labeling theorists confuse offensive misconduct with the social reactions to it. Differences between people and their actions exist and will persist independent of the names we call them. However, social labeling theorists minimize the importance of primary differences whether due to physiological, psychological or sociological influence. They preferred somewhat paradoxically political or justice systems as irresistable pressures towards criminality.

CRITICAL THEORIES

Critical theories of criminology have an extremely valuable perspective. Critical Criminology challenges liberal ideology by portraying modern capitalist society as a fiercely stratified society, in which law controls the powerless and secure the interests of the dominant class. Critical theories of criminology can be divided into two main headings viz. Traditional Marxist perspective, and Neo Marxist and Radical Perspective.

Traditional Marxist Perspective

Karl Marx argued that society is profoundly affected by its economic institution and indeed the centrality of economic activity justifies such an assumption. It logically follows that the key to the problems of a society might lie in its economic arrangements. Although Marx wrote little on crime, the criminology reaches out to his work for analytical guidance and inspiration.

Marx asserts that the owners of means of production have vast control in society not merely over working conditions but for example, legal norms. Since the ruling class dominates the creation and implementation of law, it is bound to serve their interests. Marx regarded criminals as concentrated in 'The Dangerous Classes'. He described them as unproductive parasites, living off other workers. Although he did not systematically develop his ideas about crime, he saw it as resulting from demoralization and false consciousness.

Many Marxists see crime as a natural 'outgrowth' of a capitalist society. They argue that 'capitalist economic system' generates crime. They argue that those who own means of production have the greatest power. This group of the capitalist class uses its power for its own advantage. Capitalists work for the passage of laws that criminalize and severely sanction the 'street crimes' of lower class persons, but ignore or mildly sanction the harmful actions of business and industry. They argue that a capitalist economic system generates crime for the following reasons:

1. The economic infrastructure is the major influence upon social relationships, beliefs and values. The capitalist mode of production emphasizes the maximization of profits and the accumulation of wealth.
2. Economic self-interest rather than public duty motivates behavior.
3. Capitalism based on the private ownership of property personal gain rather than collective well-being, is encouraged.
4. Capitalism is a competitive system. Mutual and cooperation for the betterment of all are discouraged in favor of individual achievement at the expense of others. Competition breeds aggression, hostility and particularly for the loser's frustration.

According to Marxists, capitalism pressurizes people to commit crimes and become deviants by making them poor in the first place. Secondly, it produces criminals by exercising coercive control over the lower classes. It tends to create resentment and forces people to engage in criminal activities. Further, the capitalistic pressure to commit crime and deviance is not confined to the lower classes but reaches upwards to affect the higher classes as well. By making possible the constant accumulation of profit, capitalism inevitably creates powerful empires of monopoly and oligopoly in the economy. These economic characteristics are an important cause of corporate crime.

Criticism

Marxist theories have been criticized for undue importance on class inequality. They have been criticized for assuming that a communist system could eradicate crime.

Before the end of communism in the Soviet Union and Eastern European countries, crime had not been eradicated. Stephen Jones (1998) points out that capitalism does not always produce high crime rates. For example in Switzerland which has long embraced a capitalist system, crime rates are very low.

Neo Marxist and Radical Perspective

Neo Marxist Sociologists of crime and deviance accept that society is characterized by competing groups with conflicting interests. Furthermore, they are all critical of existing capitalist societies and they share a concern about the unequal distribution of power and wealth within such societies. Taylor, Walton and Young were main proponents of this school. They were strongly influenced by Marxism. They accepted that the key to understanding crime lies in the 'material basis of society'. Like Marx, they saw the economy as the most important part of any society. They believed that capitalist societies are characterized by inequalities in wealth and power between individuals and that these inequalities lie at the root of crime. They supported a radical transformation of society. They suggested that Sociological theories of crime are of little use unless they contribute in a practical way to the liberation of individuals from living under capitalism.

However, in important respects they differ from traditional Marxist approach. They identified seven aspects of crime and deviance which they believed should be studied—

1. The criminologist first needs to understand the way in which wealth and power are distributed in society.
2. He or she must consider the particular circumstances surrounding the division of an individual to commit an act of deviance.
3. It is necessary to consider the deviant act itself, in order to discover its meaning for the person concerned
4. They propose that the criminologist should consider in what ways, and for what reasons other members of society react to the deviance
5. The reaction then needs to be explained in terms of the social structure.
6. They accept that it is necessary to study the effects of deviant labels.
7. The relationship between different aspects of deviance should be studied to make a complete theory.

Criticisms

Feminist Sociologists have criticized it for concentrating on male crimes and ignoring gender as a factor in criminality. They have also been accused of neglecting the impact of crime on the victims and of failing to take street crimes seriously. They have also been criticized for being too theoretical and for lacking empirical research and comparative analysis.

FEMINIST THEORY OF CRIME

Feminist perspective in criminology was developed in reaction to silences and gaps in mainstream criminology. According to the critique that feminists began to mount in the late 1960s and early 1970s, mainstream or traditional criminology was inadequate in five key respects:

1. It focused almost exclusively on male offenders;
2. It was androcentric in its understandings and interpretations of crime;

3. It paid little attention to crime victims;
4. It ignored sex differences in criminal justice processing; and
5. It disregarded the dynamics of gender and power.

The Critique of Mainstream Criminology

Feminist critics of the late 1960s and early 1970s found criminology lacking in five major respects mentioned above.

First, mainstream Criminologists have focused almost exclusively on male offenders, given that males have comprised the great majority of offenders across time and place. Feminists further argued that the use of all male samples had led to theories of offending that in fact applied only to males, even though most advertised themselves as general explanations of crime. For example, Travis Hirschi, in formulating his well-known control theory of delinquency, deliberately excluded the female subjects on whom data were available in his original sample "Since girls have been neglected for too long by students of delinquency, the exclusion of them is difficult to justify," Hirschi admitted, expressing a "hope to return to them soon". However, he has not. Titled *Causes of Delinquency*, Hirschi's book is in fact a study of the causes of male delinquency. Most other criminologists too assumed a male norm, placing boys and men at the center of their discussions and making women "invisible".

Second, Feminists have even criticized those Criminologists who had focused on female crimes for analyzing female law breakers from a patriarchal point of view. Criminologists defined the law-abiding woman as passive, obedient, chaste, and childlike while describing the criminal woman as aggressive, defiant, sexually impure, and unbecomingly adult, even masculine in nature. Feminists have objected to these stereotypes. They sexualized and condemned women criminals instead of treating them objectively. They reinforced the paternalistic view that good women are those who are submissive and docile, and they bolstered the double standard of sexual morality that accords men but not women, the sexual autonomy. Feminists stated that Criminologists have sexualized female crime while remaining silent about the economic pressures that force some women into crime.

According to them, the Criminologists have treated the women offenders as sexually abnormal and even evil while exonerating whatever males were involved. In studies of incest and domestic violence, too, mainstream criminologists interpreted crimes against women from the vantage point of the male offender, suggesting that men are more credible than women and likely to be falsely accused.

Third, Feminists have severely criticized traditional Criminologists for paying little attention to crime victims. Domestic homicide was said to be victim-precipitated in many cases, as was wife battering. Incest was a problem of seductive teenage step-daughters, not of power imbalances within the family or male views of women as sexual property, while stranger violence might be provoked by women who wore tight sweaters and drank alone in bars.

Fourth, Feminists have accused mainstream Criminologists for ignoring sex differences in criminal justice system. Taking a male norm for granted, conventional Criminologists assumed that justice officials treated women the same way as men, or more leniently. They did not investigate whether the system reacts differently to male and female defendants or to different types of female defendants. They did no research on whether women are punished more harshly than men for sex offences and public order crimes. Even though Criminologists had no empirical evidence for assuming that women fared the same as men or better in the criminal justice system, they were not interested in testing the assumption.

Fifth, Feminists further charged that traditional Criminologists had failed to investigate the interplay of male power, female economic dependency, and abusive male-female dynamics. While mainstream Criminology presented itself as an objective social science concerned with all crime, it was in fact masculinist, deeply biased against women, and riddled with hidden agendas for perpetuating male power. Thus Criminology itself served to reinforce the *status quo* and ensure continuance of female subordination.

Feminist Perspective on Criminology

Over the thirty years of their development, Feminist perspectives in Criminology have evolved through three stages, each lasting roughly a decade viz. a mobilization stage during 1968-77; a maturation stage during 1978-87; and a stage of differentiation that began around 1988 and continues into the present.

During this first developmental stage, the concepts of *sex, sexism,* and *equality* were central to Feminist work in Criminology. Arguments tended to be framed in terms of a struggle between the sexes, male and female; critiques were posed in terms of sexism, or male bias against women; and demands were based on the idea of equality, what Feminists sought was to be treated the same as men. Few noticed that this ideal involved the internalization and promotion of male standards. Moreover, Feminists assumed and fostered solidarity among women, paying little attention to divisions created by age, race, sexual orientation, or social class.

Sex, a concept that had figured prominently in the first stage, was replaced in the second stage by the concept of gender. Although differently defined, "gender" was generally used to denote socially constructed differences between males and females. Whereas first-stage theorists had been concerned about sexism, a problem that could be fixed by achieving the ideal of equality, second stage theorists were concerned about gender inequality, a more intractable problem that included the very nature of law and organizations, which now appeared to be gendered and masculine institutions. Doubts emerged about the wisdom of pursuing equality, the first-stage ideal, because it now became clear that to be equal meant to adopt masculine standards and values.

During this third stage, the concept of gender evolved even further from its roots in biological sex differences as Feminists became concerned with intersectionalities or the ways in which gender is cross-cut by such variables as age, class, race, and sexual preference, creating a multiplicity of ways of being masculine, feminine, something in between, or something entirely different. As the concept of gender fragmented, it gave rise to work on masculinities and crime. Definitions of the key criminological problems also splintered into issues of "multiple inequalities". Feminists concentrated more on crime and crime control, and less on problems presented by mainstream Criminology which despite some accommodations to the

Feminist critique has remained remarkably impervious to change.

Conceptual Framework for this Study

On the basis of above discussion on theoretical frameworks, it can be concluded that no single perspective discussed above adopts a holistic perspective with the help of which the subject of women prisoners at the individual level and at the socio-cultural level can be explained. To overcome this discrepancy a new conceptual framework using multi-dimension has been evolved and is being used to understand the problem of women prisoners in the Indian context.

Academic interest in female offending has resulted in challenges to mainstream criminological theory because existing theories have often been unable to account for the large gender ratio in offending and the differences in the types of offences committed by women and men. Instead of attempting to accommodate female offending within existing theoretical frameworks, an attempt has been made to evolve an alternative theoretical perspective. Our understanding of female offending and, in particular, of services for female offenders is relatively embryonic. The study is, for this reason, largely exploratory in nature. Crime is primarily the outcome of multiple adverse social, economic, cultural and family conditions. Creating a framework that is truly equitable requires a proper understanding of life beyond the prison life. An attempt has been made to pull together the various threads of thought regarding the relationships between gender and class to create a holistic image of females lodged in prisons.

Men since long have been regarded as the usual suspects when it comes to crime and violence. But a growing body of research on crime shows that the gender line is indeed breaking down. The past few decades have witnessed a dramatic rise in female authored crimes. Women's increased access to areas of crime formerly dominated by males, and the overall increase of violence and crime are some possible explanations for the surge. The 1970s saw a great deal of debate in the media over whether the women's movement for equal rights would produce an era of "liberated" women criminals who would venture into serious, violent criminal activities. Some academicians claimed that increased arrests of women were evidence that the Feminist movement was driving new trends in women's involvement in crime. Others countered that close analysis of arrest data indicated that increased arrests of women were largely occurring in categories conceived as traditionally female such as shoplifting, prostitution and passing bad checks. Debate about women's involvement in violent crime was freshened in the early 1990s. It is argued that as society moves towards greater gender equality and women gain more access to legitimate arsenics such as employment and education, they also gain access to once-restricted avenues of crime. As a consequence, women have involved themselves in crimes that historically have been male dominated. Women were described as responding to the same social and economic dynamics that drove increased levels of violence among men. The work of British Criminologist Pat Carlen has provided an important reference point to this research. Notably, Carlen's work *'Women, Crime and Poverty' (1988)*, the interplay of class and gender, is used to facilitate the investigation of the criminal careers of the women. For example, the role of disadvantaged class status, such as the lack of money or material goods experienced by females in specific environments, influence their deviant or law-breaking activities. The disparity in earning that still exists between women and men, in general and lower class women, in particular is also responsible for enhancement of lower class women in crime. Women are disproportionately poor (compared to men) and lower class women are far more disproportionately poor than other groups of women. Of course everyone who is poor is not going to resort to crime for survival but poverty certainly does lead to a higher probability of crime.

Meda Chesney-Lind contended that pro-arrest policies for police handling of domestic violence incidents have contributed to an unwarranted rise in arrests of women for violent offences. There is an increasing acceptance of violence in the society which has led to increase in violent crimes by women and men alike. As women achieve greater parity with men at all levels, women find that they too can engage in behavior, specifically violent behavior that once was deemed inappropriate for women. Dowry-related violence is growing and indeed spreading to communities where it earlier did not exist.

The majority of women in the prison system are sentenced for drug related offences which stems from economic marginalization. The drug war has been a major driver of female prison population growth. Women arrested for involvement in the drug trade tend to play peripheral or minimal roles, selling small amounts to support a habit of their intimates. These women have the responsibility of taking care of the entire household. Many women opt for drug smuggling as it is the easily available occupation without any specialized training which they lack. Thus most of these women come from neighborhoods that are entrenched in poverty and largely lacking in viable systems of social support. Cultural stereotypes limit their access to programs and services that could help them improve their economic circumstances, strengthen their family units, and avoid criminal involvement. It is asserted that intersection of caste, class and gender puts low-income women, especially lower caste women, in "triple jeopardy" and contributes to their disproportionate incarceration.

It is argued that much female crime stems from the fact that juvenile females are often sexually abused by family members. This high rate of sexual abuse is fostered by the power of males over females, the equalization of females' especially young females and a system that often fails to sanction sexual abuse. Abused females frequently run away but they have difficulty surviving on the streets. They are labeled as delinquents making it difficult for them to obtain legitimate work. Further, these females are frequently abused and exploited by men on the street. As a consequence, they often turn to crimes like prostitution and theft to survive. Alarmingly a large number of these women have experienced very serious physical and/or sexual abuse, often commencing when they were young children. As adults, most of these women are plagued with high levels of physical and mental health problems as well as substance abuse issues. Often these problems are combined and compounded. The great majority of the women who have suffered from these deprivations, histories of trauma and abuse, and health deficits are mothers and they are far more likely than men in the criminal justice system to be the sole support and caregivers for their children.

It is, therefore, not feasible to rely on single perspective to explain women related crime. I would recommend exploring radical and Feminist writings since they illuminate the role of women within the larger social and economic framework. Feminism has provided a great deal of understanding regarding the social conditions that impinge on women. The inequality of men and women, and their varying oppression should be considered when examining crime and law in terms of women. The role of women in the family as well as in the market place must be examined as it applies to female patterns of crime. This would mean an analysis of women's relative economic power, which is an important determinant of other inequalities. For this study social, economic and feminist framework have been collectively used to explain how prisons are being used for women, what kinds of offences are driving increases in the number of women in prison, and how the mix of female prisoners (convicts and under-trials) serving short and long sentences is affecting population levels.

Despite efforts by a handful of excellent researchers, the unique issues facing women in the criminal justice system remain poorly understood, in part because they comprise a small—if growing—share of the nation's prison population. A better understanding of this population is critical for several reasons. First, while the impact of incarcerating women is not necessarily greater than the impact of incarcerating men, it is certainly different. Women prisoners are more likely to have been primary caretakers of children prior to incarceration, and their absence can place unique strains on families. Women also respond differently to incarceration. It is often observed that correctional facilities fail to provide prisoners with the tools needed to succeed on the outside. This may be especially true for women with a history of trauma or past abuse. Second, existing research also suggests that women's pathways to prison may differ from those of men. As a consequence, strategies for improving criminal justice outcomes and reducing use of imprisonment are unlikely to succeed if these differences are not addressed.

Methodology

INTRODUCTION

The purpose of this study is to bridge a gap between what is known as exclusively feminist research to become a part of mainstream research by examining in an exploratory way, the lives of women lodged in prisons. There is an urgent need to create a research that fosters consentaneousness of both researcher and the researched. The empirical studies on criminal justice system are not always welcomed by the departments in question as it normally results in extensive criticism of their work. Further, casual visitors have always regarded prisons as undesirable places having sensational stories to tell. I understand that the work involved in running a prison is cumbersome and difficult. And the real life stories of real people deserve more respect. Understanding the sensitivity of the issue, this study was undertaken. Additionally, my interest in women issues led me to study the lives of female prisoners. As a result, this empirical research aims to penetrate deeply into the social life of women lodged in prisons.

This study has been undertaken in the states of Punjab, Haryana and Union Territory of Chandigarh. The choice of these places to study women prisoners has been done intentionally. The socio-cultural characteristics of a particular place leave an imprint on the lives of the women who belong to these places. I being familiar to this region, coupled with the fact that there has been no such collective study on women prisoners in this part of the country, I feel that it becomes my responsibility as a keen researcher, to undertake this study.

OBJECTIVES OF THE STUDY

Following were the objectives:

1. To examine the socio-economic background of the women prisoners.
2. To identify the types of crimes committed by women prisoners.
3. To explore the causal factors of female criminality.
4. To study the consequences of imprisonment on the inmates, and their relationships with their family members.
5. To examine the life of inmates in the prison and understand their relations with co-prisoners and jail staff.
6. To find out the problems faced by inmates during incarceration and to highlight the suggestions of inmates for improvements in the system.

BRIEF PROFILE OF THE STATES OF PUNJAB, HARYANA AND UT OF CHANDIGARH

A brief profile about the places undertaken for this study is provided below.

Punjab

Punjab (meaning *"Land of the five Rivers"*) is a region straddling the border between India and Pakistan. Punjab has a long history and a rich cultural heritage. The people of Punjab are called Punjabis and they speak Punjabi language. The main religions in Indian Punjab are Sikhism and Hinduism.

Ancient Punjab (or the Greater Punjab) had comprised vast territories of Northern India, eastern Pakistan and parts of Afghanistan. It once extended as far as river Yamuna in the east. The region, populated by Indo-Aryans, has been ruled by many different empires and ethnic groups, including the ancient Greeks, Persians, Arabs, Turks, Mughals, Afghans, Sikhs and British. Subsequently, in 1947, it was partitioned between India and Pakistan.

A historical region of the northwest Indian sub-continent bounded by the Indus and Yamuna rivers, it was a center of the prehistoric Indus Valley civilization, and after 1500 B.C. was the site of early Aryan settlements. The advent of Islam during the eighth century brought the region into prominence, and under the Mughals, Punjab came to light as the cultural heart of the sub-continent. The Sikh rebellion and capture of the region accelerated this development until the region was annexed by Britain. It was subsequently partitioned between India and Pakistan in 1947.

Most of the Punjab is an alluvial plain, bounded by mountains to the North. Despite its dry conditions, it is a rich agricultural area due to the extensive irrigation made possible by the great river system traversing it. The Indian Punjab is one

TABLE 2.1
State Profile—Punjab

Population (2001 census)	24289296
Males	12963362
Females	11325934
Sex Ratio (females/1000 males)	874
Density of Population (Persons/Square Km)	482
Urban Population %	33.95
Literacy Rate (census 2001) in %	69.95
Male Literacy in %	75.63
Female Literacy in %	63.55
NSDP at current prices (2002-03)	Rs. 62968 Crores
PER Capita NSDP (2002-03) at current prices	Rs. 25652

Source : Provisional Population Totals: India. Census of India, 2001.

of the wealthiest state in the country per capita, with most of the revenue generated from agriculture. Called "The Granary of India" or "The Bread Basket of India", Indian Punjab produces 1% of the world's rice, 2% of its wheat, and 2% of its cotton. Punjab's agriculture is the only source of income of farmers, who constitute almost sixty percent of Punjab's population.

Haryana

Haryana is a state in north India. Haryana was a part of both the Indus Valley Civilization and the early Vedic civilization. The Mahabharata refers to many locations which are now in Haryana, such as Kurukshetra and Gurgaon. It was carved out of the state of Punjab in 1966. It is bordered by Punjab and Himachal Pradesh to the north and Rajasthan to the west and south. Eastern border to Uttaranchal and Uttar Pradesh is defined by river Yamuna. Haryana also surrounds Delhi on three sides, forming the northern, western and southern borders of Delhi. Consequently, a large area of Haryana is included in the National Capital Region (NCR). The capital of Haryana is Chandigarh which is administered as a Union Territory and is also the capital of Punjab.

Haryana is primarily an agrarian state. The name itself means 'land covered with greenery' (The other meaning is where God comes, Hari-Aana). In addition to the river Yamuna and Ghaggar, seasonal rivers such as the Markanda and Tangri pass through the state. Numerous irrigation canals that cross the state bring water for irrigation from the perennial rivers of the Himalayas. The land is generally flat, covered with loamy soil and very suitable for agriculture. The south-western area of the state is drier and sandier. There are some hilly areas, which form part of Shivalik Hills in the north-east and Aravalli Range in the south. The climate is continental, with extremes of heat in summer. Monsoon winds bring adequate rainfall during July through September.

A number of residents, especially rural, speak Haryanyi, a dialect of Hindi that is famous for its coarseness. Hinduism is followed by a majority of people, followed by Sikhism, Islam, Jainism and Christianity.

The city of Gurgaon is emerging as a major hub for the Information Technology industry. It is a leading manufacturing hub as it is also home to Maruti Udyog Limited, India's largest automobile manufacturer, and Hero Honda Limited, the world's largest manufacturer of two-wheelers. Panipat, Panchkula and Faridabad are also industrial hubs. There is also an established steel and textile industry in the state. Despite recent industrial development, Haryana is primarily an agricultural state. About 70% of residents are engaged in agriculture. Wheat and rice are the major crops. Haryana is self-sufficient in food production and the second largest contributor to India's central pool of food grains. Dairy farming is also an essential part of the rural economy.

TABLE 2.2
State Profile—Haryana

Poopulation (2001 census)	21082989
Males	11327658
Females	9755331
Sex Ratio (females/1000 males)	861
Density of Population (Persons/Square Km.)	477
Urban Population %	29%
Literacy Rate (census 2001) in %	68.59%
Male Literacy in %	79.25%
Female Literacy in %	56.31%
NSDP at current prices (2002-03)	Rs. 57937 Crores
Per Capita NSDP (2002-03) at current prices	Rs. 26632

Source : Provisional Population Totals: India. Census of India, 2001.

Chandigarh

Chandigarh, the dream city of India's first Prime Minister, Jawahar Lal Nehru, was planned by the famous French architect Le Corbusier. Picturesquely located at the foothills of Shivaliks, it is known as one of the best experiments in urban planning and modern architecture in the twentieth century in India.

Chandigarh derives its name from the temple of "Chandi Mandir" located in the vicinity of the site selected for the city. The deity 'Chandi', the goddess of power and a fort of 'garh' lying beyond the temple gave the city its name "Chandigarh—The City Beautiful".

Chandigarh serves as the capital of two states: Punjab and Haryana. However, administratively, the city is not under the jurisdiction of either state, it is administered by the Centre government and hence classified as a Union Territory. The Governor of the Punjab is the Administrator of Chandigarh.

Chandigarh has two satellite cities (both of which share a border with it): Panchkula and Mohali. Sometimes, the triangle of these three cities is collectively called as the Chandigarh Tricity.

TABLE 2.3

Profile—Chandigarh

Population (2001 census)	900914
Males	508224
Females	392690
Sex Ratio (females/1000 males)	773
Density of Population (Persons/Square Km)	7903
Urban Population %	89.78
Literacy Rate (census 2001) in %	81.76
Male Literacy in %	85.65
Female Literacy in %	76.65
NSDP at current prices (2002-03)	Rs. 5079 Crores
PER Capita NSDP (2002-03) at current prices	Rs. 52795

Source : Provisional Population Totals: India. Census of India, 2001.

PRISONS IN THE STATES OF PUNJAB, HARYANA AND UT OF CHANDIGARH

Punjab Prisons

Table 2.4 gives the details of the various types of jails in the state of Punjab.

The authorized accommodation in these jails is for 11274 (NCRB, 2006) prisoners. However, the state prisons were over populated at 134 percent with the total inmate population of 15115. Of the total state female prisoner capacity of 420, the

TABLE 2.4
Jails in the State of Punjab

Central jails	*District jails*	*Sub-jails*
Ferozepur, Amritsar, Jalandhar, Bathinda, Gurdaspur, Ludhiana, Patiala	Hoshiarpur, Kapurthala, Sangrur, Nabha, Faridkot	Moga, Mukatsar, Fazilka, Malerkotla, Patti, Dasuya, Pathankot, Phagwara, Barnala, Ropar
Other Jails		
Women Jail Ludhiana	Open Air Jails at Kapurthala and Nabha	
Borstal Jail Ludhiana	Principal Jail Training School, Patiala	

occupancy was 776 inmates, i.e. 184.8 percent. Prison inmates in Punjab were 35.3 percent convicts, 64.5 percent under-trials and 0.1 percent detenues (NCRB, 2006).

Haryana Prisons

Table 2.5 gives the details of the various types of jails in the state of Haryana.

TABLE 2.5
Jails in the State of Haryana

Central jails	*District jails*	*Sub-jails*
Ambala, Hissar	Bhiwani, Gurgaon, Jind, Kaithal, Karnal, Kurukshetra, Mohindergarh, Rewari, Rohtak, Sirsa, Sonepat, Narnaul	Ballabgarh, Jagadhari, Palwal, Panipat
Other Jails		
Women Jail at Hissar	Borstal Jail at Hissar	

The authorized accommodation in these jails is for 10587 prisoners. However, the state prisons were over populated at 119.8 percent with the total inmate population of 12687. Of the total state female prisoner capacity of 733, the occupancy was 533 inmates, i.e. 72.7 percent. Prison inmates in Haryana were 39.3 percent convicts, 60.6 percent under-trials and 0.1 percent others (NCRB, 2006).

Chandigarh Prison Profile—The Model Jail, Burail

The Model Jail, Burail at Chandigarh had a total capacity of 1000 inmates out of which capacity of 40 inmates was for women prisoners. The women prisoner occupancy was 26 inmates, i.e. 65 percent. There were 24.4 percent convicts and 75.6 percent under-trials (NCRB, 2006).

The administration of the jails of Punjab, Haryana and Chandigarh is carried out as per provisions of the New Punjab Jail Manual which came into force w.e.f. 20-7-1996 (see Appendix 6).

SAMPLING

Criteria of Sample Selection

This study was conducted to undertake research on women prisoners lodged in various prisons in the states of Punjab, Haryana and UT of Chandigarh. For the purpose of visit formal permission from the authorities was sought. A formal request for permission to visit all the jails in the states of Punjab, Haryana and Chandigarh was made to the state authorities. However, permission was granted to visit only 7 prisons viz. four in Punjab at Amritsar, Jalandhar, Ludhiana, and Patiala; two in Haryana at Ambala and Hissar; and the Model jail of Chandigarh.

TABLE 2.6
Sampling Details

Sl. No.	*Prison*	*Total women prisoner population*			*Sample size*
		Convicts	*Under-trials*	*Total*	
1.	Amritsar	40	67	107	27
2.	Jalandhar	12	20	32	21
3.	Ludhiana	121	132	253	63
4.	Patiala	22	35	57	15
5.	Ambala	42	60	102	26
6.	Hissar	61	74	135	34
7.	Chandigarh	12	10	22	14
	Total	310	398	708	200

A total of 200 women lodged in the seven prisons were interviewed. It was decided to take 25% of the sample from the prisons where the population of female inmates was more than 50. In the cases where the population of female inmates was less than 50, at least 65% of the sample was drawn. Simple random sampling was done. The details are as under:

Of the total of 200 sample size drawn, the breakup was Amritsar jail (27); Jalandhar (21); Ludhiana (63); Patiala (15); Ambala (26); Hissar (34) and Chandigarh (14). The resultant sample was made fully representative of the prison population.

All the inmates were requested for interview. Those who willingly agreed were interviewed. Interviews were carried out within the prison premises. As the prison population is relatively transient with several inmates being released or transferred to other prisons on a daily basis, the sampling was done as close to the field-work start period as possible. It was decided to study both convicts and under-trials. There was no restriction with regards to age or length of stay of the women inmates in the prison.

Brief Description of the Prisons Under Study

Amritsar Central Jail

Amritsar central jail is one of the most important and sensitive prisons in the State of Punjab. It comprises of two separate prisons in the same complex—namely Central Jail I and Central Jail II. Central Jail II is also known as Security Jail. This prison came into existence in the present Prison Complex in the year 1957 as a District Jail. Prior to this, there was a small jail located near the Red Cross Building in the city of Amritsar. It was upgraded to Central Jail in the year 1969. In 1976, this Prison was elevated as Headquarter Jail having administrative control over all the prisons of Majha and Doaba regions namely Central jails of Gurdaspur and Jalandhar, District jails of Kapurthala and Hoshiarpur and Sub-jails of Patti, Phagwara, Dasuya and Pathankot.

Amritsar prison complex accommodates around 2200 to 2500 prisoners against a sanction capacity of 1600. Around 62% of the prisoners are under-trials. A portion of this prison has also been notified as Internee Camp for the entire state of Punjab to accommodate the foreigners awaiting deportation.

There is a separate hostel for the women inmates and their dependent children below 6 years of age.

Amritsar Central Jail has now become a Correctional Institution and a Training and Research Centre. Respect of basic human values is the core of this reform process. The prisoners are trained here in a manner so that they can share greater responsibilities to bring total reformation in the society.

Hostel No. 1 of the prison has been earmarked for the women prisoners. The Amritsar jail in association with various Government and Non-Government Organizations launched a number of projects for empowerment of women prisoners. Under the scheme, the female inmates are being taught how to weave, make toys, stitch and make embroidery items. Female inmates take keen interest in the education and health advocacy programmes. There is a separate kitchen for the female inmates.

The major partners in women empowerment projects include:

- Punjab Social Welfare Board
- Guru Nanak Dev University, Amritsar
- Krishi Vigyan Kendra, Amritsar
- India Vision Foundation
- Red Cross Society
- United Nations Office on Drugs and Crime (UNODC)

The children up to six years of age are allowed to reside in the jail along with their kith and kin. India Vision Foundation provides reading material and other support to these children. A crèche for the wards of the women prisoners has also been set-up by Punjab Social Welfare Board with the help of the India Vision foundation.

UNODC has launched this project in Amritsar Prison in collaboration with India Vision Foundation to prevent drug driven HIV. It is a peer led intervention which aims to intensify efforts to reduce drug-related HIV/AIDS amongst vulnerable high-risk groups including prisoners. Similar programme has been started for the Male Prisoners also.

Jalandhar Central Jail

The Jalandhar Central Jail is situated in the heart of

Jalandhar city with a bustling market and residential areas around it. It is almost a 100 year old building in a depilated condition. The Public Works Department had reportedly informed the jail authorities that they were continuing to use the building at their own risk. Even in the office room of Jail Superintendent, temporary arrangement using cloth was made to ensure that the plaster from the ceiling does not fall on the Superintendent's working desk. It is clearly visible that the building is not maintained. Around the entrance area there are a few rooms that would pass-off as being the administrative section of the jail. These rooms are for the Deputy Superintendent, the Deputy Jailor and the Warders on office duty. The registration of the prisoners and all those who come into and go out of the prison, the marking of the time of arrival and departure of the staff and the searches of the new prisoners or prisoners going and coming back from their hearings in the court, are all carried out in this space.

It is an overcrowded prison. Reports of hooliganism among prisoners because of in-fighting among inmates, is a routine feature. In order to enter the women prison, one has to enter through a main gate and pass through men's prison. Women prison is within the central jail for men. The prison has minimal facilities. It is an unkempt jail with both the under-trials and convicts in the same prison. There are two rooms (one big and another small) and open verandah with wash rooms on the left side. The women inmates have enough water for drinking, bathing and washing clothes. Rooms appear dull and very dingy with hardly any sunlight. There is just one light point in each room. There is a TV set and a carom board in the women cell. Women inmates spend time watching TV and playing carom. They are not engaged in any vocational activity. There is no crèche, no school room for children, and no room for imparting education to the adults.

There is one kitchen where food for both the males and females is cooked by men inmates. The food meant for women prisoners is delivered at the door of the women cell from where it is taken by the women prisoners and distributed amongst them. The menu is common and consists of *dal* and *roti* for lunch and dinner. There is a usual complaint about watery *dal* and often raw or burnt *rotis*. The *rotis* are mostly thrown away by the prisoners, leading to food wastage. Many women survive on food brought by their family members on *'mulaquat'*. Some of them cook food on earthen *chulhas* made by them. Those who can afford buy food from the canteen within the prison.

Ludhiana Women Jail

Ludhiana Women Jail in the state of Punjab is comparatively a new jail built in the year 1989. The jail is located near Ludhiana Central Jail which was once run as a part of the men's jail. It is now administered and managed as a separate entity. The main entrance is a big prison gate with a small door within the larger gate through which visitors enter. Inside is an entrance area where the visitor log is kept. The entrance gate is a part of a large administrative block where the Superintendent, Jailor, Deputy Jailer and other staff have their offices. Most of the jail staff is women.

The women jail is a modern jail with a good number of facilities like tailoring unit, school for children, play area, etc. There is no shortage of water. Each cell has a bathing and washing area as a part of the cell. Kitchen is managed by women themselves. Quality of food is not bad as in other prisons of the state. Children are given milk.

There are no regular education facilities in the jail except that classes are taken by the educated prisoners. The jail has only one pharmacist and no doctor. A male doctor from the adjoining Borstal jail take a round twice a day, once each in the morning and evening. Additionally, a Gynecologist from Government Hospital visits once a week.

Convicts and under-trials can be identified from one another on the basis of their dress code and work schedule. There is no separate wing for the under-trials. For all practical purposes, the convicts and under-trials are treated in the same way and they mix freely with each other. Educated convicts work in office. The fact that under-trials may not be compelled to do anything, not work, attend classes or attend get-togethers, makes for a different set of expectations at such places. Sometimes few under-trials do express an interest in being kept occupied.

There were 253 women in the jail (convicts and under-trials) and 22 children at the time of recording of the responses.

The women jail is overcrowded. Each day large number of convicts from different sub-jails are sent to this jail. Many inmates do not like the ides of all women's jail. They prefer to stay within the sub-jail so that they do not face the difficulty of meeting their family members. On the other hand, there were some inmates whose relatives or family members were in Ludhiana Central jail and they could meet them once in a week within the premises.

Patiala Jail

Patiala Jail was built in 1905. It is spread in an area of 94 acres. Patiala Central Jail has provision for women prisoners. It is located at a distance from the main city. The Superintendent is Incharge of the entire jail complex. There is one woman Assistant Superintendent and six women warders to look after women prisoners.

The enormous door (Colonial Structure) has the usual inset smaller gate through which most people enter. Around the entrance area there are some rooms for jail officials. A semi-open room near the entrance is for visitors. The inmates meet their visitors through barred windows. The visitors bring food items, holy books but not anything made of glass, intoxicants and other goods that are prohibited. The goods brought by visitors are thoroughly examined by staff on duty.

The prison houses both men and women. However, women enclosure is apart from men's prison. There is a Gurudwara and a temple in the prison. There is a library, and a small dispensary managed by a permanent qualified Doctor. Women inmates have no excess to the library. There is no crèche, no school for children, and no room for imparting education to women prisoners, whereas for men different educational courses are being run by Indira Gandhi National Open University. Kitchen is managed by male prisoners who are supervised by a Convict Officer. For lack of funding there are work areas only for men and not for women. Women are kept in a separate enclosure with separate entrance within the main prison. There is one big room and a small room for solitary confinement. The big room has stone floor where the women inmates sleep and there is no provision for storage. Storage of personal belongings is done in bags (plastic or cloth). There are windows all with bars and grills. In a situation of large number of inmates in the prison at a time, many have to share the outside verandah. The prisoners stay in the room having a combined foul stench of stale and damp clothes and body odours. The room has a night toilet meant only for urinating. The other toilet is located at the back of the cell. The toilets are usually clean as this task is done by women themselves and there is no shortage of water.

The women jail has an open area where most of the women have made their earthen chulhas. Women prepare their own food and use dried *rotis* as fuel.

Ambala Central Jail

Ambala Central Jail is situated in the outskirts of the city which is a non-residential area. It spreads out over large area. There is dense vegetation around the jail. It has a layout of administrative sections and residential blocks. Women prisoners are a part of the main prison. A Superintendent is Incharge of the entire jail complex. There are women constables to look after women inmates and they work in shift duties. The offices for jail staff are at the entrance. Women enclosure is attached to the men's prison. It is spacious and not in a depilated condition. The women prison gate is about 100 metres away from the men's prison. Under-trials and convicts are placed in one prison but are differentiated on the basis of their clothing. There is a large verandah with a lot of sunshine, and women regularly use it. Under-trials are not compelled to do anything, not work, attend classes, etc. Sometimes under-trials do express an interest in being kept occupied. These women anxiously wait for court orders, and one way or another always in a state of anticipation. Authorities feel that since majority of inmates are under-trials, there is no need to invest in reforming and in skill imparting. Women convicts undertake activities like cleaning pulses and cereals for the kitchen. Cooking, however, is done by the male prisoners. The menu is common and consistes of tea and rusks in the morning, dal and roti for lunch, and vegetable and roti for dinner. In between tea is served. The usual complaints about watery dal and uncooked or overcooked rotis exist here as well. Small earthen chulhas are made by women inmates. They use them to warm food or make tea for themselves. A small temple and a TV are the focus of the activity. In the prison are organized yoga and meditation classes for the inmates.

There is no crèche in the prison and no school-room for school going children of the inmates. They just loiter around with their mothers. Health facilities are also not adequate. The medical officer catering to men prisoners also pays visit to women inmates once in a while. Patients who are suffering from serious illness are often referred to the Government hospital.

Hissar Women Jail

Like Punjab, in Haryana, a separate jail exclusively for women prisoners exist at Hissar. Women convicts and inevitably also under-trials from the nearby areas are kept here. The entrance and admission area is the most innocuous space in prison. It is the area where the visitors enter the prison; it is also the place where a new prisoner gets admitted according to the rules and standards. Prisoners are brought to the jail in a police escort and admitted to the jail on warrants signed by competent authorities. There are separate cells for convicts and under-trials. After being admitted, the woman then goes to the cell allotted to her. The allotment is made on the basis of the status of the prisoner viz. an under-trial or a convict. In the prison, however, this separation is only a spatial one and for the rule of allowing under-trials to wear their own clothes. There is no separate wing for under-trials. For all practical purposes, the convicts and under-trials are treated in the same manner, and they freely mix with each other.

With 135 women in jail and 22 children, i.e. total of 157 (at the time of the study), each cell houses on an average 15 women. While this is inadequate, the situation is worse in other jails. Each cell has ceiling fans and good ventilation. There is a toilet within the cell. There are fixed hours for water supply. Storage of personal belongings is done in bags (plastic or cloth) or tin boxes. Women sleep on the stone floors.

The kitchen is managed by women convicts. A Convict Officer supervises them. She takes the food sample to the Deputy Superintendent, for tasting. The Convict Officer selects the prisoners of her choice to work in the kitchen and duties change every three months. Women are served breakfast, lunch and dinner. Twice a day they are served tea. Small children are given milk. As compared to other prisons the quality of food is relatively better. The women prisoners get a steel plate, a mug and a steel bowl as utensils of use. The women store drinking water in earthen pots.

Within the premises is located a small dispensary managed by a permanent doctor. About 10 to 20 women visit the dispensary each day for common ailments like aching limbs, cold, cough, fever, headache and also skin itches. The jail also houses a crèche and a small school room for children of the inmates. The children belong to different age groups, youngest being 2-3 years of age. The school room has many posters on the wall depicting numbers, alphabets, pictures of animals, etc. There is a nursery teacher appointed to teach the children.

Prior to the study, it is understood that there existed a small factory where the convicts got employed and were provided vocational training in furniture-making, tailoring, etc. At the time of the study, the factory had closed down and even the vocational training had discontinued.

Chandigarh Prison Profile—The Model Jail, Burail

The Model Jail, Burail at Chandigarh initially started as a sub-jail in 1972 and was later upgraded to a model jail in 1989. The jail building has been constructed in 13 acres of land and the residential complex occupies 3 acres. Further, the jail can accommodate 300 regular prisoners and 700 agitationists for a short period. There is a separate block for women prisoners. The children below the age of 6 years are permitted to stay with their mother. There is one permanent resident doctor to take care of the prisoners. Pre-detention medical examination of the prisoners is carried out at the time of their arrival. Most of the prisoner patients are treated within the prison. In case they require specialized advice or consultation, they are taken to the Government hospital(s) outside the prison. Pregnant and lactating mothers get special diet. Convict Officers, with the help of some prisoners who work in the kitchen, distribute food to the prisoners. Food is distributed to the women inmates in their cells. Special food is given on 26th January, 15th August, Holi and Diwali. There is a provision of canteen in the prison. Inmates get food and other daily needs items from the canteen on the payment basis. The constables help them to procure items from the canteen. Since these inmates are housed in the men's prison, they are denied free access to movement in the prison. Most of the time they remain confined to their cells. It is only for the visits and court trials that they are taken out. The prison houses a library from where educated prisoners borrow books for study. There is no arrangement of providing education to women prisoners and their children. The main entrance locates a visitor room where the prisoners meet their relatives. Majority of the prisoners meet their visitors at the same time, mostly causing commotion. As a consequence they can hardly listen to each other.

Technique of Data Collection

Since the present study confines to women lodged in prisons, the main sphere of activity was prisons. The main objective was to study female inmates in the prison, both convicts and under-trials, and collect all the details about them. This meant gathering both factual data and subjective information in prison. Sometimes jail staff was also present at the time of interviews.

All interviews were conducted individually, and notes recorded. The interviews with the women were held under the supervision of a guard. Visits were held on specific days, independent of regular visiting hours. All women were assured full confidentiality as required under legal and professional ethics. An elaborate interview schedule was constructed to collect quantifiable data which contained questions pertaining to prisoners' profile, family background, relations with family members, relations with jail staff and inmates, and also information regarding conditions prevailing in the jails. Women prisoners were interviewed using a set of closed and open-ended questions. Each interview lasted approximately 90 minutes. Although the emphasis was on collecting information through quantitative data, yet qualitative data could not be ignored and hence collected in the form of narratives. The repeated visits to prisons helped the researcher to develop rapport not only with the inmates but also with the jail staff. Many a times responses of the inmates were cross-examined and verified in order to collect authentic information.

Interviews with women in prison served a number of purposes, viz.

- First, they enabled the researcher to make initial contact with the women and gather information about the women's circumstances and plans whilst in prison.
- Secondly, they helped the researcher to understand the relations women developed during their custodial sentence.
- Thirdly, the interviews explored women's views about the types of services and programs that they would require enabling their problems and needs to be addressed.
- Finally, they documented women's views about existing criminal justice system and their reasons for the views they expressed.

The purpose of this study was to use double hermeneutics, i.e. interpretation of reality by the respondents at one level and interpretation by the researcher at another level. Additionally, views of police, prison staff, lawyers and those who are concerned with the lives of women prisoners have been used to draw holistic interpretation of the study.

Prison Administration in India

The word "prison" immediately evokes a stream of images viz. stark, forbidding walls spiked with watchtowers, inmates banging on the bars of their cells, and the suspicious eyes of armed and uniformed guards. It seems to be the natural end for a convicted criminal, a permanent institution stretching from the pits of the medieval dungeon to the current era of motion detectors and surveillance cameras. But centuries of development and debate lie behind the prison as we now know it—a rich history that reveals how our ideas of crime and punishment have changed over time. Penalties other than incarceration were once much more common. The nineteenth century saw the rise of the full-blown prison system in India, and along with it originated the idea of prison reforms.

In this chapter an attempt has been made to understand the prison system in the historical context. It is believed that an understanding of prison administration is essential to carry out any study on prison inmates. The prison system has been explained in this chapter under three main sections, viz. ancient period, under British rule, and post-independent India.

ANCIENT PERIOD

Numerous scholars have contributed to the revelation of crime and punishment in ancient India. P.V. Kane in "History of Dharmashastras" gives detailed information about various crimes, punishments, judicial administration, evolution of ancient Indian law and allied topics.

The early Vedic period followed by Rigveda, the later Vedic period followed by the combination of all four Vedas, while the late Vedic period was dominated by the Vedang, Smiriti. Early Vedic period was dominated by Aryans who had emigrated from Tibet plateau, Turanian Bacaricca, Pamir and other parts of the world. These communities used to administer the justice system at the family level. The family was based on the patriarchal system. The father used to dominate the family and therefore he was adjudged as the ruler of his family. His authority was final and after his death, power was transmitted to the eldest son. With the passage of time, the administering justice was based on the hierarchal basis viz. village (gram); community (vis); people (jana) and country (rashtra). The rashtra was normally ruled by the king (Rajan). Kingship was normally hereditary. This system was known as Monarchy. The main duties of monarchical system were to protect the life and property of people, maintain peace, defend the rashtra against external aggression, administer the justice, and punish the guilty. The king was helped by purohit (priest) and council of ministers. The jurisprudence of Ancient India, which was essentially Hindu-ruled, was shaped by the concept of 'Dharma', or rules of right conduct as outlined in the various manuals explaining the Vedic scriptures such as 'Puranas' and 'Smritis'. The King had no independent authority but derived his powers from 'Dharma' which he was expected to uphold. The distinction between a civil wrong and a criminal offence was clear. While civil wrongs related mainly to disputes arising over wealth, the concept of pataka or sin was the standard against which crime was to be defined. (Basham, 1967; Jois, Vol. I, 1990). Mainly murder, theft and burglary were considered as crimes. The punishment of crime differed depending upon the race, class or community to which the offender belonged to.

Manu strongly believed that the *danda, "the sceptre"*, a symbol of the power and authority was created by God and only fear alone would make the human beings to swerve not from their duties. Manu advocated the theory of deterrence as the purpose of punishment and the infliction of punishment should be according to the principles of natural justice. The king having fully considered the time and place of the offence, and the strength and the knowledge of the offender, should justly inflict punishment on the offenders. The concept of the consideration of the offence and offender for the purpose of punishment falls in line with the modern principles of justice. Manu felt that only punishment can control all the human beings on the earth and gave utmost importance to punishment. However, he is chary of punishment given without proper judgment and felt that it may destroy the country.

Manu cautions the king that if he does not punish the offenders who are worthy of punishment then the stronger would roast the weaker like fish on a spit and a situation will arise where might may overrule the right. In a country where punishment is not properly inflicted, the ownership would not remain with any one; the lower ones would (usurp the place of) the higher ones (Buhler, 1984). The whole world is kept in order only by punishment, because there is no one in the world who will always act in a just manner. Only the fear of punishment runs the world. Manu also feared that if there was no punishment then all castes (varna) would be corrupted (by intermixture), all barriers would be broken through, and all men would rage (against each other) in consequence of mistakes with respect to punishment.

Manu identified ten places on the body in which punishment may be inflicted. The sexual organ, the belly, the tongue, the two hands, and fifthly the two feet, the eye, the nose, the two ears, likewise the (whole) body are the ten places in a body fit for punishment (Buhler, 1984). From this view, we also come to know that Manu supported retributive justice. Manu was against unjust punishment and warned that unjust punishment would destroy reputation among men, and fame (after death), and would cause even in the next world, the loss of heaven. Manu provided stages of punishment for an erring person if he continues to do the crime, first by gentle admonition, afterwards by harsh reproof, thirdly by a fine, and later by corporal chastisement. However, when the offender is not able to restrain such offence even by corporal punishment, then the four modes co-jointly should be applied.

Punishment was thus four-fold viz., admonition, reproof, fine and corporal. It was awarded after considering the offenders condition and the crime committed by him. Among the physical punishments for any offence of a small nature, whipping on the back with a cord or bamboo stick was prescribed. Mutilation of limbs appeared to be one of the most common practices.

Imprisonment was also prevalent during ancient period. Hiuen-Tsang observed that imprisonment for the life was practiced. Yama suggested that instead of corporal punishment, a Brahman criminal should always be kept in prison and the king should compel him to labor. The ancient Dharmashastras do not show for what particular offences the prisoners were to be kept confined. It is also clear that the period of confinement for a particular offence has not been prescribed. Moreover, often the words used were highest punishment, etc. and it would therefore appear that it was left to the king to decide who should be sent to jail and for what period.

Prisons were generally located in an underground dungeon or in an out of the way place and were properly walled. Prisons were well protected by guards and jailors. From the Dasakumaracarita we find that occasionally jailors used to inherit the jobs from their parents. Even female criminals had their feet tied and were put in prison. The Karpuramanjari refers to the female guards of prison house. Iron fetters were generally used to bind the feet of the culprit. Wooden handcuffs were also known. From the Harsacarita, it appears that the condition of the prisoners was far from satisfactory. They bore haggard looks with long beards and their bodies looked dark due to dirt. The life of Hiuen-Tsang records that prisoners generally received harsh treatment. They were not allowed to shave and had hairy faces and matted beards.

Kautilya prescribed that a jail should be constructed in the capital, provided with separate accommodation for men and women kept apart (thus the principle of classification of men and women was in existence in the jails during ancient period), and well guarded at the entrances, (since there is no mention about jails in other parts it is evident that very few persons were sent to jail to undergo punishment). He further provided that among the duties of the Nagarka (jail officer) was to let prisoners out of the jail on the day of festival, of the birth, constellation of the king and on the full moon day (of every month). Those persons who were young, very old, suffering from diseases and helpless or those who were charitably disposed might pay the fines. Those who were not in a position to pay fines were jailed. Prisoners were released from jail (as a favor) on the conquest of a fresh territory or on the coronation of the crown prince or on the birth of a prince.

The Maurya Dynasty, which had extended to substantial parts of the Central and Eastern regions during the 4th Century B.C., had a rigorous penal system which prescribed mutilation as well as the death penalty for even trivial offences. About the 2nd or 3rd Century A.D., the Dharmashastras code was drawn up by Manu, an important Hindu jurist. The code recognized assault and other bodily injuries, and property offences such as theft and robbery. During the rule of the Gupta Dynasty (4th to 6th Century A.D.), the judicial hierarchy was formed. The judiciary was comprised of the guild, the folk-assembly or the council and the king himself. Judicial decisions conformed to legal texts, social usage and the edict of the king, who was prohibited from violating the decisions. (Pillai, 1983; Griffith, 1971; Thapar, 1990).

It is thus observed that imprisonment as a mode of punishment was not a regular feature in ancient India when compared with the modern prison system.

Mughal Period

India was subjected to a series of invasions by the Muslims beginning in the 8th Century A.D. and ending in the 15th century, when a mixed race of Persians, Turks and Mongols set-up the Mughal Empire. They occupied most of the Northern region and enforced a Mohammedan criminal law that classified all offences on the basis of the penalty which each merited. These included retaliation (blood for blood), specific penalties (as for theft and robbery) and discretionary penalties (Griffith, 1971).

The principle forms of punishment during Mughal period were capital punishment, mutilation, flogging, banishment, Tashir, fines, and imprisonment.

Although imprisonment was a very usual form of punishment in Mughal India, there were no specific rules fixed for it. The chief feature of this punishment was that no period was fixed for it. The Quazi, i.e. the magistrate had a right to send anyone to prison for the offence or crime for which the punishment could be awarded, and the accused had to show signs of repentance to secure his freedom.

There used to be three 'noble prisons' in Mughal India at Gwalior, Ranthambore and Rohtas. Criminals condemned to capital punishment were usually sent to the Fort of Ranthambore. The Gwalior Fort was reserved for "nobles that offend". To Rohtas were sent those nobles who were condemned to perpetual imprisonment from where "very few return home." Princes of royal blood were often sent to this place (Sanger, 1967).

The accounts recorded by European travellers as well as the scattered cases in the chronicles show that there were neither regular jails in the modern sense nor proper arrangements for keeping criminals and political offenders in custody.

When the prisoners were taken to the prison, they were usually loaded with iron fetters on their feet and shackles around their necks. For temporary confinement, there were police lock-ups in the cities termed as Chabutra-e-kotwali. The office in charge of Chabutra-e-kotwali used to be the Mushrif. The Chabutra-e-kotwali has resemblance with the modern police lock-ups where the accused persons are kept, prior to being produced before the Magistrates. Even though there were no jails in the modern sense during Mughal period, the practice of releasing the prisoners on bail from jail was in existence.

To summarize the main features of prison system as they prevailed in pre-British period, we find that:

1. There were no prisons in the modern sense.
2. There is no description about the internal administration of prison.
3. There was no separation of prison service from the civil service.

4. There is no description about the types of prisoners sent to prison and the relation of prisoners with the outside world.
5. Courts were not the feeding centers for prisons.
6. Imprisonment was not the normal feature of punishment and most of the punishment were metted out outsides the prison.
7. Some forts were used for keeping certain types of prisoners. In such "Fort prisons" there were no rules for the recruitment of the staff, or rules and regulations for the treatment of prisoners.

MODERN PRISON SYSTEM UNDER THE BRITISH RULE

India became a nation under the British who arrived in the early 17th Century as traders of the East India Company. The Company slowly acquired territory across the sub-continent, strictly for commercial operations in the beginning, but gradually assumed considerable powers of governance. Considering the Muslim criminal law to be irrational, the Company brought about several reforms through a series of regulations which modified or expanded the definitions of some offences, introduced new offences and altered penalties to make them more logical and reasonable (Jois, Vol. II, 1990). In 1857, the large possessions and the authority enjoyed by the Company were transferred to the British Monarch by an Act of Parliament. Until this time, India was a loose collection of kingdoms, interactions between whom were nominal, though cultural links were quite pronounced.

The prison system as it operates today in our country is a legacy of the British rule. It was established as a result of the attempts of the former British rule in consolidating their administration in this country. Prisons on the Western model were established during the regime of the East India Company. Though much material is not available on the early prison system, yet the minutes submitted by Lord Macaulay to the legislative council of India at Fort William on December 21, 1835, clearly indicates the thinking which patterned the systematic development of the prison system in this country. Macaulay considered this problem of utmost importance and opined that the best criminal code was of very little use to a community unless there was good machinery for the infliction of punishment. He propagated that imprisonment is the punishment to which we must chiefly trust. It will probably be resorted to in ninety nine cases out of every hundred. It is, therefore, of the greatest importance to establish such regulations as shall make imprisonment a terror to wrong doers, and shall at the same time prevent it from being attended by any circumstances shocking to humanity.

Macaulay's ideas clearly indicated that Penal code was to rely chiefly on imprisonment as a method of punishment. The prison sentence should inspire terror in the people yet it should not be inhumane. A system based on such an approach was considered beneficial by the then rulers of the land for their native subject. Macaulay drew attention of the legislative council of India to the deplorable conditions of the Indian jails and proposed to appoint a committee "for the purpose of collecting information as to the state of Indian prison and of preparing an improved plan of prison discipline and to suggest such reforms as may make the place a model for other prison", which was readily received by Sir C. Metcalfe, the then acting Governor-General. A Committee was appointed to report upon the subject. The report was presented in the early part of 1838. The committee handled the aspects of housing of prisoners, discipline, health, diet, remunerative theory, rewards and punishments, education, labour and recommended a series of suggestions. The committee in its recommendations deliberately rejected, "all reforming influences such as moral and religious teaching, education or any system of rewards for good conduct and suggested the building of central prisons where the convicts might be engaged not on manufactures which it condemned but in some dull, monotonous, wearisome and uninteresting work" (Howell, 1936). In regard to central prisons, the committee recommended that they should be constructed to accommodate prisoners sentenced to a term of over one year. Each central prison should accommodate up to 1000 prisoners.

In pursuance of this recommendation, a network of central prisons was constructed in the North Western Province, now comprising the major portion of Uttar Pradesh. In view of the terrible conditions as in Alipore jail, referred to by Macaulay in the minute of 1835, it was recommended that sufficient buildings should be provided for the proper and orderly housing of the prisoners.

Sir John Lawrence, the Governor of India reviewed the position in 1864 and appointed the Second Prison Commission to minimize the high death rates in prison, and for considering other aspects of jail management. The committee of 1864 found that during the preceding ten years no less than 46309 deaths had occurred within walls of the Indian prisons (Howell, 1936). The committee came to the conclusion that the sickness and mortality may be considered as mainly attributable to overcrowding, bad ventilation, bad conservancy, bad drainage, insufficient clothing, sleeping on the ground, deficiency of personal cleanliness, bad water, extraction of labor from unfit persons and insufficient medical inspection.

The committee also considered the aspects of juvenile delinquents, female prisoners, dietary, jail discipline (Superintendence, labor, rewards, punishments, and education), classification of convicted prisoners, habitual prisoners, and recommended a series of suggestion in the prison system. Due to implementations of the recommendations of the committee, the death rate in prisons was considerably reduced.

The Third Committee was appointed in 1877. It reviewed jail administration and made important recommendations pertaining to the receipts of supplies and maintenance of accounts. The committee was composed entirely of officials actually engaged in prison work. It reviewed the jail management generally and mostly concerned itself more with the matters of detail prison work than with the general aims and principles of administration.

The Fourth All India Jail Committee was appointed in 1889. In addition to the review of prison administration, its major contributions were the separation of under-trial prisoners and the classification of the prisoners into casual and habitual. This committee also recommended the establishment of a hospital in each jail. Most of the recommendations of the committee were incorporated in the jail manuals of various provinces. The work of the committee was supplemented by the All India Jail Committee, 1892. It re-examined the whole prison administration in India and drew up proposals on the subject of prison offences and punishment. The report of the committee was accepted by the Government of India which passed the Prisons Act, 1894. The Act fixed 9 hours labour a day for a criminal prisoner sentenced to labour or employed on labour at his own desire. It further defined what constitutes prison offences and laid down punishment for the same. Since these efforts were confined to the material side of prison administration, the Indian jails appeared to have achieved considerable material progress during this period. Buildings had been gradually provided, dietaries laid down, systems of labour elaborated, a rational remission system developed, unsanitary conditions partly corrected and death rates reduced. Despite such material progress, the jail administration in India still lacked on its reformative side. The administrators were still in no mood to regard the prisoners as a human being and seek to reform him by humane methods, as opposed to methods of torture of either body or mind. All emphasis was given to the material well-being of a prisoner, his diet, health and labour and totally ignoring the possibility of his moral or intellectual reclamation.

The Fifth Committee was appointed in 1919. The Indian Jails Committee, 1919 gave expression to the new ideas. The committee made an extensive tour of England, Scotland, U.S.A., Japan, Philippines, Hong Kong and Andaman's (where Indian political prisoner were detained), studied prison systems there, and submitted a comprehensive report suggesting far reaching changes in the various aspects of the prison system. The committee made 584 recommendations (some of which have not been implemented even today in most of the Indian jails).

The changes in the prison system in India received a sudden setback due to the constitutional changes brought about by the Government of India Act, 1919. The enforcement of this Act affected the transfer of the jail department from the control of the Government of India to that of the provincial government.

As regards the general objectives of prison administration, the report of the committee of 1919-20 observed: "there is very general agreement that crime is an anti-social act and that it is the task of the prison administrator so to deal with the offender that he and others may be deterred from the commission of such acts in future. It is also generally admitted by modern authorities that the aim of the prison administration should further be to effect such a reformation in the character of the criminal as well as fit him again to take his place in society and to become a useful citizen."

For the fulfilment of the objectives mentioned above, the committee of 1919-20 recommended following measures as the essentials of prison administration:

1. As far as possible, every prison should be under the superintendence of a trained expert who should devote his whole time and attention to the subject, and the number of prisoners who can properly be entrusted to the care of a single superintendent must not exceed a certain maximum.
2. The prison staff, from the Jailor down to the Warder, should be recruited with care, properly trained and paid a salary sufficient to secure and retain faithful service.
3. Prisoners in jail shall be so classified and separated that the younger or less experienced shall not be contaminated or rendered worse by communication and associated with the older or more hardened offender.
4. The prisoners, while in prison, should be brought under such humanizing and improving influences as will not only deter them from committing further crimes but will also result in a real reformation of their character.
5. It is desirable, as far as practicable, to help such prisoners as may need help on their release from prison, so that they may be given a reasonable chance of securing an honest living.
6. Since imprisonment is generally an evil, measures such as extension of the probation systems, prohibition of petty sentences of imprisonment, extension of the period for payment of fine in reasonable cases as determined by the court and the practice of payment by installments should be adopted as far as possible.

7. Measures for revision of every sentence of long imprisonment and grant of increased remission for good behavior should be taken to shorten imprisonment.

It goes without saying that by recommending these valuable measures for prison reform, the Indian Jails Committee of 1919-20 gave an impetus to modernization of jail administration in this country. In practice, however, not much had been done by the alien governments on the reformative side of prison system during the next quarter of a century that ended with the transfer of power to Indian hands in 1947.

INDIAN PRISON ADMINISTRATION POST-INDEPENDENCE

After the advent of freedom a new phase of humanitarian prison administration began in India. Ideas regarding punishment and functions of prisons changed. The changing circumstances on the socio-economic scene of the country after independence had also inspired a few conscientious prison administrators of our country to undertake some innovative experiments through their own individual efforts. Since such efforts and innovations were only sporadic and short lived, their total impact on prison administration was not discernible up to any appreciable extent.

In the constitution of Republic of India, prison administration has been included in the state list. In view of the changed penological ideology from custodial security to correction and rehabilitation of offenders, the Ministry of Home Affairs, Government of India, set-up a committee in 1957 to prepare an All India Skeleton Jail Manual, to examine the Prison Acts and other central legislation on the subject, and to recommend prison reform to be applied uniformly throughout the country. The committee was further directed to examine and make recommendations regarding the classification of prisoners on scientific lines, abolition of short-term sentences and provision of alternative measures to consider the question of care of children and of women offenders, etc.

The committee divided its recommendations as under:

1. Provision of Jail Manual
   - Part I—Department of Prison and Correctional Services.
   - Part II—Personnel
   - Part III—Treatment of prisoners
   - Part IV—Special categories
2. Classification of prisoners and diet-scale, short-term sentence, children of women offenders, smoking and use of hand cuffs and fetters.
3. Prison reforms.
4. Legislation.
5. Other items, such as Planning of Correctional Administration, Five Year Plan, Annual Conference of Correctional Administration and revision of the Draft Manual and follow-up of the recommendation.

The committee recommended that the prevention and control of crime, treatment of offenders and after care of prisoners should be treated as a unified programme. The Department of Prisons and Correctional Services should exercise jurisdiction over prisons juvenile delinquency, probation and after-care services. The Inspector General should be a departmental officer, as far as possible. There should be a proper classification on the bases of sex, age, criminal record, security conditions and need of training and treatment. There should be separate institutions for women, adolescents and recidivistic offenders, mental cases, and under-trials. Tuberculoses and leprosy inflicted prisoners should be provided with separate institutions. The maximum strength of prisoners should not exceed 750 in a central prison and 400 in a district jail.

With regards to the personnel, the committee recommended that executive, clerical and accounts functions should be separated. There should be an All India Service Cadre from whose ranks the top executive of the prison and correctional administration should be drawn. The staff training should comprise initial basic training, refreshers and specialization courses and preparation of an All India Training Manual.

With respect to the treatment of prisoners, the committee recommended the classification of prisoners into Division A and Division B. The Divisions may be abolished as the social strata would get merged. The classification of prisoners for the purpose of treatment should be on the basis of age, physical and mental health, length of sentence, degree of criminally and character, antecedents, background and on the basis of the possibilities of rehabilitations.

The committee recommended a compulsory educational programme for all prisoners. The programme should comprise physical and health education, vocational and cultural education. The aim of education should be both literacy and correction.

Under-trial prisoners should be housed in separate institutions located near the courts. Women, adolescents and habitual offenders should be segregated. Their detention should not be too long and when necessary additional courts should be set-up for quick disposal of cases.

Women offenders should be provided a separate institution where the daily average exceeds 50. Habituals, prostitutes, and brothel keepers should be separated from other women. Certain categories of these offenders should be placed in state homes and *Mahila Ashrams*.

Life convicts should be examined by the classification committee on the expiry of their five years of imprisonment. The classification of habitual offenders should be made by the court of law and where necessary by the Inspector General of Prisons. The committee also recommended the extension of wall-less prisons or open institutions.

The committee recommended the amendment of certain sections of the Indian Penal Code and Criminal Procedure Code. The classification of imprisonment as "simple" and "rigorous" and "solitary confinement" as a form of punishment should be abolished.

In consonance with its radical approach to the prime objective of the problems of crime and delinquency, and of correctional administration, the All India Jail Manual Committee furnished a detailed report containing necessary principals for modernization of prisons together with a Model Prison Manual in 1960 as a broad guidelines for the states to revise their outdated prison manuals.

The valuable recommendations of the committees appointed by these governments were not implemented in an effective manner. Official apathy and bureaucratic bungling continued so much so that even after the end of another decade (1961-70) the general state of prison administration in the country was described by an official committee as "Depressing". In 1972, the Government of India's Ministry of Home Affairs appointed a working group on prisons:

1. To examine the physical and administration conditions of the jails in the country, and suggesting ways and means of their improvement.
2. To lay down standards in respect of different services and facilities in the jails.
3. To lay down an order of priorities for the prison development schemes.
4. To consider other allied matters concerning prisons and prisoners.

A year later, the group submitted its report in which it emphasized the need for a National Policy on Prison and Correctional Administration. Discarding the traditional prison-based policy, the report of the group identified the main elements of the proposed National Policy; the more important of them are as follows:

1. A suitable system should be established for coordination among the three organs of the criminal justice system, i.e. the police, the judiciary and the prison and correctional administration for the effective prevention of crime and treatment of offenders.
2. The supreme aim of punishment should now be the protection of society through the rehabilitation of offenders. The re-assimilation of the offenders in society and the prevention of crime should be the principal aim of the prison administration.

3. The concepts of deprivation of liberty and segregation from society should be limited mostly to the habitual, the incorrigible and the dangerous criminals and the Government should make fullest possible use of various alternatives to imprisonment as a measure of sentencing policy. Non-institutional and semi-institutional forms of treatment should be resorted to as far as possible.
4. There should be close coordination between the prison and the probation and other correctional services. It follows that the prison administration should be treated as an integral part of the social defense component of the national planning process.
5. Free legal aid should be provided to all indigent prisoners.
6. Under-trial prisoners should be lodged in separate institutions as far as possible and facilities should be provided to them for work on a voluntary basis.
7. The Union and State Governments should declare unequivocally that there will be no bar or restriction on the employment of ex-convicts of specified categories in the public services after a due scrutiny of the prison reports certifying to their abilities and qualities.
8. The prison administration should systematically involve enlightened individual citizens, association, societies and other community agencies in the treatment, after care and rehabilitation of offenders.

In order to usher in the desired changes in the prison administration as a whole, the group recommended that the highest priority should be given to the adoption of the National Policy on Prisons as suggested by them along with the inclusion of certain aspects of the prison administration in the Five Year Plan, the amendment of the constitution to include the subject of prisons and allied institutions in the concurrent list, the enactment of suitable legislation by the centre as well as the states, and the revision of the State Prison Manuals.

Government of India in 1978 requested the seventh Finance Commission to submit report on upgrading the standards of jail administration. The commission in its report admitted that jails had been neglected for too long and that there had been practically no improvement in their environments or in the methods of dealing with inmates. The commission recommended that priority should be given: firstly, to ensure that adequate direct expenditure was incurred on the prisoners; secondly, to bring improvements in amenities in respect of water supply, sanitary facilities, electrification, etc. and thirdly, to provide for the construction of additional jail capacities in states where these were found short of the minimum requirements.

While the planning and monitoring of the schemes recommended by the seventh Finance Commission were being assigned to the National Institute of Social Defense through the ministry of Home Affairs, the Government of India appointed another committee (the All India Committee on Jail Reforms) in July 1980 for making a comprehensive review of prison administration in the country and suggesting suitable measures for its improvement. Though total overhauling has not taken place, yet as a result of recommendations made by various committees, some of the better amenities have been extended to the prison inmates. The Committee was headed by Justice Anand Narain Mulla and it submitted its reports in 1983. It gave suggestions on various aspects of jail administration including those relating to modernization of jails and segregation of young prisoners from the hardened criminals. Basic objective of the Committee was to review the laws, rules and regulations keeping in view the overall objective of protecting the society and rehabilitating the offenders. The Committee has suggested that the existing hierarchy of prison administration at Union and State-level should be removed. The Committee specially recommended a total ban on the heinous practice of clubbing together juvenile offenders with the hardened criminals in prisons. Consequently, a comprehensive legislation has been enacted for the security and protective care of delinquent juveniles. The Committee also suggested segregation of mentally disturbed prisoners to mental asylums.

The committee recommended that protection of society is universally accepted objective of punishment which can be achieved through reformation and the rehabilitation of offenders. In order to keep out of circulation of harmful, habitual, dangerous recidivists, the committee emphasized correction and rehabilitation along with protection. The recommendations of the Mulla Committee touched upon legislative, operational, security aspects besides matters like classification of prisoners, living condition in prison, medical and psychiatric services, treatment programs, vocational training for prison inmates, problems related to under-trials and other non-convicted prisoners, and problems of women prisoners, etc. The report laid emphasis on the management of prisons to be entrusted to a cadre of professionals.

Again in 1987, the Government of India appointed Justice Krishna Iyer Committee to undertake a study on the situation of women prisoners in India. It has recommended induction of more women in the police force in view of their special role in tackling women and child offenders. The following are some of the more important aspects of their recommendations:

1. Women prisoners, like men, should be informed of their rights under the law.
2. Women constables should conduct searches.
3. Medical check ups of women prisoners or under-trials should be done by women doctors as soon as they come to prison.
4. Women prisoners should be allowed to contact their families and communication with their lawyers, women social workers and voluntary organization.
5. Women prisoners should be allowed to keep their children with them.
6. Voluntary organizations of women should be encouraged to be associated with women prisoners.
7. Separate jails should be provided for women.
8. Special prosecution officers should be available to present the case of women prisoners.

The Mulla Committee, Justice Krishna Iyer Committee and the National Human Rights Commission have made numerous valuable recommendations to bring about not only improvements and reform in the jail administration but in the entire criminal justice system itself. In spite of so many efforts, conditions of prison and prisoners have not improved. Prisons in India are not governed uniformly. Every state applies a different set of rules and regulations. In 1960, Model Prison Manual was prepared for the purpose of updating and revising the state manuals. It was also meant to lend uniformity to rules and regulations as to the procedures and punishments. It needs to be still adopted and implemented in many states.

'Prisons' being a State subject, Prison Administration is the responsibility of the State Governments. The provisions of The Prisons Act, 1894 and the Jail Manuals framed by State Governments are the bedrock of the prison administration. The State Governments may undertake legislation, and make rules and regulations on the subject. Although 'Prisons' is a State subject, keeping in mind the pressing need for improving the prevailing conditions inside prisons, Government of India has been providing central assistance to the State Governments to supplement their efforts in improving the condition of prisons and prisoners under the scheme of Modernization of Prisons since 1987.

As the efforts made till 2001 did not bring significant improvements, and in order to reduce the continuing overcrowding and improving the condition of prisons, prisoners and the prison staff, and also to ensure certain basic minimum standards for keeping the prisoners in healthy and hygienic conditions, Central Government launched a new non-plan scheme in the year 2002-03 with much higher outlay for construction of additional jails, repair and renovation of existing jails, improvement in sanitation and water supply, and construction of living accommodation for prisons staff. The scheme which is known as 'Modernization of Prisons' was implemented over a period of five years (2002-07) with an outlay of Rs. 1800 Crore on cost sharing basis with the State Governments in the ratio of 75:25. During 2002-03, 2003-04 and 2004-05, the Central share amounting to Rs. 270 Crores, Rs. 197 Crores and Rs. 191.38 Crores respectively were released to the State Governments. The scheme was closely monitored to ensure its desired impact on the conditions of prisons and lives of prisoners.

The above discussion on prison administration in post-independence period reflects that various committees have been formulated by the Government of India, from time to time, to improve the conditions of prisons and the prisoners. At national level a research bureau, i.e. National Crime Records Bureau (NCRB) has been formed to provide a comprehensive database on various prisons and prisoners, which can be of immense use to prison authorities in planning various activities connected with prison administration. Below are the brief excerpts of jail data, as presented by NCRB at the end of 2006.

PRISON DISTRIBUTION IN INDIA

Prison and its administration is a State subject as it is covered by item 4 under List II in Schedule VII of the Constitution of India. Prison establishments in different States/UTs comprise of several tiers of jails.

The most common and standard jail institutions which are in existence in the States/UTs are better known as Central Jails, District Jails and Sub-Jails. The other types of jail establishments are Women Jails, Borstal Schools, Open Jails and Special Jails.

Total number of jails in the States/UTs shows that Maharashtra has the highest number (210) of jails among the States/UTs followed by Andhra Pradesh (141), Tamil Nadu (134), Madhya Pradesh (116), Rajasthan (105) and Karnataka (98). Arunachal Pradesh does not have any jail of its own. It's convicts and undertrial prisoners are kept in jails of Assam, therefore, prison statistics in respect of Assam include prisoners of Arunachal Pradesh also.

Central Jail

The criteria for a jail to be categorised as a Central Jail differs from State to State. However, the common features observed in all the States/UTs are that the prisoners sentenced to imprisonment for a longer period are confined in the Central Jails, which have larger capacity in comparison to other jails.

These jails also have rehabilitation facilities. Meghalaya, Orissa, Uttaranchal, Andaman and Nicobar Islands, Chandigarh, Dadra and Nagar Haveli, Daman and Diu and Lakshadweep do not have any Central Jail in their territories. Tamil Nadu has the highest number of 9 Central Jails followed by Madhya Pradesh, Maharashtra, Rajasthan and Delhi (8 each).

The available information regarding capacity for Prison Inmates in Central Jails in respect of States/UTs indicate that Tamil Nadu (12356), Maharashtra (11382), West Bengal (10957) and Bihar (10459) have comparatively larger capacity followed by Madhya Pradesh (8290), Punjab (8236), Rajasthan (8118), Andhra Pradesh (6632), Jharkhand (6558), Uttar Pradesh (5974), Karnataka (5222) and Delhi (4800).

The capacity to accommodate female prisoners in Central jails is comparatively higher in Madhya Pradesh (567), followed by Maharashtra (389), West Bengal (305), Punjab (252), Karnataka (250), Kerala (239), Chhattisgarh (230), Andhra Pradesh (204) and Rajasthan (191).

District Jail

District Jails serve as the main prisons in some of the States/UTs. States which have considerable number of District Jails are Uttar Pradesh (50), Rajasthan (25), Bihar and Maharashtra (23 each), Madhya Pradesh (22), Jharkhand (19), Assam (18), Orissa (13), Haryana and West Bengal (12 each). Andaman and Nicobar Islands, Delhi and Pondicherry have one District jail each among UTs.

The District Jails in Uttar Pradesh (28874), Bihar (9702), Haryana (7732), West Bengal (5803), Madhya Pradesh (5261), Maharashtra (5022), Rajasthan (4929), Orissa (4430) and Jharkhand (4147) have the capacity of lodging a large number of inmates with an average capacity of 577, 422, 644, 484, 239, 218, 224, 341 and 218 inmates per jail, respectively.

Comparatively higher accommodation for female inmates was also provided in District Jails in Uttar Pradesh (1271), West Bengal (528), Haryana (504), Madhya Pradesh (378), Bihar (350), Maharashtra (289) and Assam (254).

Sub-Jail

10 States have reported comparatively higher number of sub-jails revealing a well organized prison set-up even at lower formation. These States are Maharashtra (172), Andhra Pradesh (120), Tamil Nadu (113), Madhya Pradesh (86), Karnataka (81), Rajasthan (59), Orissa (52), West Bengal (29), Kerala (26) and Bihar (25).

Madhya Pradesh had the highest capacity of inmates (6704) in various Sub-Jails followed by Karnataka (4589), Bihar (4248), Tamil Nadu (3832), Rajasthan (3611), Orissa (3370), Andhra Pradesh (3304), Maharashtra (2361), West Bengal (1751), Gujarat (1292) and Kerala (1192).

Women Jail

There are only 15 women jails in 12 States/UTs functioning exclusively for women prisoners. Andhra Pradesh, Rajasthan and Tamil Nadu have 2 women jails each followed by Bihar, Kerala, Maharashtra, Orissa, Punjab, Tripura, Uttar Pradesh, West Bengal and Delhi (1 each). The total capacity of women inmates was highest in Tamil Nadu (513) followed by Delhi (400), Rajasthan (350), Andhra Pradesh (320), Maharashtra (262), Punjab (150), West Bengal (100), Uttar Pradesh (90), Bihar (83), Kerala (60), Orissa (55) and Tripura (30).

Borstal School

The primary objective of Borstal Schools is to ensure care, welfare and rehabilitation of young offenders in a different environment suitable for children and keep them away from contaminating atmosphere of the prison. Borstal schools cannot be treated as either a miniature jail or a substitute for it. The delinquents detained in Borstal Schools are provided various vocational trainings. They are also given education with the help of trained teachers.

Ten States namely, Andhra Pradesh, Haryana, Himachal Pradesh, Jharkhand, Karnataka, Kerala, Maharashtra, Punjab, Rajasthan and Tamil Nadu have reported 1 Borstal School each in their respective jurisdiction.

Haryana had the highest capacity for keeping 462 inmates followed by Tamil Nadu (405) and Punjab (300). Haryana (195) and Himachal Pradesh (15) have also reported female inmates in their Borstal School. Existence of Borstal Schools was not reported from any of the UTs.

Open Jail

Prisoners with good behaviour satisfying certain norms prescribed in the prison rules are admitted in open prisons. Minimum security is kept in such prisons and prisoners are trained in agriculture. Only 13 States have reported about the functioning of Open Jails in their jurisdiction. Rajasthan amongst these States reported the highest number of 10 open jails. Maharashtra had 3 followed by Andhra Pradesh, Gujarat and Kerala (2 jails each). The remaining 8 States—Assam, Himachal Pradesh, Karnataka, Orissa, Punjab, Tamil Nadu, Uttaranchal and West Bengal had one Open Jail each. Existence of such jail was not reported from any of the UTs.

The highest capacity of inmates in open jails was reported from Maharashtra (722), Rajasthan (456), Andhra Pradesh (430), Kerala (350), Uttaranchal (300), Punjab (200), Assam, Gujarat, Orissa and Tamil Nadu (100 each), Himachal Pradesh and Karnataka (80 each) and West Bengal (70).

Special Jails

Special Jail means any prison provided for the confinement of a particular class or particular classes of prisoners which are broadly as follows:

1. Prisoners who have committed serious violations of prison discipline.
2. Prisoners showing tendencies towards violence and aggression.
3. Difficult discipline cases of habitual offenders.
4. Difficult discipline cases from a group of professional organized criminals.

Kerala has the highest number of Special Jails (5) out of the 9 States having Special Jails followed by West Bengal (4), Gujarat, Karnataka, Orissa and Uttar Pradesh (2 each), Assam, Maharashtra and Tamil Nadu (1 each).

As far as the available capacity in these jails is concerned, the highest capacity for keeping the prisoners was available in Orissa (1,073) followed by West Bengal (1,041), Uttar Pradesh (594), Kerala (424), Assam (372), Karnataka (250), Maharashtra (246) and Gujarat (186) in their Special Jails. Provision for keeping female prisoners in these special jails was available in West Bengal (95), Kerala (47), Orissa (30), Assam and Karnataka (12 each), Gujarat (10) and Maharashtra (3).

Other Jails

Some States/UTs have other jails also besides the jails discussed above. Goa has reported 3 such jails. Karnataka, Maharashtra, Orissa, Tamil Nadu and UT of Chandigarh each have reported one such jail in their jurisdiction. The capacity of inmates (male and female) reported by various States in such jails was Karnataka (250), Orissa (97), Goa (91), Tamil Nadu (40) and Maharashtra (28). UT of Chandigarh has reported one such jail termed as 'Model Jail' having capacity of lodging 1000 inmates (960 for males and 40 for females).

(See Appendix 1 through 5 for further information on prisons.)

CONCLUSION

Prison Institutions are one of the three main constituents of the Criminal Justice System. Prisons are no longer regarded only as places for punishment with the changing perception towards prisoners. They are now being considered as reformatories and greater attention is being given to ameliorate the conditions in jails so that it has a healthy impact on prisoners in developing a positive attitude towards life and society.

A review of the existing prison administration in India shows that though numerous efforts have been made through the formulation of various jail regulations and recommendations of committees from time to time, the ground reality, however, presents a diagonally opposite picture. An overwhelming majority of the prison population is not even convicted. The inmates are mostly under-trial or even uncommitted to trial, with only a few criminals in their early criminal careers. As mentioned earlier, several committees have recommended classification of inmates on the basis of their status which is not being followed. Prisons are still following the concepts as prevalent in colonial India. When imprisoned, men and women do not cease to be human beings. Therefore, the material and moral standards by which society lives must apply to them as far as possible. As a consequence to this fact, it follows that what happens to people in custody must always have regard to their likely conditions during as well as after release. Apart from the humane and secure containment of inmates, the prison environment should provide controlled conditions in which they can move towards a better understanding of themselves and learn to accept and deal responsibly with the consequences of their own behavior. Since the inmates are to be reformed, it becomes essential to provide them with a built environment that gives them a chance to introspect, and not an environment that leads to a loss of self-control, self-confidence and self-esteem.

Characteristics of the Inmate Population in the Prison

To understand the nature of the social groupings inside the prison it is essential to understand the background of the inmate population. Research on female offenders in India has been very limited. One main reason is under-reporting. Further, there is a paucity of literature and empirical data on women lodged in prisons. Women have, historically, comprised a relatively small proportion of criminal population. However, this proportion has been increasing over time putting new demands on the police, courts and correctional facilities. For instance, because of the small number of females in the inmate population, accommodations and programme planning may be more of a challenge than it is for males. A better understanding of the characteristics of female inmates can help policy-makers to decide how to best utilize limited budgets to address the needs of this population. As well, it may help to identify areas for prevention which could reduce the incidence of crimes committed by females.

As stated earlier, this field study was carried out in seven prisons not only for the purpose of comparison of different prisons, but also to describe the variations of inmate behaviors under different institutional settings. There is a wrong assumption that prisoners form a single homogeneous category of law violators. Prisoners belong to different categories, their offences, their backgrounds and circumstances, their age, their awareness all make them different from one another. It is, therefore, essential to understand the socio-economic background of the female prisoners.

STATUS OF PRISONERS—STATE-WISE

TABLE 4.1

State-wise Distribution of Prisoners

Status of Prisoners	*State*			*Total*
	Chandigarh	*Punjab*	*Haryana*	
Under-trial	11 78.6%	75 59.5%	35 58.3%	121 60.5%
Convict	3 21.4%	51 40.5%	25 41.7%	79 39.5%
Total	14	126	60	200

The present study has been undertaken in states of Punjab, Haryana and Union Territory of Chandigarh. There were 14 female inmates from Chandigarh, 126 female prisoners from Punjab and 60 from the state of Haryana, who had been undertaken as a sample for the present study. In Union Territory of Chandigarh, out of 14, 11 were under-trials. In Punjab 59.5 percent, and in Haryana 58.3 percent had the status of under-trials. In all there were 60.5 percent female prisoners who were under-trials and 39.5 percent convicts in all the three places. Findings of the present study indicate that sample drawn is quite close to prison population in the country. NCRB (2006) report shows that the number of under-trial prisoners has increased by 3.4 percent in 2006 over 2005. The percentage of under-trial prisoners to the total prisoners in jails is 65.7 percent in the country and the share of convict prisoners is 31.3 percent.

STATUS OF PRISONERS—PRISON-WISE

Table 4.2
Prison-wise Distribution of Inmates

Status of Prisoner	*Jail*							*Total*
	Burail	*Ludhiana*	*Jalandhar*	*Patiala*	*Amritsar*	*Hissar*	*Ambala*	
Under-trial	11 78.6%	31 49.2%	14 66.7%	12 80.0%	18 66.7%	17 50.0%	18 69.2%	121 60.5%
Convict	3 21.4%	32 50.8%	7 33.3%	3 20.0%	9 33.3%	17 50.0%	8 30.8%	79 39.5%
Total	14	63	21	15	27	34	26	200

There were approximately 61 percent female prisoners who had the status of under-trials in the sample. Maximum under-trials, i.e. 80 percent were from Patiala Central Jail in Punjab followed by 78.60 percent from Burail Modal Jail at Chandigarh. Lowest number of under-trials, i.e. 49.2 percent was from Ludhiana Women Jail. There were approximately 39.5 percent convicts in the sample. Ludhiana and Hissar Jails had half of the population of convicts, i.e. 50 percent each. Lowest convicts, i.e. 20 percent were in Patiala Central Jail in Punjab. The various State Governments have come with an idea of all women's jail to accommodate only women prisoners. These prisons are managed by all women staff, from lowest-level to top position. Since these women jails are newly constructed with a good accommodation for large number of prisoners, they accommodate more number of convicts. District jails in the states serve the purpose of accommodating under-trials.

LENGTH OF STAY IN THE PRISON

Even if it is short, a prison sentence has disastrous effects on women because it seriously disrupts their family life. Since most of the women in the prison are mothers and sole charge of the children, the prison sentence the mother serves affects the children and other members of the family.

The length of time that an inmate has spent in the prison irrespective of their prison status shows the lacunae of our

TABLE 4.3
Distribution of Inmates on the Basis of Length of Stay in the Prison

Since When	*Jail*							*Total*
	Burail	*Ludhiana*	*Jalandhar*	*Patiala*	*Amritsar*	*Hissar*	*Ambala*	
< 1 Yr.	7 50.00%	20 31.70%	9 42.90%	7 46.70%	12 44.40%	11 32.40%	9 34.60%	75 37.50%
1 to 5 Yrs.	6 42.90%	32 50.80%	12 57.10%	7 46.70%	11 40.70%	17 50.00%	15 57.70%	100 50.00%
5 to 10 Yrs.	1 7.10%	11 17.50%		1 6.70%	4 14.80%	6 17.60%	2 7.70%	25 12.50%
Total	14	63	21	15	27	34	26	200

criminal system. There were 25 prisoners who had spent more than 5 year in prison, and there were 75 prisoners who had spend less than one year in the prison. Half of the female prisoners had spent 1 to 5 years in prison, out of which 57.7 percent were from Ambala Central Jail followed by 57.1 percent from Jalandhar Central Jail. Short sentences were more common among prisoners in Burail Jail, while Ludhiana, Hissar and Amritsar jails contained more women with long-term sentences.

TERM OF PUNISHMENT

Available penalties include most severe as capital punishment (death sentence) followed by life imprisonment, imprisonment, forfeiture of property, and fines as the least severe. Under certain circumstances, a person under 21 years of age who is convicted of an offence punishable with a fine or with imprisonment for 7 years or less may be released on probation. A death sentence can be imposed for murder and for specified offences against the State which include waging war against the Government of India, attempting or abetting war or mutiny. Special reasons have to be given for imposing the death penalty. For instance, in addition to the above circumstances, the death penalty can be imposed for abetting the suicide of a child, an insane or delirious person, an idiot, or an intoxicated person. The death penalty can also be imposed when an individual serving a life sentence attempts to murder, even if a non-fatal injury results from the attempt.

TABLE 4.4
Distribution of Inmates on the Basis of Term of Punishment

Term of Punishment	*Jail*							*Total*
	Burail	*Ludhiana*	*Jalandhar*	*Patiala*	*Amritsar*	*Hissar*	*Ambala*	
Not decided as yet	2 14.3%	5 7.9%	3 14.3%	3 20.0%	4 14.8%	2 5.9%	3 11.5%	22 11.0%
< 5 Yrs.	1 7.1%	8 12.7%	3 14.3%	3 20.0%	1 3.7%	1 2.9%	5 19.2%	22 11.0%
5 to 10 Yrs.	2 14.3%	34 54.0%	9 42.9%	1 6.7%	13 48.1%	13 38.2%	7 26.9%	79 39.5%
>10 Yrs.	6 42.9%	11 17.5%	4 19.0%	4 26.7%	4 14.8%	12 35.3%	8 30.8%	49 25.50%
Life/Death Sentence	3 21.4%	5 7.9%	2 9.5%	4 26.7%	5 18.5%	6 17.6%	3 11.5%	28 14.0%
Total	14	63	21	15	27	34	26	200

Out of 14 inmates of Burail Jail, 42.90 percent were imprisoned for more than 10 years. In Ludhiana jail 54 percent of female inmates had been sentenced for 5 to 10 years. Maximum number of inmates had been sentenced for the period of 5 to 10 years. In all the prisons there were 22 cases scattered whose sentence was not decided at the time of study. Out of 28 cases of death sentence/life imprisonment, 11 were awarded death sentence and the remaining 17 life imprisonment. Of 11 cases of capital punishment, it was only in one case from Ambala Central Jail where an inmate had been given death sentence by the Supreme Court. The remaining 10 cases were awarded capital punishment by the lower courts and the convicts had appealed in the higher courts. There were, however, 17 cases of life sentence out of which 3 each were from Burail and Patiala Jails, 5 from Ludhiana Jail, 4 from Hissar Jail, and 1 each from Amritsar and Ambala jails. Findings indicate delayed justice and long period of trials are a part of Indian judicial system. In most of the cases under study term of punishment was decided by the lower court. Women prisoners were however, planning to file cases in the higher court at the time of study since they were not satisfied with the decision of the court.

MARITAL STATUS OF THE INMATES PRIOR TO IMPRISONMENT

A number of researchers have reported that most of women inmates were likely to be unattached at the time of arrest. Garg (2006) reported that married women committed more crime. Borbora *et. al.* (2008) also mentioned that marital status was found to be crucial factor as the majority of the convicted women criminals were found to be married. Whether marriage has anything to do with commission of crime is not conclusively established so far but description of the inmate's martial background, however, always forms a part of the mode of sociological analyses of prison inmates.

For the purpose of analysis marital status has been divided into three main categories viz. never married i.e. single, married, and once married but presently single. The last category included widows, divorced and separated women.

TABLE 4.5
Distribution of Inmates on the Basis of their Marital Status Prior to Imprisonment

Marital Status	*Jail*							*Total*
	Burail	*Ludhiana*	*Jalandhar*	*Patiala*	*Amritsar*	*Hissar*	*Ambala*	
Never married	2 14.3%	12 19.0%	1 4.8%	2 13.3%	2 7.4%	3 8.8%	4 15.4%	26 13.0%
Married	10 71.4%	37 58.7%	16 76.2%	9 53.3%	21 77.8%	25 73.5%	11 46.2%	129 64.5%
Once married, presently single	2 14.3%	14 22.2%	4 19.0%	5 33.3%	4 14.8%	6 17.6%	10 38.5%	45 22.5%
Total	14	63	21	15	27	34	26	200

Most of the inmates were married before coming to prison. The data on the marital status of the inmates revealed that the married women constituted more than half of the inmate's population, i.e. 64.5 percent. Maximum married inmates belonged to Amritsar Central Jail and the least number, i.e. 46.2 percent were in Ambala Central jail. The next largest category was made up of women who were either widows, separated or divorced, i.e. single at the time of study with maximum, i.e. 38.5 percent in Ambala Central jail. Distribution of table shows there were 26 never married single women out of which 12 were in Ludhiana Women jail, followed by 4 in Ambala Central Jail. Out of 10, there were 2 cases of deserted women and 1 of divorcee and 7 of separated women in Ambala Central Jail who had been included under "once married" category. Findings of this study endorses the results of Garg and Borbora *et. al.*

NUMBER OF CHILDREN OF THE INMATES

Presence or absence of children in the family is likely to affect the behaviour of the mother. Research worldwide has shown that both the imprisonment of children with their mothers and their separation from them at an early age, have extremely harmful effects on the children. Thus, the imprisonment of the mother entails punishment for their children as well. Children of incarcerated parents suffer due to social stigma. They face difficulties in adjustment, low self esteem, aggressive behaviour and general emotional dysfunctions. Beck *et. al.* (1993) reported that children of incarcerated parents are five times more likely to land up in prison when they become adults, because of the negative role models. Sociological and Criminological theories point to three prominent ways in which the effects of parental imprisonment on children might be understood. These involve the strains of economic deprivation; the loss of parental socialization through role modeling, support, and supervision; and the stigma and shame of societal labeling.

Those respondents, who were married, were further asked to report the number of children. There were 19 respondents who were married and had no child. Majority of the respondents, i.e. 39 percent had more than 3 children. There was 23.5 percent respondent who had two children. In Burail Jail, 42.90 percent of the respondents had two children. In Ludhiana

TABLE 4.6
Distribution of the Number of Children of the Inmates

Number of Children	*Jail*							*Total*
	Burail	*Ludhiana*	*Jalandhar*	*Patiala*	*Amritsar*	*Hissar*	*Ambala*	
Not Applicable	2 14.3%	12 19.0%	1 4.8%	2 13.3%	2 7.4%	3 8.8%	4 15.4%	26 13.0%
Up to 2	6 42.9%	13 20.6%	5 23.8%	3 20.0%	11 40.7%	5 14.7%	4 15.4%	47 23.5%
3	3 21.4%	4 6.3%	3 14.3%	4 26.7%	4 14.8%	6 17.6%	6 23.1%	30 15.0%
> 3	3 21.4%	27 42.9%	7 33.3%	5 33.3%	9 33.3%	17 50.0%	10 38.5%	78 39.0%
No Child	0 0%	7 11.1%	5 23.8%	1 6.7%	1 3.7%	3 8.8%	2 7.7%	19 9.5%
Total	14	63	21	15	27	34	26	200

jail, 20.6 percent had two children and 42.90 percent had more than three children. In Patiala Jail, 33.3 percent inmates had more than three children. In Hissar Jail, 50 percent of the inmates had more than three children. In Ambala Jail also maximum number of inmates had more than three children. Majority of inmates in the sample had children and they were staying with them before their arrest. Imprisonment was disrupting their family life and producing anxiety for both mothers and children.

SEX OF THE INMATE'S CHILDREN

In the patriarchal society like India, greater importance is given to the male child. The high female foeticide reinforces the sex preferences prevalent in our society. Since daughters are considered to be the reflection of the mother, it is essential to know whether presence of female child in the family affects their criminal behaviour or not. The problems of children differ according to the sex of the child. Hagan and Dinovitzer (1999) noted that children of incarcerated mothers in which 40 percent of the boys aged between 12 to 17 were delinquents, while the rate of teenage pregnancy was 60 percent.

TABLE 4.7
Distribution of the Sex of Children of the Inmates

Sex of Children	*Jail*							*Total*
	Burail	*Ludhiana*	*Jalandhar*	*Patiala*	*Amritsar*	*Hissar*	*Ambala*	
Not Applicable	2 14.3%	19 30.2%	6 28.6%	3 20.0%	3 11.1%	6 17.6%	6 23.1%	45 22.5%
Only Male	3 21.4%	7 11.1%	1 4.8%	1 6.7%	2 7.4%	2 5.9%	0 0.0%	16 8.0%
Only Female	3 21.4%	2 3.2%	2 9.5%	2 13.3%	3 11.1%	2 5.9%	1 3.8%	15 7.5%
Both	6 42.9%	35 55.6%	12 57.1%	9 60.0%	19 70.4%	24 70.6%	19 73.1%	124 62.0%
Total	14	63	21	15	27	34	26	200

The inmates were asked to specify the sex of the children. Majority of the respondents, i.e. 62 percent had children of both the sexes. In Burail Jail 42.90 percent respondents had children of both the sexes and 21.40 percent respondents had male children and equal number of the respondents had only female children. In Ludhiana Jail 11.10 percent of respondents had only male children, whereas in Jalandhar Jail 9.50 percent of respondents had only female children. In Patiala Jail 13.30 percent of respondents had only female children and similarly in Amritsar Jail also more inmates had only female children. Such a distribution clearly indicates that women indulge in criminal behaviour without realizing the repercussions of their behaviour on their female children.

AGE OF THE INMATE'S CHILDREN

Age of the child is a very significant variable. Absence of parents especially mother results in different problems for children at different age groups. Fuller (1993) reported that disruption of the adjustment bond between mother and child is particularly deleterious between ages of 6 months and 4 years. Adolescent children, however, develop delinquent behaviour and there are often complaints of poor school performance, truancy, use of drugs or alcohol (Dressel and Barnhill, 1994). A number of children display post traumatic stress disorders namely depression, feelings of anger and guilt, flash backs about their mother's crime or arrest, and the experience of hearing their mother's voice (Hagan and Dinovitzer, 1999).

TABLE 4.8

Distribution of the Age of the Inmate's Children

Age of the Children	*Jail*							*Total*
	Burail	*Ludhiana*	*Jalandhar*	*Patiala*	*Amritsar*	*Hissar*	*Ambala*	
Not Applicable	2 14.3%	19 30.2%	6 28.6%	3 20.0%	3 11.1%	6 17.6%	6 23.1%	45 22.5%
Very Small	1 7.1%	2 3.2%	3 14.3%	1 6.7%	1 3.7%	1 2.9%	1 3.8%	10 5.0%
Small	2 14.3%	8 12.7%	1 4.8%	1 6.7%	6 22.2%	6 17.6%	1 3.8%	25 12.5%
Adolescents	3 21.4%	5 7.9%	5 23.8%	5 33.3%	4 14.8%	7 20.6%	9 34.6%	38 19.0%
Adults	3 21.4%	9 14.3%	3 14.3%	1 6.7%	4 14.8%	5 14.7%	1 3.8%	26 13.0%
Mixed	3 21.4%	20 31.7%	3 14.3%	4 26.7%	9 33.3%	9 26.5%	8 30.8%	56 28.0%
Total	14	63	21	15	27	34	26	200

For the purpose of analysis, the children of incarcerated mothers have been divided into five categories on the basis of their age. The first category included children of less than 5 years of age labeled as 'very small'. Children in the age group of 6 to 10 years have been included in the second category as 'small children'. Children in the age group of 11 to 19 years have been included in the third category of 'adolescents'. Those who were above 20 years of age have been treated as 'adults' and have been included in the fourth category. The fifth category is of the 'mixed' age groups where children from very young to small to adolescents and to adults have been grouped.

Age of the children plays an important role because responsibility of taking care of younger children lies with the mother and many a times inmates bring their small children to the prison. The authorities allow only children younger than 6 years to stay with their mothers. Children above 6 years remain away from their mothers. During incarcerated period their lives are disrupted. Maximum number of inmates with 'very small' children were in Jalandhar jail, and maximum number of inmates with 'small children' were in Amritsar jail. A large number of women inmates in Patiala jail had only 'adolescent' children. Burail jail inmates had maximum 'adult' children followed by inmates of Amritsar, Ludhiana and Jalandhar jail. Majority of inmates, i.e. 28 percent were in the mixed category. They had children of all age groups ranging from very small to adolescents to adults. Very few inmates, i.e. 5 percent had very young children, and 13 percent inmates had adult children only. There were however, 45 respondents who did not have any child out of which 26 were single and 19 were married but had no child.

LODGING OF THE INMATE'S CHILDREN

Recently, a lot of research is being carried out on the children of female offenders in the prison. Chatto Raj (2000) stated the miserable conditions of children who were staying in prisons along with their mothers and suffered due to seclusion

TABLE 4.9
Stay of the Inmate's Children

Children Stay	*Jail*							*Total*
	Burail	*Ludhiana*	*Jalandhar*	*Patiala*	*Amritsar*	*Hissar*	*Ambala*	
Not Applicable	2 14.3%	19 30.2%	6 28.6%	3 20.0%	3 11.1%	6 17.6%	6 23.1%	45 22.5%
In Prison	0 0.0%	3 4.8%	3 14.3%	0 0.0%	2 7.4%	6 17.6%	1 3.8%	15 7.5%
With Husband	5 35.7%	17 27.0%	7 33.3%	3 20.0%	11 40.7%	4 11.8%	6 23.1%	53 26.5%
With Others	5 35.7%	12 19.0%	1 4.8%	5 33.3%	6 22.2%	10 29.4%	7 26.9%	46 23.0%
On their own	2 14.3%	12 19.0%	4 19.0%	4 26.7%	5 18.5%	8 23.5%	6 23.1%	41 20.5%
Total	14	63	21	15	27	34	26	200

from the normal familial environment. Other studies have shown that children of male prisoners tend to stay in the care of their mother whilst their fathers serve a prison term, whereas the children of female prisoners frequently end up in the care of immediate or extended family (Gabel, 1992; Sheridan, 1996; Healy *et. al.*, 1999).

An attempt was made to explore the whereabouts of the inmate's children. In the present study, there were only 15 inmates whose children were in prison out of which 6 children were in the Hissar jail, 3 each in Ludhiana and Jalandhar jail, 2 in Amritsar and 1 in Ambala jail. Of these 15 children, 2 children were infants, i.e. less than one year of age. They were with their grandmothers who were being imprisoned for burning their daughter-in-laws for dowry. Although very few children were staying with their mothers and grandmothers, they continued to suffer without any fault of their. Just how the problem of imprisoned women is related to their children and how it should be addressed are not easy questions to answer. There is no prison system in the world that has found a satisfactory answer to the problem of the children accompanying their mother to prison. There were 53 children who were staying with their fathers. In the absence of their mothers, their father had taken the responsibility of care takers for their children. The results do not endorse the findings of Gabel and Schindledecker (1993) who found that approximately 75 percent of the children of imprisoned mothers were cared for by the women's parents or other relatives, with less than 10 percent cared for by husband's and 15 percent by friends or in foster homes. In 46 cases children were taken care of by extended kins, i.e. paternal/maternal grandparents, uncles/aunts or friends. There were 41 children who had no one to care for. Majority of the inmates in the Ludhiana women jail had children with no one to care for. They were left to fend for themselves. These children were staying alone mainly because neither of the parents was available. Their mothers were in the prison for murdering their fathers.

PRESENT MARITAL STATUS OF INMATES

Most of the respondents were married before being lodged

TABLE 4.10
Distribution of Inmates on the Basis of their Marital Status during Imprisonment

Present marital status	*Jail*							*Total*
	Burail	*Ludhiana*	*Jalandhar*	*Patiala*	*Amritsar*	*Hissar*	*Ambala*	
Never married	2 14.3%	12 19.0%	1 4.8%	2 13.3%	2 7.4%	3 8.8%	4 15.4%	26 13.0%
Married	6 42.9%	32 50.8%	12 57.1%	8 53.3%	20 74.1%	24 70.6%	10 38.5%	112 56.0%
Once married, presently single	6 42.9%	19 30.2%	8 38.1%	5 33.3%	5 18.5%	7 20.6%	12 46.2%	62 31.0%
Total	14	63	21	15	27	34	26	200

in the prison. The number of married women decreased from 64.5 percent to 56 percent during imprisonment. Bhadauria and Mathur (1981) investigated the effects of long detention before trial. One of the effects was marital dissolution. Men were deserted by their wives once they were imprisoned. If this is the situation with regard to men, we can understand the fate of women inmates as their chances of desertion are likely to be much more. The increase in the number of divorced, separated and deserted women suggests that stigma gets attached to women who are imprisoned. Men are not ready to continue their marital life with the women who have been imprisoned. Such a trend was seen in all the prisons. Further, the number of singles in all the prisons remained same which reinforces the idea that women who are imprisoned get labeled and it becomes difficult for them to get married. Further, interaction between male and female prisoners was not allowed in the prison premises. As such chances of getting married while staying in prison were minimal.

EDUCATION OF THE INMATES

Education not only widens the horizon but also facilitates in developing rational outlook towards life. The role of education in preventing persons from falling an easy prey to criminality is well known but crime in the 21st century has become far more complex phenomenon and there has emerged a new class of educated offenders all over the world, including India. Ahuja (2006) indicated that 79 percent female criminals were illiterate and 11 percent could read and write though they had no formal education and 10 percent had some school education. Fassaei and Kendall (2001) using official data in Iran prisons reported that compared to general population, imprisoned women are likely to be uneducated and illiterate. Kim *et. al.* (2007) reported that over half of incarcerated women in South Korea prisons did not complete school education. Borbora *et. al.* (2008) on the basis of their study of women criminals in Assam mentioned that majority of women came from very low educational background. Keeping this in mind, relationship between education and presence of inmates in different prisons has been looked into.

TABLE 4.11
Distribution of Inmates Based on their Education

Education Status	*Jail*							*Total*
	Burail	*Ludhiana*	*Jalandhar*	*Patiala*	*Amritsar*	*Hissar*	*Ambala*	
Illiterate	7 50.0%	18 28.6%	15 71.4%	11 73.3%	15 55.6%	27 79.4%	11 42.3%	104 52.0%
Up to 10+2	4 28.6%	35 55.6%	5 23.8%	4 26.7%	11 40.7%	6 17.6%	8 30.8%	73 36.5%
Graduate	1 7.1%	9 14.3%	1 4.8%	0.0%	1 3.7%	1 2.9%	5 19.2%	18 9.0%
Post Graduate/ Professional	2 14.3%	1 1.6%	0 0.0%	0 0.0%	0 0.0%	0 0.0%	2 7.7%	5 2.5%
Total	14	63	21	15	27	34	26	200

The actual educational qualification of the inmates prior to their current inmate status in prison is shown in the Table 4.11. The illiterate inmates constituted more than half of the inmate's population, i.e. 52 percent. There were 36.5 percent respondents who were educated up to high school. There were only 5 inmates, i.e. 2.5 percent, who were highly qualified. In Burail Jail at Chandigarh there were three respondents one each in the category of Graduate, Post Graduate/Professionals. Such a scenario indicates that women who did not belong to educated segment of the society were lodged in prisons. The findings somehow confirm the notion that under the present system of crime detection and criminal justice, apprehension at the hands of the police and subsequent conviction at the hands of the judges, the educated women for the best known reasons, escape punishment. Only the poor, the resources less and illiterate almost always get caught and are condemned to prison incarceration. The results are congruent to Ahuja, Fassaei and Kendall, Kim *et. al.* and Borbora *et. al.*

OCCUPATION OF THE INMATES

Occupation is an important indicator of a person's position in society. In most of the societies around the world men have taken up the role of provider and women act as the housekeeper. It is argued that since housewives are perceived to contribute less to the family's subsistence, consequently they are less valued. Changing scenario especially deteriorating economic conditions are pushing women to the brink faster than men. As the primary caretakers of children, women may be driven by poverty to engage in more crimes, for survival. Most of these women are unemployed or with few marketable job skills. Hampton (1993) outlined the data from New South Wales in Australia that majority of women prisoners were unemployed at the time of arrest. Persistent unemployment often creates a sense of despair and can provoke angry expression, including crime. Keeping this in mind an effort was made to know the occupational status of the women lodged in prisons. For the purpose of analysis occupation has been divided into five main categories viz. housewives and/or unemployed; menial occupations that included maids, servants, daily wage labourers, etc., middle level occupations including school teachers, clerks, nurses, etc., professionals, and miscellaneous that included singers, sex workers, folk dancers, thieves, etc.

Majority of the inmates were housewives, i.e. they were not engaged in outside paid work. Results coincide with the findings of Hampton (1993). There were 34 percent respondents

TABLE 4.12
Distribution of Inmates Based on their Occupation

Occupation	Jail							Total
	Burail	Ludhiana	Jalandhar	Patiala	Amritsar	Hissar	Ambala	
Housewife/ Unemployed	2 14.3%	38 60.3%	9 42.9%	5 33.3%	15 55.6%	21 61.8%	11 42.3%	101 50.5%
Menial	7 50.0%	14 22.2%	8 38.1%	7 46.7%	11 40.7%	11 32.4%	10 38.5%	68 34.0%
Middle	1 7.1%	6 9.5%	0 0.0%	0 0.0%	0 0.0%	1 2.9%	1 3.8%	9 4.5%
Professional	1 7.1%	0 0.0%	0 0.0%	0 0.0%	0 0.0%	0 0.0%	0 0.0%	1 0.5%
Miscellaneous	3 21.4%	5 7.9%	4 19.0%	3 20.0%	1 3.7%	1 2.9%	4 15.4%	21 10.5%
Total	14	63	21	15	27	34	26	200

who were engaged in menial types of occupation. In Burail Jail 50 percent of respondents were engaged in menial types of occupation. Findings indicate that majority of the inmates were not working, and most of the working women were engaged in menial types of jobs. There were 10.5 percent of the inmates who have been grouped under miscellaneous types of occupation. They were in sex trade, worked as troupe dancers, folk singers, even as thieves as they belonged to notified criminal tribes. In Ludhiana Jail there were 3 respondents who reported that they were from Sansi tribe engaged in stealing. One respondent from Jalandhar Jail and 3 from Patiala Jail also mentioned stealing as their occupation. There were in all 7 respondents who stated that they were sex workers, one each from Burail Jail, Ludhiana and Jalandhar, Amritsar and Hissar, and 2 cases belonged to Ambala Jail. All these respondents were grouped under miscellaneous category. There was only one case of Doctor in the sample that belonged to Burail jail.

RELIGION OF THE INMATES

It is believed that religion is instrumental in preaching, developing and maintaining morality in people. It influences the behaviour of an individual and refrains him/her from following the path of immoral behaviour. The question arises as to why some people take up wrong course in life? Is it that for them religion carries no meaning or that they make a distinction between practice and preaching? Borbora *et. al.* (2008) found a close relationship between religious dogmas and criminal behaviour as many convicts were imprisoned for brutally killing victims through witchcraft.

TABLE 4.13

Distribution of Inmates Based on their Religion

Religion	*Jail*							*Total*
	Burail	*Ludhiana*	*Jalandhar*	*Patiala*	*Amritsar*	*Hissar*	*Ambala*	
Hindu	8 57.1%	19 30.2%	10 47.6%	6 40.0%	8 29.6%	30 88.2%	13 50.0%	94 47.0%
Sikh	4 28.6%	38 60.3%	7 33.3%	6 40.0%	18 66.7%	4 11.8%	7 26.9%	84 42.0%
Muslim	1 7.1%	4 6.3%	2 9.5%	—	1 3.7%	—	4 15.4%	12 6.0%
Any other	1 7.1%	2 3.2%	2 9.5%	3 20.0%	—	—	2 7.7%	10 5.0%
Total	14	63	21	15	27	34	26	200

Table 4.13 shows the distribution of respondents according to their religion. There were 47 percent of the respondents who were Hindus, followed by 42 percent Sikhs and 6 percent Muslims. Maximum number of Muslim respondents was in Ambala jail followed by 9.5 percent in Jalandhar jail. Maximum number of respondents belonging to Sikh religion was from the Ludhiana Jail. Punjab is a Sikh dominating state. There were 10 cases who have been included under 'any other' category as they mentioned that they believed in different sects like Radhasoami, Nirankaris, Deras, etc.

CASTE OF THE INMATES

Indian caste system is based on hierarchical gradations which incorporates ascribed lower and upper social positions to people. Various studies have established relationship between violence and caste in rural areas. It is important to mention here that caste though an important variable in Indian criminality has no genetic specificity for one's vulnerability to commit crimes. It only relates to sub-culture of violence which certain criminal tribes and caste share as matter of family tradition. Ahuja (1969) observed that crime rate was low in the lower caste groups. Pandey (2004) on the other hand found that majority of women prisoners belonged to the lower caste.

TABLE 4.14

Distribution of Inmates Based on their Caste

Caste	*Jail*							*Total*
	Burail	*Ludhiana*	*Jalandhar*	*Patiala*	*Amritsar*	*Hissar*	*Ambala*	
Upper	3 21.4%	6 9.5%	1 4.8%	1 6.7%	2 7.4%	1 2.9%	2 7.7%	16 8.0%
Middle	4 28.6%	15 23.8%	3 14.3%	4 26.7%	7 25.9%	10 29.4%	7 26.9%	50 25.0%
Backward	2 14.3%	17 27.0%	5 23.8%	1 6.7%	4 14.8%	6 17.6%	6 23.1%	41 20.5%
Lower	5 35.7%	25 39.7%	12 57.1%	9 60.0%	14 51.9%	17 50.0%	11 42.3%	93 46.5%
Total	14	63	21	15	27	34	26	200

Caste is an important indicator of status in an Indian set-up. Caste and class many a time coexists. For the purpose of analysis the respondents have been divided into four main caste categories, i.e. upper, middle, backward and lower caste. It is believed that lower the caste lower the class, higher will be the crime. Such a view was found to be true in the present study. Results indicate that maximum women lodged in the prisons belonged to lower caste. There was less number of women from upper caste who were in the prisons. In Ludhiana Women Jail and Jalandhar Central Jail, the numbers of women prisoners increased as we moved down the caste hierarchy. In Burail Jail at Chandigarh, Patiala, Ambala, Amritsar and Hissar Jails, fairly large number of women belonged to middle categories of caste groups. Results indicate that there is an over representation of the backward and lower caste respondents in the prisons under study. The results of this study are aligned with the findings of Pandey but not with Ahuja.

AGE OF THE INMATES

Criminological research tells that young people are the most likely group to commit crimes (Blumstein *et. al.* 1985; Gottfredson and Hirschi, 1990). As people age they tend to commit fewer crimes. Ahuja (1969) showed that out of 325 offenders 5.7 percent female offenders were very young (below 16 years of age), 52.8 percent were young (16-30 years of age), 35.8 percent were middle aged (30-50 years of age) and 5.7 percent were old (above 50 years of age).

TABLE 4.15
Age-wise Distribution of Inmates

Age	*Jail*							*Total*
	Burail	*Ludhiana*	*Jalandhar*	*Patiala*	*Amritsar*	*Hissar*	*Ambala*	
Up to 18 Yrs.	0	3	0	0	2	1	0	6
	0.0%	4.8%	0.0%	0.0%	7.4%	2.9%	0.0%	3.0%
18 to 25 Yrs.	3	14	2	4	1	7	5	36
	21.4%	22.2%	9.5%	26.7%	3.7%	20.6%	19.2%	18.0%
25 to 35 Yrs.	2	9	2	0	7	6	4	30
	14.3%	14.3%	9.5%	0.0%	25.9%	17.6%	15.4%	15.0%
35 to 45 Yrs.	4	18	11	5	6	6	6	56
	28.6%	28.6%	52.4%	33.3%	22.2%	17.6%	23.1%	28.0%
45 to 55 Yrs.	5	11	5	5	9	8	9	52
	35.7%	17.5%	23.8%	33.3%	33.3%	23.5%	34.6%	26.0%
55 + Yrs.	0	8	1	1	2	6	2	20
	0.0%	12.7%	4.8%	6.7%	7.4%	17.6%	7.7%	10.0%
Total	14	63	21	15	27	34	26	200

Findings show that, inmates were found in the age group of 18 to 55+ years. There were 3 inmates of up to 18 years in Ludhiana Jail, 2 in Amritsar Central Jail and 1 in Hissar Jail. All these inmates were unmarried. In Burial Jail the inmates ranged from 18 to 55 years. In Ludhiana Jail the inmates were found in all the age groups of up to 18 to 55+ years. The maximum numbers of respondents were in 35 to 45 years age category. In Jalandhar the inmates were from 18 to 55+ years. In Patiala Jail 4 inmates were in the 18 to 25 years, 11 cases in 35 to 55 years category. In Amritsar less than 18 to 55+ year there were 27 inmates. In Hissar Jail and Ambala Jail maximum inmates were in the age group of 45 to 55 years. In these prison inmates were involved in dowry-related offences. That is why many aged women who were mothers-in-law were in the prison. Out of 200 respondents, majority were in 35 to 45 years age category followed closely by 45 to 55 years. Such a scenario indicates that female criminality is related to middle age since maximum number of female prisons in the present study were found in the age group of 35 to 55 years. Such results do not endorse the findings of those researchers who reported that young people commit most of the crimes.

BACKGROUND OF THE INMATES

Poor housing often amplifies poor parental supervision, marital disharmony, inconsistent care, poor nutrition, poor schooling and thus greatly increases the risk of turning to crime. Further, it is important to know whether the inmates were from large metropolitan and other urban area or rural background in order to assess accurately the kinds of environmental factors to which they must adjust when they return to the society. Therefore an attempt was made to know the residential background of the women inmates.

TABLE 4.16
Inmate's Background

Background	*Jail*							*Total*
	Burail	*Ludhiana*	*Jalandhar*	*Patiala*	*Amritsar*	*Hissar*	*Ambala*	
Rural	5 35.7%	28 44.4%	14 66.7%	8 53.3%	18 66.7%	27 79.4%	10 38.5%	110 55.0%
Urban	9 64.3%	35 55.6%	7 33.3%	7 46.7%	9 33.3%	7 20.6%	16 61.5%	90 45.0%
Total	14	63	21	15	27	34	26	200

In Table 4.16, accurate information is presented of each inmate's residential background. The vast majority were from rural areas, i.e. 79.40 percent from Hissar Jail, 66.70 percent each from Jalandhar and Amritsar Central Jail. There were 90 respondents who belonged to urban background. Maximum inmates were housed in Burail jail which is located in urban area. Such distribution highlights over-representation of women in prisons from rural background.

COMPOSITION AND SIZE OF THE INMATE'S FAMILY

In poor communities, spousal unions are fragile and extended kin are important. It is often the extended kin who come to the rescue of the inmates after their arrest. It is for this reason it is essential to know the family composition of the inmates.

TABLE 4.17
Distribution of Inmate's Family Composition

Family Composition	*Jail*							*Total*
	Burail	*Ludhiana*	*Jalandhar*	*Patiala*	*Amritsar*	*Hissar*	*Ambala*	
Nuclear	11 78.6%	30 47.6%	16 76.2%	8 53.3%	16 59.3%	18 52.9%	16 61.5%	115 57.5%
Joint/Extended	2 14.3%	26 41.3%	3 14.3%	7 46.7%	10 37.0%	15 44.1%	10 38.5%	73 36.5%
Alone	1 7.1%	7 11.1%	2 9.5%	—	1 3.7%	1 2.9%	—	12 6.0%
Total	14	63	21	15	27	34	26	200

To provide a more complete picture of the inmate's home situation, an attempt was made to investigate the family composition and family size. In-spite of the fact that most of the respondents belonged to rural background, it was found that most of the respondents belonged to nuclear household. Maximum respondents from the nuclear family were lodged in Burail and Jalandhar Jails. There were 12 cases of respondents who were staying alone. Maximum respondents, i.e. 11.1 percent, who were staying alone, belonged to Ludhiana Jail.

TABLE 4.18
Distribution of Inmate's Family Size

Family Size	*Jail*							*Total*
	Burail	*Ludhiana*	*Jalandhar*	*Patiala*	*Amritsar*	*Hissar*	*Ambala*	
Small (4)	7 50.0%	17 27.0%	7 33.3%	2 13.3%	7 25.9%	7 20.6%	2 7.7%	49 24.50%
Medium (6)	4 28.6%	24 38.1%	10 47.6%	10 66.7%	13 48.1%	9 26.5%	11 42.3%	81 40.5%
Large (10)	3 21.4%	16 25.4%	3 14.3%	3 20.0%	5 18.5%	15 44.1%	12 46.2%	57 28.5%
Very Large (10+)	—	6 9.5%	1 4.8%	—	2 7.4%	3 8.8%	1 3.8%	13 6.5%
Total	14	63	21	15	27	34	26	200

Presence of more children puts a lot of stress on the limited resources of the family. Family plays an important role in socialization of the child. Sociological and Criminological theories commonly emphasize the importance of parental supervision, role modeling and support. Lack of parental supervision, parental rejection and parent-child involvement are consistent indicators of delinquent behaviour. Parenting that features inconsistent, incoherent, overly punitive or too permissive methods of discipline also increase the risk of delinquency. Ineffective parenting encourages youth to associate with peers who are involved in criminal activities. Thus, there is a direct relationship between the size of family and criminal behaviour. Parents in large families fail to provide individual attention to each and every child. For these parents survival is more important, thus resulting in neglect of the child. Most of the respondents came from families with 5-6 members. Only 24.50 percent were from small families. There were also respondents who had very large family size. They were in Ludhiana, Jalandhar, Amritsar, Hissar and Ambala Jails.

EMPLOYMENT STATUS OF THE HEAD OF INMATE'S FAMILY

Employment status of the head of the family gives an idea

TABLE 4.19
Distribution of the Inmates Based on the Employment Status of the Head of the Family

Employment status of the Head of inmate's family	*Jail*							*Total*
	Burail	*Ludhiana*	*Jalandhar*	*Patiala*	*Amritsar*	*Hissar*	*Ambala*	
Full Time	2 14.3%	25 39.7%	6 28.6%	6 40.0%	9 33.3%	9 26.5%	12 46.2%	69 34.5%
Part Time	5 35.7%	26 41.3%	9 42.9%	6 40.0%	11 40.7%	18 52.9%	10 38.5%	85 42.5%
Disabled/ Retired/ Unemployed	7 50.0%	12 19.0%	6 28.6%	3 20.0%	7 25.9%	7 20.6%	4 15.4%	46 23.0%
Total	14	63	21	15	27	34	26	200

about the economic condition of the inmate's family. Economic factor is an important cause for opting criminal lifestyle. There were 34.5 percent of the inmates whose heads of the household were engaged in full time jobs. In majority of the cases, i.e. 42.5 percent, the heads of the household were engaged in part-time job. Most of these inmates belonged to Hissar jail. In the Burail Jail 35.7 percent of head of inmate's family were employed part time. It is only in Ambala Jail that more members were employed full time and less were employed part time. There were 23 percent cases where the head of the household was not working. A few of them were old enough to work or find a job. Others were disabled and some never wanted to work. The overall picture indicates that majority of the respondents belonged to poor economic background, where the burden of fulfilling the family obligations rested with the inmates.

TOTAL FAMILY INCOME OF THE INMATES

Though the traditional explanation that poverty breeds crime had been rejected by the Criminologists as a major explanation of criminality in the rich countries, the contention still holds good in the context of the large majority of offenders in India who go to prison. In the context of the present study, it was clear that poverty appeared quite a significant factor to be reckoned with.

Table 4.20
Distribution of the Inmates Based on their Total Family Income

Total Family Income	Jail							Total
	Burail	Ludhiana	Jalandhar	Patiala	Amritsar	Hissar	Ambala	
Up to Rs. 5000 p.m.	6 42.9%	36 57.1%	15 71.4%	10 66.7%	16 59.3%	21 61.8%	12 46.2%	116 58.0%
Rs. 5000 to 10000 p.m.	5 35.7%	15 23.8%	5 23.8%	4 26.7%	9 33.3%	7 20.6%	12 46.2%	57 28.5%
Rs. 10000 to 15000 p.m.	2 14.3%	6 9.5%	1 4.8%	—	—	4 11.8%	1 3.8%	14 7.0%
> Rs. 15000 p.m.	1 7.1%	6 9.5%	—	1 6.7%	2 7.4%	2 5.9%	1 3.8%	7 3.5%
Total	14	63	21	15	27	34	26	200

Total family income highlights the socio-economic status of the respondents. Income is inversely related to the crime. Higher the income lesser the number of respondents, and lower the income more is the number of respondents. Many researchers propagated that poverty forces individual to indulge in anti-social activities. As stated by Tonry (1997) that whilst there is a clear relationship between socio-economic disadvantage and crime, 'that not all disadvantaged groups exhibit high crime rates'. As any reasonable person would acknowledge, this suggests that whilst socio-economic disadvantage is a strong predicator of criminal activity, other factors also influence criminality. In the present study, more than 50 percent of the respondents whose total family income was less than Rs. 5000 per month were in Ludhiana Jail, 71.4 percent in Jalandhar Central Jail and 66.70 percent in Patiala Jail. There were 7.1 percent of respondents in Burail Jail whose family income was above Rs. 15000 per month. Majority of the respondents belonged to the lower strata. Findings indicate that women who were lodged in prisons belonged to the households with meager assets and heavier familial liabilities.

CONCLUSION

The present analysis covering several dimensions of social, demographic and economic background of the inmate population unmistakably reveals that a large proportion of women prisoners consist of under-trials, married women with familial responsibility of children (77.5 percent). Most of the imprisoned women belonged to the age group of 35 to 55 years which indicates that there were more aged women in the prison. Adults under age group of 25 represented only 21 percent. More than half of the inmates were illiterate. Majority of them were not engaged in any productive work outside the home. Those who were employed had menial types of occupations at their disposal. Women belonging to lower class backgrounds represented a good number of incarcerated women. Additionally, poor economic background and large family size were other important characteristics of women prisoners. The culture of poverty along with other socio-environmental factors played a significant role in putting these women behind bars. After getting a profile of the women lodged in prison, criminal background of the inmates has been discussed in the next chapter.

5

Types of Crime

There is little agreement, even among specialties, about the definition of "Crime" although it is essential to a scientific approach that a precise conception of the subject under examination be understood, even through its basic assumptions by their definition impose limitations and procedural restrictions for its investigation. The fact that the meaning of "Crime" is open to so many interpretations has led inevitably to claims and counter claims by specialists dealing with differing realms within Criminology. Much of the confusion arises from the fact that the vantage points from which specialists, Sociologists, lawyers, Psychiatrists, social workers and Criminologists view crime, differ and therefore their fundamental conceptions of what crime is, or should be, also differ.

In common usage "Crime" is referred to as "multitude of sins". It includes acts that are proscribed by law, acts that deviate from the imperatives of various ethical systems and innumerable other forms of human behaviors that, at one time or another and in some guise, appear to some persons and by some standard to represent improper behavior.

In the border sense, crime refers to certain acts that are legally defined as crimes, for example, although they do not include positive forms of action, but rather constitute a future to act on occasions when the law insists upon a certain standard of performance.

Italian Criminologist Francesco Carrarra noted that crime constitutes "not action . . . but infraction". Behavior defined as "failure to act" can of course be analyzed in essentially the same manner as other forms of action, since failure to behave in a prescribed way includes selection of a course of action other than the required pattern.

It is apparent that although crime is a condition that all men seem to recognize, but it is not easy to formulate definition of crime. Since a diverse and wide range of behavior is included in the category of crime because of the increasing realization, however, that crime refers to a great variety of behaviors. Criminologists have in recent years turned their attention to the study of particulars types of crime.

Criminologists have constructed and utilized various kinds of classification and typologies of crime and criminals. The task, however, has not been an easy one. The most commonly used classifications and typologies have been the legalistic, individualistic and social.

LEGALISTIC CLASSIFICATION

The oldest and still the most frequently used forms of classification are based on the legal definition of the offence. A familiar legalistic classification is in terms of the seriousness of the offence as indicated by the kind of punishment provided for the behavior. The most serious offences are called felonies and are usually punishable by confinement in prison for life or by death. The less serious offences are called misdemeanors and are usually punishable by fines or confinement in prison for a limited time.

It is common to identify the criminal act in terms of a legal category. Thus criminals are referred to as murderers, burglars, robbers, embezzlers and rapists in terms of specific offences defined in the criminal code. The category of crimes against the person includes such illegal acts as murder, assault and rape, crimes against property include burglary, larceny, forgery and automobile theft, and crime against public order consist of such behaviors as prostitution, gambling, drunkenness, disturbing the peace and the use of narcotics.

Critique

This method of classifying criminals suffers from a number of disadvantages. For example :

1. It tells nothing about the person and the circumstances associated with the offence nor does it consider the social context of the criminal act.
2. It creates a false impression of specialization by implying that criminals confine themselves to the kind of crime for which they happen to be caught or convicted.
3. The legal definition of a criminal act varies according to time and place, the legal classification of crime presents problems for comparative analysis.

INDIVIDUALISTIC CLASSIFICATIONS

Those who belong to this school of thought relate criminal behavior to individuals. Lombroso (1835-1909) for example, identified to his satisfaction at least, a "born criminal" with a unique and inferior physique. Later, Lombroso recognized other types of criminals, including :

1. The insane criminal,
2. The criminal by passion, and
3. The occasional criminal, a type which emphasized the social aspects of the offender as well as individualistic characteristics.

Garofalo (1852-1934) maintained that criminals are characterized by psychological anomalies. He divided these defectives into four categories:

1. Typical criminals or murderers who kill for enjoyment.
2. Violent criminals.

3. Criminals deficient in pity and probity, and
4. Lascivious criminals.

In a not too different fashion, Ferri (1856-1929) distinguished between five types of criminals, namely:

1. The insane,
2. The born,
3. The habitual,
4. The occasional, and
5. The passionate.

Criminal Psychologists and Psychiatrists have attempted to classify criminal offenders by utilizing either a single personality trait or a syndrome or grouping of traits. Accordingly, criminal offenders have been grouped according to whether they are "immature", "emotionally insecure", "dependent", "hostile", "anti-social", "non-conformists", or "aggressive". Sometimes a single treat has been used to apply to a variety of criminal careers differing in both the nature and the seriousness of the activity. Consequently, personality trait syndromes by themselves have little meaning for distinguishing either type of criminal careers on the behavior of criminals from non-criminals who also may have these traits. Individualistic classifications have limited diagnostic possibilities for treatment as they have little utility for the construction of Sociological theories of criminal behavior.

TYPOLOGIES BASED ON SOCIAL BEHAVIOR SYSTEM

If crime is to be studied as a social phenomenon, it is necessary to delineate types of criminal behavior according to the social context of the criminal offender and the criminal act.

Mayhew and Moreau proposed criminal types based on the way in which crime is related to the various activities of the criminal. Mayhew distinguished between professional criminals who earn their living through criminal activity and accidental offenders who commit criminal acts as a result of unanticipated circumstances. Moreau added one another type of "habitual criminal" who continues to commit criminal acts for such diverse reasons as deficiency in intelligence and lack of self-control.

Lindesmith and Dunham (1941) devised a continuum of criminal behavior ranging from the individualized criminal to the social criminal. The criminal acts of the individualized criminal are committed for diverse and personal reasons with the behaviors finding little cultural support. The criminal behavior of the social criminal on the other hand, are supported and prescribed by group norms. The social criminal through has criminal behavior achieves status and recognition within a group.

Gibbons and Garrity (1963) suggested that a significant difference between criminals is the chronological age at which the offender is defined by the society as a criminal. They expressed these differences as a dichotomy :

1. that group of offenders defined as criminals from the time of their first criminal act, and
2. that group of offenders not defined as criminal until late in life, through committing criminal acts early in life.

A significant typology of criminal offenders has been constructed by Gibbons (1965) in terms of offence patterns, self-image, normative orientation and other social psychological characteristics. A uniform frame of reference employing the criteria of "definitional dimensions" and "background dimensions" is used by Gibbons. The definitional dimensions consist of:

1. The nature of the offence behavior.
2. The interactional setting with others in which the offence takes place.
3. Self-concept of the offender
4. Attitudes towards society and agencies of social control such as the police.
5. The steps in the role carriers of the offender.

There are four aspects of the background dimensions of each type :

1. Social class,
2. family background,
3. peer group associations, and
4. contact with defining agencies such as the police, courts and the prison.

On this basis Gibbons (1971) sets up 15 adult types and 9 juvenile types:

Adult Type	*Juvenile Type*
1. Professional thief	1. Predatory gang delinquent
2. Professional "heavy" criminal	2. Conflict gang delinquent
3. Semi-Professional property criminal	3. Casual gang delinquent
4. Property offender—"One-time loser"	4. Casual delinquent—Non-gang members
5. Auto mobile thief—"joy rider"	5. Automobile thief—"Joy rider"
6. Naïve check forger	6. Drug use—heroin
7. White collar criminal	7. Overly aggressive delinquent
8. Professional "fringe" violator	8. Female delinquent
9. Embezzler	9. "Behavior problem" Delinquent
10. Personal offender—"One time loser"	
11. Psychopathic assaulter	
12. Violent sex offender	
13. Non-violent sex offender	
14. Non-violent sex offender—Statutory rape	
15. Narcotic addict—heroin	

Gibbons provided a description of each type. Unfortunately, some of his types are not sharply delineated and tend to overlap or be unclear as to their specific characteristics.

Clinard and Ohlin (1960) have given six types of crimes:

1. *Violent personal crime*—This crime is based on the use of

violence and is committed by a person who does not have an earlier record of crime against him. Murder, rape, assault are some examples of this crime.

2. *Occasional property crime*—This crime is violation of individual property rules, for example, shop lifting.
3. *Occupational crime*—This crime is committed during the course of one's occupation, with an economic motive. The criminals who commit this crime accept the traditional norms of society except that of honesty. Embezzlement, black-marketing, misleading advertisements are some examples of this crime.
4. *Political crime*—This is committed by an individual with vested political and economic interests. Treason, spying, passing secrets to enemy country are examples of this crime.
5. *Public order crime*—This crime is one in which an individual violates the rules of conduct in society. Some examples of this crime are alcoholism, vandalism, prostitution, homosexuality and violation of traffic rules.
6. *Conventional crime*—This is a crime in which an individual violates the sacred norms of individual property. Theft, robbery, dacoity, kidnapping are some examples of this crime. Individuals commit these crimes on part time basis and these crimes are not the main source of their income.

Legal Classification

The Indian Penal Code (IPC) divides an estimated 300 offences into two classes, viz. cognizable and non-cognizable.

Cognizable crimes are those in which a police officer may arrest the accused or a suspect without a warrant, and includes murder, rioting, rape, kidnapping and abduction, robbery, dacoity, organized robbery, house-breaking and theft.

Non-cognizable crimes are those in which a warrant is required for arrest and are generally of a more trivial nature. Crimes can be classified as "bailable" or "non-bailable", depending on their severity (Rao, 1991).

For the present study on attempt has been made to develop a typology keeping in mind the social and legal aspects. It is however expected that we cannot achieve a typological system which can be agreed upon by all as being the most desirable. Since the present study is confined to female offenders, it is expected that the types of crimes committed by women will be different from male offenders. In the present study the 5 main types of crime include:

1. Property-related crimes
2. Violent crimes
3. Sex crimes
4. Drugs-related crimes
5. Miscellaneous crimes

1. Property-related Crimes

There are a large number of economic offences, some are cognizable and others non-cognizable in nature. In the present study theft, robbery and land disputes have been treated as property-related crimes. These crimes are done in an organized manner with or without associates or gangs with an intent to earn wealth through illegal means and earn out illicit activities violating the laws of land, other regulatory, statutory provisions governing the economic activities of the government and its administration. Property-related crimes affect all strata of society and must be taken seriously.

2. Violent Crimes

The crimes with an intention to physically harm another human being or leading to homicide are referred to as violent crimes. Killing a person either by smothering, poisoning, drowning, burning, etc. has been included under violent crimes. Emotional reasons such as jealousy, spite, revenge and hatred are strong enough to cause women to resort to violent crimes. Broken nuptial engagements, extra-marital relations, domestic quarrels, dowry, an unwanted child, a feeble parent blocking the taking over of family property, etc. are various reasons for women to indulge in violent crimes.

3. Sex Crimes

Sex crimes mainly involve crimes concerning prostitution. Selling or buying minors for purposes of prostitution, accomplice in kidnapping and abduction of women with an intent to outrage her modesty, adultery have been included in sex crimes.

4. Drugs-related Crimes

Drug abuse is spreading fast in the country. Women in large number indulge in drug trafficking for monetary purpose. The burden of increased incarceration for drug sales has fallen more heavily on women of poor economic background than on rich women. Most of the times these women sell small qualities to support the habits of the partner or they are living with the inmates who are engaged in drug sale.

5. Miscellaneous Crimes

Different crimes which cannot be included in the above four types have been grouped under miscellaneous category. It includes cheating, fraud, creating false evidence, bouncing of cheque, etc.

TYPES OF CRIME COMMITTED BY WOMEN IN INDIA

FIG. 5.1
Types of Crime

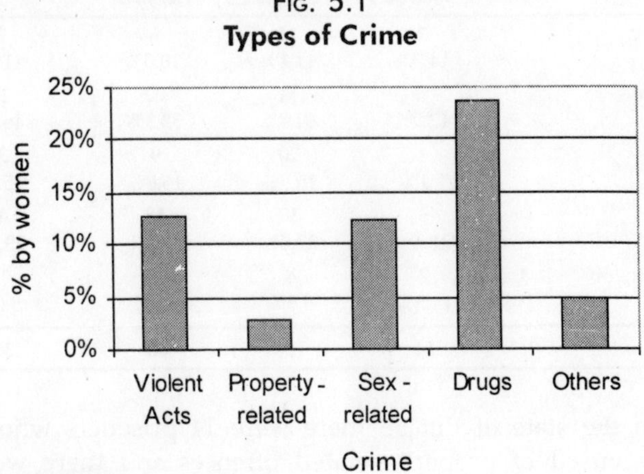

Source : NCRB, 2007.

Through the graphical presentation, an attempt has been made to indicate different types of crimes committed by women at all India level. Maximum number of women inmates are involved in drug-related offenses, followed equally by violent acts and sex-related offences. The assumption that women are mostly arrested for property-related offences does not appear to be true in an Indian set-up.

TYPES OF CRIME BY THE INMATES IN DIFFERENT STATES

Different researchers have indicated that prisoners serving time for violent crimes are a majority (just over 50 percent) of the prison population, and their share is growing, followed by drug offenders. However, majority of women most often serve time for property crimes. Greenfeld and Snell (1999), on the basis of Bureau of Justice Statistics reported that women account for about 14 percent of violent offenders.

TABLE 5.1
State-wise Distribution of Types of Crimes by Inmates

Crime Related to	*State*			*Total*
	Chandigarh	*Punjab*	*Haryana*	
Property	2	14	6	22
	14.3%	11.1%	10.0%	11.0%
Violence	6	54	32	92
	42.9%	42.9%	53.3%	46.0%
Sex	1	20	9	30
	7.1%	15.9%	15.0%	15.0%
Drugs	3	30	13	46
	21.4%	23.8%	21.7%	23.0%
Miscellaneous	2	8	—	10
	14.3%	6.3%		5.0%
Total	14	126	60	200

In the state of Punjab there were 14 prisoners who had been accused of property-related offences and there were 6 prisoners from Haryana who had been in prison because of property-related offences. There were 2 inmates who had been lodged in Burail jail at Chandigarh due to property-related offences. Maximum inmates were involved in homicide and assaults, i.e. 46 percent. In Chandigarh highest numbers of inmates were in prison because of homicide and assaults. In the state of Punjab maximum number of respondents had been involved in homicide and assaults, followed by drug smuggling and then sex-related offences. There were 15.9 percent respondents who were involved in sex-related offences in the state of Punjab. In the state of Haryana maximum inmates were involved in homicide and assaults, followed by drug smuggling and sex-related offences. There were 15 percent respondents who were involved in sex crimes. Changing values in the society with more emphasis on consumerism and individualistic outlook has brought changes in the types of crime. The results indicate that similar trend in crimes existed in the state of Punjab and Haryana. In Chandigarh, however, except sex and miscellaneous crimes, other types of crimes showed similar trend. Findings of the present study indicate that majority of women in prison served time for violent offences followed by drug-related offences, sex offences and then property offences. The results indicate that similar trend in crime existed in the states of Punjab and Haryana. In Chandigarh, however, except sex and miscellaneous types of crimes, other types of crime showed similar trend.

TYPES OF CRIME BY THE INMATES IN DIFFERENT PRISONS

TABLE 5.2
Prison-wise Distribution of Types of Crimes by Inmates

Crime related to	*Jail*							*Total*
	Burail	*Ludhiana*	*Jalandhar*	*Patiala*	*Amritsar*	*Hissar*	*Ambala*	
Property	2 14.3%	8 12.7%	3 14.3%	3 20.0%	—	1 2.9%	5 19.2%	22 11.0%
Violence	6 42.9%	26 41.3%	8 38.1%	8 53.3%	12 44.4%	20 58.8%	12 46.2%	92 46.0%
Sex	1 7.1%	10 15.9%	3 14.3%	2 13.3%	5 18.5%	3 8.8%	6 23.1%	30 15.0%
Drugs	3 21.4%	13 20.6%	6 28.6%	2 13.3%	9 33.3%	10 29.4%	3 11.5%	46 23.0%
Miscellaneous	2 14.3%	6 9.5%	1 4.8%	—	1 3.7%	—	—	10 5.0%
Total	14	63	21	15	27	34	26	200

In additions to the information on types of crime at State level, it has been further explained in terms of types of prisons. In Burail Jail at Chandigarh, there were 42.9 percent inmates who were in the prison due to homicide and assaults-related crimes. In Ludhiana women jail, majority of the respondents were involved in homicide and assaults-related offences, followed by drug and then sex-related offences. In Jalandhar Central Jail, 38 percent of respondents were involved in homicide and assaults followed by 28.6 percent in drug-related crimes. In Patiala Jail there were 3 cases of property-related crime and 8 cases of violent crimes out of total 15 inmates under study. In Amritsar prison, there were 33.3 percent inmates who were involved in drugs-related crimes, 12 inmates were involved in violent crimes, followed by 18.5 percent in sex-related offences. In Hissar jail maximum numbers of inmates were involved in violent offences, followed by drug-related crimes. In Ambala Central jail 46.2 percent respondents were involved in violent offences, followed by 23.1 percent in sex-related offences. Such findings indicate that maximum numbers of women in all the prisons were engaged in violent crimes which included homicide and assault of their family members. This is very horrifying since women who are considered to be meek, submissive and responsible for the welfare of the family, indulge in violent crimes against their own family members.

TYPES OF CRIME ACCORDING TO THE STATUS OF THE PRISONERS

The status of prisoners can be divided into two main categories, i.e. convicts and under-trials. Convicts are those whose term of punishment has been decided by the court of law. Convicts however, keep on filing cases in higher courts for change in their detention. Under-trials are those who are accused in criminal cases and are under detention awaiting trial in the court of law. Such persons are detained in prison as they may escape trial and consequent punishment, if awarded, at the end of the trial. This is not the case with non-bailable offences only but it is true in numerous other cases also. These unfortunate women are denied justice for long spells of time and pass major part of their fruitful period of life in prisons without even knowing the type of crime they have committed.

TABLE 5.3
Distribution of the Types of Crime Based on Inmate Status

Crime Related to	*Status of Prisoner*		*Total*
	Under-trial	*Convict*	
Property	16 13.2%	6 7.6%	22 11.0%
Violence	43 35.5%	49 62.0%	92 46.0%
Sex	24 19.8%	6 7.6%	30 15.0%
Drugs	34 28.1%	12 15.2%	46 23.0%
Miscellaneous	4 3.3%	6 7.6%	10 5.0%
Total	121	79	200

Table 5.3 highlights the status of prisoners according to types of crime. As stated earlier there were more under-trials in all the prisons than convicts. In property-related crimes there were 16 inmates who were under-trials. Out of 46 female inmates involved in drug-related offences 34 were under-trials and 12 were convicts. Out of 92 inmates in prison due to violent crimes, there were more women convicts than under-trials. Out of total under-trials more inmates were involved in violent crimes. The overall picture highlights the fact that there is a shift in type of crime; more and more women are being involved in violent and drug-related crimes.

TYPES OF CRIME AND THE MARITAL STATUS OF THE INMATES PRIOR TO IMPRISONMENT

Marital status plays a significant role in regulating a women's life. The nature of marital status she enjoys exerts a serious influence over her behavioural patterns. Adwani (1978) found that the highest rate of offenders in her study was of married women and the lowest rate was found to be among deserted and divorced women. Mathews (1999) noted that 60.7 percent of females engaged in sex-related offences were separated from their husbands. 37.5 percent of the divorced females engaged in theft offences and 40.6 percent of married women were involved in violent crimes. Garg (2006) reported that women killed their husbands mainly for extra-marital affairs. Thus more married women committed violent crimes than single woman.

TABLE 5.4

Distribution of the Types of Crime on the Basis of the Inmate's Marital Status Prior to Imprisonment

Crime Related to	*Marital Status*			*Total*
	Never married	*Married*	*Once married, presently single*	
Property	4 15.4%	13 10.1%	5 11.1%	22 11.0%
Violence	10 38.5%	58 45.0%	24 53.3%	92 46.0%
Sex	2 7.7%	17 13.2%	11 24.4%	30 15.0%
Drugs	5 19.2%	38 29.5%	3 6.7%	46 23.0%
Miscellaneous	5 19.2%	3 2.3%	2 4.4%	10 5.0%
Total	26	129	45	200

As nature of marital status influences the type of crime, it is essential to know the marital status of inmates according to the types of crime. Results show that maximum number of widows/divorced/deserted women, i.e. 53.3 percent were involved in violent crimes, followed by married women, i.e. 45 percent and then never married, i.e. 38.5 percent. Even with regard to sex-related crimes, similar trend was noticed. However, fewer married women were involved in property-related crimes. Maximum number of married women, i.e. 29.5 percent were involved in drugs-related offences. The findings do not endorse the results of Adwani (1978).

TYPES OF CRIME AND THE NUMBER OF CHILDREN OF THE INMATES

The presence or absence of marital partner does not influence the types of crime a female offender would indulge in. Women prisoners, no doubt, are worried about their family, particularly the children. Yet the foremost thought which exists in their mind at all times is about their future. Women prisoners also remain perturbed about the future of their children. Children whose parents are in prison face a number of difficulties. Imprisonment of the mother affects every aspect of their lives. It is similar to bereavement, but with added stigma and often less support from the new care-takers, teachers and others. Children of imprisoned parents have an increased tendency to exhibit aggressive and anti-social behavior compared to the general population.

TABLE 5.5

Distribution of the Types of Crime and the Number of Inmate's Children

Crime Related to	*Number of Children*					*Total*
	Not Applicable	*Up to 2*	*3*	*> 3*	*No Child*	
Property	4 15.4%	5 10.6%	—	11 14.1%	2 10.5%	22 11.0%
Violence	10 38.5%	22 46.8%	22 73.3%	32 41.0%	6 31.6%	92 46.0%
Sex	2 7.7%	8 17.0%	4 13.3%	8 10.3%	8 42.1%	30 15.0%
Drugs	5 19.2%	11 23.4%	4 13.3%	25 32.1%	1 5.3%	46 23.0%
Miscellaneous	5 19.2%	1 2.1%	—	2 2.6%	2 10.5%	10 5.0%
Total	26	47	30	78	19	200

Presence of children, at times, forces a woman to follow wrong means to fulfil her goals. Since majority of inmates in the present study belonged to lower strata of the society, they did not hesitate to get involved in anti-social activities in order to fulfil the needs of the family members. There were 26 prison inmates who were single and there were 19 inmates who were married but had no issue. There were 155 respondents who had children, out of which 78 inmates had more than 3 children. They were involved in all types of offences. Majority was involved in violent crimes (41 percent), drug-related crimes (32.1 percent), and followed by in property-related crimes (14.1 percent). More mothers with 3 children were involved in violent crimes. There was no difference with regard to sex and drug-related offences in this category. More women with 2 children were involved in violent crimes, and less in sex-related offences. Married women with no child were involved in sex-related offences. Presence or absence of children influences women's decision to get involved in sex-related crimes. In a society where women's identity is traced through her father, brother, husband and son, it becomes very difficult for a single woman to survive.

TYPES OF CRIME AND EDUCATION STATUS OF THE INMATES

A large number of researchers reported that criminality among females' increases as the level of education decreases and *vice versa* (Ahuja, 1969; Mishra and Gautam, 1982; Parsad, 1982). It is often pointed out that illiterate women tend to commit more crimes due to lack of awareness of criminal justice system.

In order to find the role of education in the lives of female offenders, a table highlighting educational status and type of crime was formulated. It was found that more educated women were involved in violent crimes. With regard to the other crimes it was noticed that as the educational status improved, the number of crimes decreased. One professional doctor, one Ph.D., and one college lecturer were involved in violent offences. Majority of respondents were illiterate. A few researches have reported that lack of awareness about law and criminal activity among women results in offensive behavior. It came to be true especially in case of tribal women who were involved in theft and drug smuggling without realizing the consequences of their behavior. On the other hand, more the

TABLE 5.6
Distribution of the Types of Crime and the Education Status of the Inmates

Crime Related to	*Education Status*				*Total*
	Illiterate	*Up to 10+2*	*Graduate*	*PG/ Professional*	
Property	8 7.7%	6 8.2%	7 38.9%	1 20.0%	22 11.0%
Violence	49 47.1%	33 45.2%	7 38.9%	3 60.0%	92 46.0%
Sex	11 10.6%	17 23.3%	2 11.1%	—	30 15.0%
Drugs	33 31.7%	13 17.8%	—	—	46 23.0%
Miscellaneous	3 2.9%	4 5.5%	2 11.1%	1 20.0%	10 5.0%
Total	104	73	18	5	200

awareness of legal loopholes, more was the tendency to get involved in white collar crimes. Results show involvement of educated women in personal one to one relationships which were violent in nature, whereas illiterate women were involved in property and drug-related offences. The results of the study coincide with the findings of Ahuja, Mishra, Gautam and Parsad.

TYPES OF CRIME AND OCCUPATION OF THE INMATES

Chapman (1980) studied the connection between labour force participation and revealed an increase in female criminal activity during times of economic hardship. The smallest increases in arrest coincided with the periods of the greatest increase in economic activity with the most common offence being that of shop lifting. These findings support the theory of a relationship between employment and crime. Hagan (1993) argued that the relationship between crime and unemployment is embedded in elements of the larger social structure.

The present study revealed that there was a significant influence of occupation on the offenders. Out of 200

Table 5.7
Distribution of the Types of Crime and the Occupation of the Inmates

Crime Related to	*Occupation*					*Total*
	Housewife/ Unemployed	*Menial*	*Middle*	*Profe-ssional*	*Misce-llaneous*	
Property	8 7.9%	3 4.4%	6 66.7%	—	5 23.8%	22 11.0%
Violence	57 56.4%	28 41.2%	3 33.3%	1 100.0%	3 14.3%	92 46.0%
Sex	8 7.9%	17 25.0%	—	—	5 23.8%	30 15.0%
Drugs	26 25.7%	14 20.6%	—	—	6 28.6%	46 23.0%
Miscellaneous	2 2.0%	6 8.8%	—	—	2 9.5%	10 5.0%
Total	101	68	9	1	21	200

respondents 101 were not engaged in any paid work outside. There is also an exceptionally close relationship between unemployment and crime. Ragib (1987) similarly concluded that there was a significant correlation between unemployment and property crime. Sabri (2002) showed that the effects of unemployment to property crime could be seen by the rise in property crimes. Property crimes offenders were mainly unemployed or hold low paying jobs and thus got involved in crime to supplement their income. Fassaei and Kendall (2001) found that women with higher social class status were more often imprisoned for forgery, fraud as well violent offences.

The economic necessity forced them to indulge in crime to fulfil their families as well as their own requirements. These housewives were, however, involved in all types of criminal activities. There were 68 inmates who were engaged in menial work like maid servants and labourers. Sex-related offences were found to be more among women engaged in menial and miscellaneous types of occupations like sex workers, folk dancers, singers, etc. Women engaged in middle level of occupations showed more inclination towards property-related offences. Women in the higher status occupation were imprisoned for violent offences. Results of the present study, however, did not show the endorsement of the findings of Ragib, Fassaei and Kendall. All violent offences by women occurred in the context of intimate relationships, many of which were abusive. In the present study women inmates who were engaged in middle and higher level occupation were also involved in homicide.

TYPES OF CRIME AND RELIGION OF THE INMATES

Little information is available regarding the comparative criminality of religious groups. Whatever information is available discloses that criminality of women in Muslim, Hindu or Buddhist societies is very little. In these societies offences committed by women are, in general, dealt within the family group rather than by the courts.

TABLE 5.8
Distribution of the Types of Crime and Religion of the Inmates

Crime Related to	*Religion*				*Total*
	Hindu	*Sikh*	*Muslim*	*Any other*	
Property	8 8.5%	9 10.7%	1 8.3%	4 40.0%	22 11.0%
Violence	50 53.2%	41 48.8%	1 8.3%	—	92 46.0%
Sex	15 16.0%	10 11.9%	2 16.7%	3 30.0%	30 15.0%
Drugs	19 20.2%	23 27.4%	3 25.0%	1 10.0%	46 23.0%
Miscellaneous	2 2.1%	1 1.2%	5 41.7%	2 20.0%	10 5.0%
Total	94	84	12	10	200

In the present study, majority of inmates were Hindus, followed by Sikhs. Muslims constituted only 12 cases. There were, however, 10 respondents who believed in different sects, thus, have been grouped under "Any other" category. All religions refrains a person from following a sinful path. Results seem to indicate that the religious teachings have no effect on the lives of the inmates. There was hardly any difference between Hindus and Sikhs with regard to types of crime. Large number of Hindu and Sikh women were involved in violent crimes, i.e. 53.2 and 48.8 percent respectively. In case of Muslims, more women, i.e. 25 percent were involved in drug smuggling and 16.7 percent were involved in sex-related offence. It was the economic status rather than religious background which influenced the types of crime.

TYPES OF CRIME AND CASTE OF THE INMATES

In spite of the ideals of a casteless society in India, caste still act as a potent factor in determining stereotypes, social relationships and socio-economic role of men and women. It is presumed that each caste will have certain behavioural characteristics which do influence the types of crime. Indian castes have been divided into four main categories for the purpose of analysis viz. upper, middle, backward and lower.

TABLE 5.9
Distribution of the Types of Crime and Caste of the Inmates

Crime Related to	*Caste*				*Total*
	Upper	*Middle*	*Backward*	*Lower*	
Property	1 6.3%	3 6.0%	5 12.2%	13 14.0%	22 11.0%
Violence	12 75.0%	30 60.0%	19 46.3%	31 33.3%	92 46.0%
Sex	—	8 16.0%	7 17.1%	15 16.1%	30 15.0%
Drugs	3 18.8%	7 14.0%	6 14.6%	30 32.3%	46 23.0%
Miscellaneous	—	2 4.0%	4 9.8%	4 4.3%	10 5.0%
Total	16	50	41	93	200

Caste background has been studied in relation to the types of crime. As reported earlier, lower the caste, more the number of inmates; higher the caste, lesser the number of inmates. Women belonging to upper caste were involved in violent and drug-related offences. In the middle caste group, majority, i.e. 60 percent were involved in violent offences, mostly pertaining to dowry. In backward castes, majority, i.e. 43.6 percent inmates were involved in homicide and assaults. In lower caste, majority of the inmates were involved in violent crimes and drug-related offences. With regards to homicide and assaults, more inmates of the upper caste were involved. There was less number of women in the upper caste who were involved in the property crimes. It can be concluded that caste background plays an important role in determining the type of crimes an individual is likely to commit.

TYPES OF CRIME AND AGE OF THE INMATES

It is particularly difficult to come to any firm conclusions regarding the age at which women indulge in crime. According to Youth Lifestyle Survey, almost one in five youth admitted committing at least one offence in the previous twelve months, and nearly three quarters of all offences committed were property offences (Flood-Page *et. al.*, 2000). A few researchers reported that young girls who indulge in deviant behaviour are often protected by their family members because of strictness of social customs. It is for this reason that there is a predominance of women in higher age groups in prisons. Various researchers have reported higher incidence of criminality among women in the age group of 20 to 30 years (Nagla, 1991; Saxena, 1994). According to NCRB crime data for 2007, majority of women in the age group of 30 to 45 years were imprisoned for violent acts (39.3 percent); property-related offences (42.8 percent); and drug-related offences (48.4 percent). Majority of women in the age group of 18 to 30 years were involved in sex-related offences (54.7 percent). A large number of aged women were imprisoned for dowry deaths and were incarcerated under Dowry Prohibition Act.

Table 5.10 highlights the distribution of age of the inmates and types of crime they were involved in. Out of 6 inmates

TABLE 5.10
Distribution of the Types of Crime and Age of the Inmates

Crime Related to	Age				Total
	Very Young (below 18)	Young (18-35)	Middle Aged (35-55)	Old (55 plus)	
Property	—	8 12.1%	14 13.0%	—	22 11.0%
Violence	4 66.7%	23 34.8%	46 42.6%	19 95.0%	92 46.0%
Sex	—	19 28.8%	11 10.2%	—	30 15.0%
Drugs	2 33.3%	9 13.6%	34 31.5%	1 5.0%	46 23.0%
Miscellaneous	—	7 10.6%	3 2.8%	—	10 5.0%
Total	6	66	108	20	200

below the 18 age group, 4 were involved in violent offences and 2 were imprisoned for drug-related offences. Majority of imprisoned inmates were in the age group of 35 to 55 years. If we club 18 to 55 years categories, we find that 174 inmates out of 200 in this age group. These are the most productive years in the life of any individual. These women spent their crucial years in anti-social activities. More young women, i.e. in the age group of 18 to 35 years were involved in sex-related offences and middle aged women, i.e. 35 to 55 years were involved in violent and drug-related offences. Elderly women were involved in dowry-related offences in the present study. Results are quite close to the NCRB findings where maximum women in the age group of 18 to 45 years were involved in criminal offences. The social control, theories by Emile Durkheim and Robert Merton which depended on the weakening moral guidelines and the blurring of the distinction between right and wrong, could explain the above as unfeasible aspirations that are capable of generating disillusionment which thus leads to deviance, in general.

TYPES OF CRIME AND BACKGROUND OF THE INMATES

A number of researchers have drawn attention to the higher crime rates in urban area generally as compared to rural areas mainly due to the obvious temptations and opportunities for crime offered by city life. Female crimes of petty theft tend to be concentrated in cities, especially those crimes that are performed outside the women's place of work or residence. Prostitution is also considered to be a city-based crime. The proportion of crimes against property always tends to be highest in urban districts, whereas the proportion of violent crimes against persons is highest in rural areas (Taft, 1950). Trikett *et. al.* (1992) discovered that prevalence of property offences was four times greater in the worse inner city areas than in sub-urban areas and the prevalence of offences against the person was eleven times as great.

TABLE 5.11

Distribution of the Types of Crime and Background of the Inmates

Crime Related to	*Background*		*Total*
	Rural	*Urban*	
Property	9 8.2%	13 14.4%	22 11.0%
Violence	56 50.9%	36 40.0%	92 46.0%
Sex	10 9.1%	20 22.2%	30 15.0%
Drugs	30 27.3%	16 17.8%	46 23.0%
Miscellaneous	5 4.5%	5 5.6%	10 5.0%
Total	110	90	200

Table 5.11 focuses on the background of the prison inmates and types of crime. The table indicates that the higher number of inmates belonged to the rural background. More women

from rural areas as compared to from urban areas, i.e. 55.9 percent to 40 percent were involved in violent crimes. More women from urban areas, i.e. 14.4 percent as compared to 8.2 percent from rural areas were imprisoned for property offences. More women from urban areas, i.e. 22.2 percent as compared to 9.1 percent from rural areas were involved in sex-related offences. More drug offenders belonged to rural areas as compared to those from urban areas. Results indicate that violent and drug-related offences are more in rural areas, and sex and property related offences are more in urban areas. These findings endorse the results of Trickett *et. al.* (1992).

TYPES OF CRIME AND FAMILY COMPOSITION OF THE INMATES

Family composition has some influence on the type of crime. The spouse killings are more in nuclear families. Drunken husbands, wife beating and adultery are more common in nuclear families where the wife is defenseless and in the event of domestic violence no one is likely to come to her rescue. More dowry deaths occur in joint families. Mothers-in-law has clearly defined role of the "power holder" in the household where the new wife has no chance.

TABLE 5.12
Distribution of the Types of Crime and Family Composition of the Inmates

Crime Related to	*Family Composition*			*Total*
	Nuclear	*Joint/Extended*	*Alone*	
Property	18 15.7%	4 5.5%	—	22 11.0%
Violence	45 39.1%	46 63.0%	1 8.3%	92 46.0%
Sex	16 13.9%	9 12.3%	5 41.7%	30 15.0%
Drugs	35 30.4%	10 13.7%	1 8.3%	46 23.0%
Miscellaneous	1 0.9%	4 5.5%	5 41.7%	10 5.0%
Total	115	73	12	200

Majority of female inmates in the present study belonged to nuclear household. In joint family 63 percent women were involved in violent offences. Dowry-related offences and land dispute homicides were more common in the joint family. 39.1 percent women from nuclear families were involved in homicide of their spouse. Most of these women were the victims of abusive relationship. Drug-related offences were found more in the nuclear family. It is believed that most of the women who were the main care takers of their children and elderly parents took to economic offences to support their families. Women who were living alone, i.e. 41.7 percent were engaged in sex-related offences. Whether family was nuclear or joint, it had some effect on the offending women. Property and drug-related offences were common across both types of families but were more in nuclear families.

TYPES OF CRIME AND FAMILY SIZE OF THE INMATES

TABLE 5.13
Distribution of the Types of Crime and Family Size of the Inmates

Crime Related to	*Family Size*				*Total*
	Small (4)	*Medium (6)*	*Large (10)*	*Very Large (10+)*	
Property	5 10.2%	15 18.5%	1 1.8%	1 7.7%	22 11.0%
Violence	21 42.9%	34 42.0%	32 56.1%	5 38.5%	92 46.0%
Sex	11 22.4%	8 9.9%	8 14.0%	3 23.1%	30 15.0%
Drugs	7 14.3%	23 28.4%	14 24.6%	2 15.4%	46 23.0%
Miscellaneous	5 10.2%	1 1.2%	2 3.5%	2 15.4%	10 5.0%
Total	49	81	57	13	200

Family size is stated to be related to type of crime. Larger the size, more the money-related crimes would be. Majority of those females who belonged to large families were engaged in violent offences followed by sex-related offences. Similarly, women who belonged to small families, majority, i.e. 36.7 percent were engaged in homicide and assaults; followed by sex-related offences, i.e. 22.4 percent. Those women, who had medium family size, i.e. 6 members per unit, more inmates were involved in violent offences followed by drug-related offenses and then property-related offences.

REASONS FOR CRIME

Presumed changes in the patterns of crime by females are drawing the attention of popular media as well as that of Sociologists and Criminologists. There are a number of diverge views advanced by various social scientists for explaining the reasons for women to indulge in crime. Increase in the rate of crime by the women is commonly attributed to the emergence of women's liberation movement. Others argue that increasing criminal opportunities, group support for illegal behaviour and weakening social controls, especially parents are the main reasons for women to indulge in crime. Bilmoria (1983) reported that domestic factors played an important role in compelling many women to adopt criminal behavior. Daniel and Kashani (1983) discussed Sociological and Environmental factors that might have contributed individually or collectively to the causation of crime. They noted that a majority of female violent crimes were intra familial and related to life experiences. Davies (1999) mentioned that some types of criminal activity that women take part are strictly financially motivated. Prostitution is pursued purely for money. Shoplifting, theft, fraud and forgery and drugs-related offences are the principal crime categories that women contribute to. All of those crimes may be seen as crimes which are committed as a rational response to a lack of money or ability to obtain sufficient money from traditional and legitimate sources. Morash *et. al.*. (1998) reported that more than 43 percent of women inmates had been physically or sexually abused before their admission to prison. Willis and Rushforth (2003) reported that women incarcerated had experienced higher levels of abuse, economic hardships and other adversity in their lives. Such research studies indicate that multiple variables are responsible for female criminality.

TABLE 5.14
Distribution of the Inmates on the Basis of Reasons of Crime

Response	*Jail*							*Total*
	Burail	*Ludhiana*	*Jalandhar*	*Patiala*	*Amritsar*	*Hissar*	*Ambala*	
Personal	1 7.1%	14 22.2%	2 9.5%	1 6.7%	5 18.5%	1 2.9%	4 15.4%	28 14.0%
Familial	7 50.0%	13 20.6%	6 28.6%	3 20.0%	8 29.6%	12 35.3%	8 30.8%	57 28.5%
Economic	4 28.6%	25 39.7%	8 38.1%	5 33.3%	9 33.3%	13 38.2%	8 30.8%	72 36.0%
Falsely implicated	2 14.3%	11 17.5%	5 23.8%	6 40.0%	5 18.5%	8 23.5%	6 23.1%	43 21.5%
Total	14	63	21	15	27	34	26	200

Inmates were asked to specify the main reasons for their criminal behaviour. Majority of the inmates, i.e. 36 percent reported that they were the main care takers of their children and family. It was poverty which drove them towards criminality. Out of 72 inmates who gave economic reasons for their crime, 39.7 percent belonged to Ludhiana women jail followed equally by Jalandhar and Hissar jails. There were 25.8 percent inmates who mentioned that familial environment especially abusive behaviour of the partner forced them to crime. A few respondents in Patiala and Amritsar jail reported that their relatives and spouses socialized them to follow criminal lifestyle. There were others who mentioned that crime was a part of their family and they were born in the culture of crime. There were 43 inmates who refused to accept the fact that they were offenders. They stated that they were falsely implicated by their relatives to get their scores right. There were 28 inmates, out of which maximum belonging to Ludhiana jail stated personal reasons for their criminal behaviour. They mentioned that they were over-ambitious and in order to fulfil their wishes, they did not mind deviation from the socially sanctioned limits. Consumerism and vengeful nature were other explanations given under personal causes. The findings of the study endorse the results of Davies, and Willis and Rushforth.

WERE THE INMATES PUNISHED RIGHTLY FOR THE CRIME?

Table 5.15

Inmate's Response to the Punishment assigned to them

Crime Related to	*Punished Rightly*		*Total*
	Yes	*No*	
Property	2 22.2%	20 10.5%	22 11.0%
Violence	3 33.3%	89 46.6%	92 46.0%
Sex	—	30 15.7%	30 15.0%
Drugs	2 22.2%	44 23.0%	46 23.0%
Miscellaneous	2 22.2%	8 4.2%	10 5.0%
Total	9	191	200

Out of 200 female prison inmates under study, 191 showed no regret for their criminal behaviour as they asserted that they were falsely implicated, out of which 89 women prisoners were involved in violent crimes related to homicide or dowry-related offences. They argued that they were innocent. Those women who were involved in sex-related offences argued that since it was the only means of livelihood available to them, they had not done any wrong. Similarly with regard to drug-related offences, out of 46 cases 44 respondents had no grudge about their crime. They stated that they were only working for money. They opined that if government was serious enough to check the problem of drugs in the society it should control the demand by enhancing the awareness efforts. Similarly, with regard to property-related offences, out of 22 cases 20 respondents felt that they were not punished rightly. Such responses clearly indicate that majority of women lodged in prison showed resentment against the punishment.

INVOLVEMENT OF OTHER FAMILY MEMBERS IN CRIME

According to Differential Association theory, individual gets inspired by the immediate environment. Role of kinsmen, family members is very crucial in influencing the behaviour of women inmates. Bailey and Hayes (2006) reported that more than half of women in California prison had an immediate family member (mother, father, brother, spouse or child) who had also been imprisoned. Mathews (1999) also mentioned association of family members in different types of crimes. Hence an attempt was made to enquire about other family members staying in the prisons.

TABLE 5.16

Other Family Members Arrested for Criminal Activities

Crime Related to	*Anyone else arrested in family?*		*Total*
	Yes	*No*	
Property	8 9.9%	14 11.8%	22 11.0%
Violence	49 60.5%	43 36.1%	92 46.0%
Sex	3 3.7%	27 22.7%	30 15.0%
Drugs	16 19.8%	30 25.2%	46 23.0%
Miscellaneous	5 6.2%	5 4.2%	10 5.0%
Total	81	119	200

Out of 200 respondents under study, 81 female prisoners reported that there were other members in their family who have also been imprisoned. Such a response indicates that these women were not solely responsible for criminal outlook. Other members of their families were also involved in criminal activities. The results of the study endorse the findings of Bailey and Hayes as well as Mathews. There were maximum respondents, i.e. 60.5 percent whose family members were involved in violent crimes followed by drug-related offences at 19.8 percent. Those females whose family members were not arrested were involved in sex-related offences, i.e. 3.7 percent. Many a times their parents were unaware of their daughter's misdemeanors.

CONSEQUENCES OF CONFINEMENT

Imprisonment represents an involuntary interruption of normal life. There may be negative psychological effects of imprisonment (low self-esteem, distrust, defensiveness, aggressive mannerism) that forms barriers to seeking employment and performance on the job. The length of imprisonment also influences the intensity of the effects. It may be that both the positive and negative effects get magnified, the longer one remains in the prison. Just as there are possible negative and positive affects on the incarcerated individuals, there are mixed implications for their family members and significant others. The personal behaviour of the individuals before they came to prison obviously mediates the impact of their incarceration on their families and friends. Some will have been abusive and negligent in their intimate relations. They may feel that there is no negative effect. Those who have been responsible, caring spouses and parents may feel otherwise. According to them, their household would loose economic resources and social and emotional capital. Thus, we know that these consequences and implications are about to be felt in unprecedented ways by these women, and their families, especially children. Kingi (1993) has predicted that "imprisonment will become the most significant factor contributing to the dissolution and breakdown of families during the decade of the 1990s". There will be more single parent families (Chambliss, 1994).

Stress levels may increase at the end of an inmate's sentence due to anticipation and feelings of uncertainty about one's ability to adjust and cope in the outside world again, after having adjusted to prison life (Bartol and Bartol, 1994). Clinical studies have shown that imprisonment can have devastating effects, and may lead to a 'psycho-syndrome' which includes a loss of memory, clouding of comprehension, apathy, infantile regressions, hopelessness and the appearance of various psychotic characteristics such as obsession and major depression. This is most common amongst those prisoners who endure long sentences, have unstable personalities, the inability to maintain normal relations with members of non-prison society, a readiness or desire to integrate into the sub-culture, and a close proximity to other individuals that are already integrated. On an overall, the results from studies indicate that individuals react differently to confinement. While some find their experience of prison extremely stressful, at the other extreme those who are dependent, passive, and generally incompetent may find that the prison structure offers them a positive experience.

TABLE 5.17
Consequences of Confinement

Response	*Frequency*	*Percent*
Loss of self-esteem	52	26.0%
Loss of Family prestige	89	44.5%
Loss of Social prestige	42	21.0%
Unaffected	17	8.5%
Total	200	100.0%

Keeping these reasons in mind, respondents were asked how the confinement had affected them. The effects of incarceration vary from individual to individual and are often reversible. Not everyone who is imprisoned is harmed by it. But few people are completely unchanged or unscathed by the experience. At the very least, prison is painful and incarcerated persons often suffer long-term consequences from having been subjected to pain, deprivation and extremely atypical patterns and norms of living and interacting with others. There were 89 inmates who reported that they had lost relations because of their confinement. Women prisoners who were responsible for the care of their children and maintenance of home showed concern about their family members. These women felt that they would be held responsible by their family members as they brought bad name to the family. The pains of imprisonment produced negative long lasting consequences for them. There were, however, 17 cases who stated that confinement did not affect them at all. They continued to lead a normal life. The most negative consequences of prison may first occur in the form of internal chaos, disorganization, stress, and fear. The results coincide with the findings of Bartol and Bartol. Yet, institutionalization has taught most people to cover their internal states, and not to openly or easily reveal intimate feelings or reactions. So, the outward appearance of normality and adjustment may mask a range of serious problems in adapting to the free world. A diminished sense of self-worth and personal value was reported by 42 inmates. They developed a feeling of helplessness and stated that they deserved such treatment. For 52 women prisoners, imprisonment had resulted in serious disruption in their lives. Rejection from society was feared by these respondents. Findings indicate that societal rejection was feared as the most important consequence of imprisonment by these inmates. Such findings clearly indicate that society continues to play a significant role in acting as an agency of social control for its members. Social ridicule, ostracism, stigma, neglect are the most common reactions which deviants receive from the society because of their anti-social behaviour. In the list of priority, these women gave least importance to their self-image.

CONCLUSION

One of the major findings of the present study is that more incarcerated women have been behind bars for violent crimes. They indulged in homicide and in majority of the cases the victim was the member of the family, either husband or daughter-in-law. The researcher endorses the feminist argument that most of the women are likely to kill in self-defense in response to their male partner's physical aggression and threats. However, the issue of killing daughter-in-laws for dowry does not fit into the above explanation, since it is fundamentally a different sort of act. The lower middle class families preferred to fulfil their economic aspirations by seeking dowry. In case their demands are not fulfilled, it results in physical abuse of the young bride and in extreme case life threatening situation.

The region (Punjab, Haryana and Chandigarh) has become a drug haven and it has targeted women, and in part explains the huge increase in women's imprisonment due to drug-related offences. A large number of women who were offended for drug-related offences had large families and poor economic background. A maximum number of unattached women were involved in sex-related offences. Those inmates who were illiterate, unemployed or working in lowly paid jobs were involved in property-related offences. Economic necessity forced them to indulge in crime to fulfil their needs as well as of their dependent family members.

Another important finding was that majority of women inmates lodged in prisons did not feel that they were punished rightly. They rather blamed the socio-economic circumstances for their conviction. Such an attitude highlights the changing connotations of moral values in society when women prisoners do not hesitate to put onus of their blame on others.

Close to half the women lodged in prison had other family members involved in violent crimes and were also in jail. Women have a unique life experiences, occupy different familial and social roles, their incarceration have negative impact on their self-image, family and society at large. After explaining the relationship between the types of crime with various socio-economic variables and causes of criminality, an effort has been made to get an insight into the lives of inmates in the prison:

Life of Inmates in the Prison

The prison community, being a microcosm of the larger society shares in varying measures all those social processes, patterns and parameters of human relationship that operate in a free society. The people in prison like the people outside, constitute a small dynamic society of their own—"*the society of captives*". Despite heterogeneity in terms of their age, educational attainments, caste, religion, socio-economic and criminal background, inmates have a feeling of belongingness to each other—a feeling generated by the "community character" of the prison milieu. Clemmer (1940) proposed the concept of prisonization to explain the formation of prison sub-culture. When a new inmate enters the prison, he or she begins the process of prisonization. This process is not the same for all the inmates and may be affected by the inmate's personality, environment and relationships outside the prison; whether the inmate joins a primary group in prison; and the degree to which the inmate accepts the codes of prison life. The prison is not a closed system, and in exploring the inmate culture, we must examine the quality of contacts with people outside the walls, relationships with staff and fellow inmates, and immediate problems of adjustment. It is in this context that it becomes essential to study the life of female inmates in the prisons

In this chapter, an attempt has been made on the following:

- To study the relationships of inmates with
  - their family members,
  - co-prisoners, and
  - jail staff
- To find out the problems faced by inmates and their suggestions to improve the system.

Upon arrival at the prison, the inmates are bewildered with the surroundings, unless they have been in prison earlier, and are faced with problems with adjusting and learning the rules in dealing with both the staff and other inmates. Few prisoners develop coping strategies that shield them from prison problems. The starting point for exploring the ways in which inmates adjust in prison has been Goffman's analysis of adaptation. There is a traditional gap between the ruling group (prison staff) and the subordinate group (prisoners) in the prison system. Goffman provided one of the brilliant analysis, "there is a basic split between a large class of individuals who live in and who have restricted contact with the world outside the walls, conveniently called inmates, and the small class that supervises them, conveniently called staff, who often operate on an eight hour day and are socially integrated into the outside world. Each group tends to conceive off members of other in terms of narrow hostile stereotypes: staff often seeing inmates as bitter, secretive and untrustworthy; while inmates often see staff as condescending, high handed and mean. Staff tends to feel superior and righteous: inmates tend, in some way at least, to feel inferior, weak, blameworthy and guilty. Social mobility between the two strata is grossly restricted; social distance is typically great and a special tone of voice. The restrictions on contact presumably help to maintain the antagonistic stereotypes. In any case, two different social and cultural worlds develop, tending to job along besides each other, with points of official contact but little mutual penetration." (Goffman, 1961) It was expected that different inmates employ different strategies to cope up with the other inmates and jail staff. Moreover, it was envisaged that inter-prison would reveal differences in the proportions of the inmates adhering to one or the other line of adaptations.

LIFE AFTER INCARCERATION

The pain of confinement is limited to certain psychological deprivations. This includes the loss of liberty which prisoners experience as a limitation of movement. There is also the pain of moral rejection implied in confinement. Confinement applies that the prisoner is not trusted or respected therefore s/he should not be able to move freely amongst other citizens (Johnson, 2003). The biggest problem identified by the women was re-establishing the bond with their children, badly damaged by the separation and the negative impacts of trying to keep contact during the sentence-serving period. Morris and Wilkinson (1995) in another study observed that women faced housing problems. Only a few women were able to retain their accommodation and when this did occur, it was through family assistance. Further, of those in relationships, a number of inmates described them as 'abusive' but felt considerable pressure to return mainly for financial reasons. It is believed that even if prison inmates try hard to lead a normal life after completing their sentence, the life spent in the prison leaves its imprint in their later life.

TABLE 6.1
Life of Inmates after Incarceration

Lead a normal life	*Jail*							*Total*
	Burail	*Ludhiana*	*Jalandhar*	*Patiala*	*Amritsar*	*Hissar*	*Ambala*	
Yes	5 35.7%	18 28.6%	12 57.1%	8 53.3%	11 40.7%	13 38.2%	10 38.5%	77 38.5%
No	9 64.3%	45 71.4%	9 42.9%	7 46.7%	16 59.3%	21 61.8%	16 61.5%	123 61.5%
Total	14	63	21	15	27	34	26	200

It is not necessary that all inmates would see themselves as negatively as others view them. Perhaps there would be those inmates who would have high self-esteem in prison than other inmates. 38.5 percent of prisoners reported that they would lead a normal life after completing their sentences. In Burail jail there were 35.7 percent respondents who felt that they would lead a normal life. In Jalandhar and Patiala Jails more than half of the respondents felt that they would lead a normal life. Yet, the psychological effects of incarceration vary from individual to individual and are often reversible. To be sure, then, not everyone who is incarcerated is disabled or psychologically harmed by it. But few people are completely unchanged or unscathed by the experience. At the very least, prison is painful, and incarcerated persons often suffer long-term consequences from having been subjected to pain, deprivation, and extremely atypical patterns and norms of living and interacting with others.

However, majority, i.e. 61.5 percent felt that they would not be able to lead a normal life. In Ludhiana women jail 71.4 percent respondents felt that they would not be able to lead a normal life. In Amritsar jail 59.3 percent, 61.8 percent inmates in Hissar jail and 61.5 percent inmates in Ambala jail felt that they would not be able to lead a normal life. Rejection by society and family would not permit them to lead a normal life.

REASONS FOR NOT LEADING A NORMAL LIFE AFTER CONFINEMENT

Criminologists have paid particular attention to imprisonment as stigma that attaches to inmates and the groups to which they belong, especially their families. Braithwaite (1989) draws an important distinction between the kind of stigma imposed by imprisonment and alternative processes of "re-integrative shaming", which are intended to bring the person back into the group after being punished. The stigma of imprisonment is intended to result in exclusion from the social group, while re-integrative shaming includes rituals of re-acceptance and re-absorption that are designed to encourage a return to group membership. Well-functioning families are prominent sites of re-integrative shaming, but Braithwaite's point is that this kind of response to anti-social behaviors can be adopted in broader societal settings as well. In the absence of efforts to encourage reacceptance and re-absorption, the stigma of imprisonment risks not only making parents into outlaws, but their children as well.

TABLE 6.1.1

Reasons for not Leading a Normal Life after Confinement

Reasons	*Jail*							*Total*
	Burail	*Ludhiana*	*Jalandhar*	*Patiala*	*Amritsar*	*Hissar*	*Ambala*	
Not Applicable	5 35.7%	18 28.6%	12 57.1%	8 53.3%	11 40.7%	13 38.2%	10 38.5%	77 38.5%
Stigmatized	4 28.6%	16 25.4%	4 19.0%	—	5 18.5%	4 11.8%	4 15.4%	37 18.5%
Life will be over	4 28.6%	16 25.4%	3 14.3%	4 26.7%	6 22.2%	9 26.5%	4 15.4%	46 23.0%
Family life disrupted	1 7.1%	13 20.6%	2 9.5%	3 20.0%	5 18.5%	8 23.5%	8 30.8%	40 20.0%
Total	14	63	21	15	27	34	26	200

There were 123 respondents who reported that they would not be able to lead a normal life after staying in prison. These female prisoners were further asked to specify the reasons for their not being able to lead a normal life. There were 18.5 percent respondents who reported that they would be stigmatized. Societal rejection would not allow them to lead a normal life. People would terminate all the relations with them. There were 30.7 percent respondents in Ambala jail who reported that their family life would be ruined. There were 13 respondents in Ludhiana jail, 8 in Hissar jail, and 8 in Ambala jail who stated that their children won't accept them. As a consequence their family would be disintegrated. These respondents stated that they were in prison because of ill fate but they would be blamed and stigmatized throughout their lives and thus not be able to lead a normal life. There were 46 respondents who mentioned that life outside would continue and their lives had come to standstill, *it would create a gap in their lives*. These respondents felt that after getting imprisoned they would be labeled as 'deviants' that reduces their worth as a person. It is submitted that lack of ability to perform the proper role was greatly felt by them as a 'personal defacement'.

RELATIONS WITH THE FAMILY MEMBERS

There are a few prisons exclusively for women, where women tend to be imprisoned far away from their homes; the distance separating them from their children, families and friends increases their isolation and can be a source of additional stress such as economic hardship and anxiety, for both the women concerned and their families. In the study undertaken, two women jails—one in Ludhiana and other in Hissar have been included. According to Healy *et. al.* (1999), "Families can play a vital role in reintegrating the prisoners into meaningful social lives. Positive ties between an inmate and their family, either family of origin or their current family, are strongly associated with reduced recidivism." Harrison (1997) found that inmates who maintained family relationships while in prison have indicated reduced disciplinary problem whilst serving their prison sentence and improved mental health.

TABLE 6.2
Respondent's Family Relations

Relations with family members	*Jail*							*Total*
	Burail	*Ludhiana*	*Jalandhar*	*Patiala*	*Amritsar*	*Hissar*	*Ambala*	
Congenial	9 64.3%	35 55.6%	15 71.4%	12 80.0%	24 88.9%	21 61.8%	12 46.2%	128 64.0%
Non-congenial	3 21.4%	10 15.9%	3 14.3%	2 13.3%	2 7.4%	1 2.9%	9 34.6%	30 15.0%
Workable	2 14.3%	18 28.6%	3 14.3%	1 6.7%	1 3.7%	12 35.3%	5 19.2%	42 21.0%
Total	14	63	21	15	27	34	26	200

In our society, family continues to remain an important institution. Acceptance or rejection of family affects the life of an individual. Inmates were asked to mention the type of relations they maintained with their family members after coming to prison. However, 64 percent of inmates reported that they maintained cordial relations with their family members. 64.3 percent inmates of Burail jail, 55.6 percent of Ludhiana jail, 71.4 percent of Jalandhar jail, 80 percent of Patiala jail, 88.9 percent of

Amritsar jail, 61.8 percent of Hissar jail and 46.2 percent inmates of Ambala jail had congenial relations with their family members. There were very few inmates who reported that they had non-congenial relations with their family members. Maximum inmates, i.e. 34.6 percent who had non-congenial relations with their family members were from Ambala jail. Their family members did not maintain any contact with them when they went astray. Further, those women who were involved in homicide acts of their partners did not get any support of their husband's family of orientation.

VISITS BY THE FAMILY

All the prisons allow inmates to meet their family members twice a week. Different days are fixed for convicts and under-trials. Family members frequently pay visit to prison to inquire about their well-being and deliver items of daily needs. Visiting prisons can be a daunting and frustrating experience for adults. Travelling a long distance, entering a grim building, being searched by strangers, to spend a short time with the inmate may be distressing especially for the child. This in turn may make the child substitute care taker less inclined to undertake this arduous task. Furthermore, the new care taker may have their own family responsibilities as well as financial constraints, which put strains on taking in additional children and in particular adding to the financial, time and emotional burdens of taking children to visit their imprisoned mother.

In prison, visit by family members is a pleasant experience for inmates. In almost all the prisons under study, for two days in a week prisoners were allowed to meet the visitors. The states of Punjab and Haryana have one each women prisons, located in Ludhiana and Hissar, respectively. Most often women convicts are kept in these jails. Therefore many a times place of residence is far off from the prison. As a consequence number of visits by family members declare. Inmates were asked whether their family members come to visit them. There were 125 respondents who stated that their family members came to visit them. It made them feel that they were cared for. It provided them an opportunity to meet and hear the loved ones face to face. Further, *mulaquats* were the source or channel through

TABLE 6.3
Distribution of the Inmates on the Basis of Visits by the Family

Response	*Jail*							*Total*
	Burail	*Ludhiana*	*Jalandhar*	*Patiala*	*Amritsar*	*Hissar*	*Ambala*	
Yes	10 71.4%	42 66.7%	13 61.9%	9 60.0%	16 59.3%	20 58.8%	15 57.7%	125 62.5%
No	4 28.6%	21 33.3%	8 38.1%	6 40.0%	11 40.7%	14 41.2%	11 42.3%	75 37.5%
Total	14	63	21	15	27	34	26	200

which inmates procured many items of daily needs (soap, toothpaste, sweets, fruits, pickles, bidis, cigarettes, etc). There were 37.5 percent respondents who stated that their family members didn't come to visit them. There were some respondents who didn't have cordial relations with their family members. Severances of social connections and emotional ties with family members aggravated the inmates' sense of alienation and made them feel completely rejected. There were a few respondents who stated that their family members were unaware of the fact that they were in prisons as they belonged to another state. Majority of the inmates, i.e. 42.3 percent whose family members did not pay visits belonged to Ambala Central Jail followed by 41.2 percent from Hissar jail and 40.7 percent from Amritsar Central Jail. A few respondents stated that their family members were poor, worked as daily wagers and were not in a position to spend on travel. This led to scarcity of material goods. As a consequence, some of them worked for rich inmates and got supply of certain daily need items. There were a few respondents whose family members were in some other prisons and thus could not pay visits.

RELATIONSHIP OF INMATES WITH JAIL AUTHORITIES

The prisoners and prison authorities constitute a group within which their behaviour with each other as well as with the authorities is of great importance. When most inmates first enter the prison, they find that they are being forced to adapt to an often harsh and rigid institutional routine. They get deprived of the privacy and liberty, are subjected to a diminished and stigmatized status, and extremely sparse material conditions leading to stress, unpleasantness and difficulties. However, in the course of becoming institutionalized, women inmates gradually become more accustomed to the restrictions. Some inmates, however, choose not to accept the system and consciously decide not to allow the transformation. Jensen and Jones (1976) mentioned that younger educated inmates with urban background were more hostile towards the institution and its staff than older, lesser educated and non-urban inmates. A traditional jail environment cultivates a fear-hate syndrome, which means that the inmates and the staff hate each other and at the same time are afraid of each other. This happens because of the fact that in the traditional jail setting, the basic inequality between the prisoners and the staff is emphasized, and there is undue subjugation of the personality of the inmates.

TABLE 6.4
Distribution of Inmates on the Basis of their Relationship with Jail Authorities

Response	*Jail*							*Total*
	Burail	*Ludhiana*	*Jalandhar*	*Patiala*	*Amritsar*	*Hissar*	*Ambala*	
Congenial	10 71.4%	36 57.1%	9 42.9%	8 53.3%	18 66.7%	10 29.4%	12 46.2%	103 51.5%
Non-congenial	—	3 4.8%	3 14.3%	—	—	—	2 7.7%	8 4.0%
Workable	4 28.6%	24 38.1%	9 42.9%	7 46.7%	9 33.3%	24 70.6%	12 46.2%	89 44.5%
Total	14	63	21	15	27	34	26	200

The practice of discriminatory treatment of prisoners, which was instituted during the colonial period, continues in independent India. The prison as an institution has become a site of contention between the privileged and the deprived. Inmates were asked to specify the relationships with the jail staff. Out of 200 inmates, 103 reported that they had congenial relations with the jail staff. There were 89 inmates who mentioned that since they were at the mercy of jail staff, they didn't want any conflict. As a result their response was 'workable'. There were, however, 8 inmates, 3 each were from Ludhiana and Jalandhar jails and 2 from Ambala jail that had non-congenial relations with the jail staff. These respondents felt that prison officials misused their authority and also indulged in favoritism which was not tolerated leading to protest by these inmates. As a consequence they were not in the good books of the authorities. On the contrary, persistence defiance and constant rebellion against the authorities made them important in the eyes of other inmates.

ARGUMENTS WITH JAIL AUTHORITIES

Different researchers have discussed the problem of indiscipline in the prisons. The prison authorities find maintaining law and order as one of the most difficult and problematic task in the men prisons. However, the problem of indiscipline is not severe in the women prisons. There are majority of female inmates who conduct themselves according to the rules of the prison, mainly to avoid degradation of punishment and to be in good books of prison officials. In the light of such observations, relationships of inmates with jail authorities have been studied.

TABLE 6.5
Distribution of Inmates on the Basis of Arguments with Jail Authorities

Response	*Jail*							*Total*
	Burail	*Ludhiana*	*Jalandhar*	*Patiala*	*Amritsar*	*Hissar*	*Ambala*	
Yes	5 35.7%	18 28.6%	6 28.6%	4 26.7%	4 14.8%	12 35.3%	12 46.2%	61 30.5%
No	9 64.3%	45 71.4%	15 71.4%	11 73.3%	23 85.2%	22 64.7%	14 53.8%	139 69.5%
Total	14	63	21	15	27	34	26	200

When asked if the inmates had arguments with the jail staff, 61, i.e. 30.5 percent responded in affirmation. Out of 14 inmates at Chandigarh jail 35.7 percent reported that they had arguments. Therefore it is assumed that not all inmates would see themselves more negatively inside than outside. Perhaps there would be those who would have high self-esteem in prison (particularly inmates who have nowhere to turn to outside) and these inmates may tend to see the staff more favourably or nearer to themselves than others; thus being identified with the staff they would wish to win their approval by conforming to the rules. Out of all the jails, in Ambala jail maximum respondents, i.e. 46.2 percent reported that they had arguments with authorities. In Patiala central jail only 26.7 percent, in Amritsar 14.8 percent, and in Hissar 35.3 percent respondents reported that they had argument with jail staff. In Ludhiana and Jalandhar jail a great majority, i.e. 71.4 percent reported that they had no arguments with the jail authorities. These inmates may tend to see the staff more favorably or nearer to themselves than others. Thus being identified with the staff they would wish to win their approval by conforming to the rules.

ISSUES OF ARGUMENTS WITH JAIL AUTHORITIES

TABLE 6.6
Issues of Arguments

Response	*Frequency*	*Percent*
Not Applicable	139	69.5%
For rights	21	10.5%
For situations	5	2.5%
Treatment by staff	35	17.5%
Total	200	100.0%

Those respondents who reported that they had arguments with authorities were asked to specify the issues on which they had arguments. A close examination of these incidents reveal that majority of inmates had problem with the jail staff when they showed partiality towards some inmates or when they were looked down upon. Withholding prisoner's rights, favoritism, unfairness or victimization are a few causes of friction and confrontation between inmates and staff. According to respondents most of the prison officials in their behaviour with the ordinary inmates were offending and discourteous. They were arrogant and high headed. They always relied on their own sources of information and seem to think that whatever they knew was perhaps the only truth. Conflicts and arguments were accentuated when inmates were not provided the facilities like hygienic food and living conditions to which they were entitled. There were 21 respondents who reported that material deprivation in the prison demoralized inmates that they resorted to stealing. Further, poor quality of food, shelter and absence of healthy living due to corrupt measures led to arguments with authorities. In 5 cases denial of the right to privacy and expression forced the inmates to follow the conflicting path with authorities.

CHECK ON MOVEMENT OF THE INMATES

Imprisonment imposes restrictions and deprives prisoners of their individual liberty and comforts of a free life. Sykes contended that of all the painful conditions of imprisonment imposed on the inmates, none is more obvious than the loss of liberty.

TABLE 6.7
Check on Movement of the Inmates in Different Prisons

Response	*Jail*							*Total*
	Burail	*Ludhiana*	*Jalandhar*	*Patiala*	*Amritsar*	*Hissar*	*Ambala*	
Yes	14 100.0%	63 100.0%	10 47.6%	15 100.0%	13 48.1%	33 97.1%	26 100.0%	174 87.0%
No	—	—	11 52.4%	—	14 51.9%	1 2.9%	—	26 13.0%
Total	14	63	21	15	27	34	26	200

Table 6.7 shows the extent of restrictions on the movement of female inmates in the prison. Results indicate that 87 percent of respondents reported that there was a constant check on their

movement in the prison. All the inmates of Burail, Ludhiana, Patiala and Ambala jail reported that there was always a female police staff to check their movement within the cell. The inmates had to live in a restricted environment where freedom of movement was denied. In Jalandhar, Amritsar and Hissar jail there were 52.4 percent, 51.9 percent and 2.9 percent respondents respectively, who reported that there was no constant check on their movement. In Jalandhar jail inmates were dumped together like animals and in Ambala jail male staff was frequently entering female wards.

DO INMATES SHARE THEIR PROBLEMS WITH JAIL STAFF?

TABLE 6.8
Inmates Sharing their Problems with Jail Staff

Response	*Jail*							*Total*
	Burail	*Ludhiana*	*Jalandhar*	*Patiala*	*Amritsar*	*Hissar*	*Ambala*	
Yes	5 35.7%	38 60.3%	12 57.1%	12 80.0%	13 48.1%	23 67.6%	17 65.4%	120 60.0%
No	9 64.3%	25 39.7%	9 42.9%	3 20.0%	14 51.9%	11 32.4%	9 34.6%	80 40.0%
Total	14	63	21	15	27	34	26	200

The prisoners are faced with many problems of adjusting and learning the rules of the jail life. Many a times they discuss their problems with jail staff in order to seek some help. Findings indicate that 60 percent of the respondents tried to discuss their problems with jail staff and 40 percent of the respondents did not talk to authorities on the subject. Some of them felt that prison officers were very arrogant. They were partial and unjust to those prisoners who were weak, poor, simple and resourceless. These inmates were pinched at the inhumanity of certain officials as they felt that it was below the officials' dignity to properly talk to the inmates. All these reasons stopped inmates from sharing their problems with jail authorities. In Burail jail only 35.7 percent respondents reported that they discussed their problems with jail staff. In Ludhiana jail 60.3 percent, in Jalandhar 57.1 percent, in Patiala 80 percent, in Amritsar 48.1 percent, in Hissar 67.6 percent and in Ambala 65.4 percent respondents stated that they discussed their problems with the jail staff. Except Burail jail at Chandigarh, in all six prisons, majority of the inmates discussed their problems with the jail staff. These problems ranged from their personal problems to inter-personal interactional problems. In continuation with issue of sharing problems with jail staff, a few inmates in the present study informally admitted that they had been regularly informing the staff about the activities of other inmates.

REACTIONS OF THE JAIL STAFF TOWARDS INMATE'S PROBLEMS

Table 6.8.1
Reaction of the Jail Staff

Response	*Frequency*	*Percent*
Not Applicable	80	40.0%
Ignored/avoided	45	22.5%
Sympathized/consoled	47	23.5%
Helped/Guided	9	4.5%
Showed helplessness	19	9.5%
Total	200	100.0%

Those respondents who discussed their problems with jail authorities were further asked to report the reactions of the jail staff towards their problems. 22.5 percent reported that authorities ignored them. Most of the prison officers listened to their problems in a very casual manner. Others avoided them as they did not want to waste their time in listening to the problems. Out of 200 cases, only 9 cases reported that the authorities tried to help them. The jail staff tried to guide these inmates. There were 47 cases who reported that authorities sympathized with them and tried to console them. There were 19 respondents who reported that the jail authorities showed their helplessness and disclosed their own personal problems.

Such variations in reactions of the jail staff indicate individual variations in society in general.

LIVING CONDITIONS IN THE PRISONS

The basic necessity that preserve human life, i.e. food, clothing and shelter is one of the most important tasks that prison administration is expected to perform after security. This aspect of prison has a direct bearing upon the attitudes and morale of inmate population. For the inmates too, these services represent the basic few things which concern their immediate life. The desire to safeguard the present is far important for long-term prisoners who usually do not hopefully look forward to a very happy future life beyond walls. This down to earth thinking of some prisoners made them vocal on the grievances that concern the administration of these services. To highlight the living conditions of female inmates, this aspect has been studied.

Overcrowding is one of the major problems of prisons in India. According to NCRB (2006) Punjab jails are overcrowded. Against authorized capacity of 11274 prisoners with 420 for females there are 15115 prisoners including 776 female inmates in jails in the state. Similar is the case with the state of Haryana where against the available space to accommodate 10587 prisoners with 733 for females are packed with 12687 prisoners including 533 females. One reason for overcrowding of women jail in Punjab is mentioned that women who are being held for trivial offences are incarcerated in the maximum security institutions for lack of other facilities. Jails are overcrowded with 20 to 30 inmates sharing the same cell. Crowding can also affect the psychological state of an inmate due to the fact that crowded institutions have reduced work and activity programs available for fewer inmates or for shorter time periods. Therefore, this increases the amount of time that an inmate is left with nothing to do which generates a great deal of stress and boredom (Bartol and Bartol, 1994). The physical condition of the prison cells is stuffy and suffocating. Most of the prisons are so built that inhibited the flow of fresh air and sunlight. The caged windows make sunshine and breeze difficult to reach the cells. Inmates sleep on raised cement floor in a close proximity

TABLE 6.9
Distribution of the Inmates in One Cell

No. of inmates in one cell	*Jail*							*Total*
	Burail	*Ludhiana*	*Jalandhar*	*Patiala*	*Amritsar*	*Hissar*	*Ambala*	
10 to 15	14	63	—	—	—	—	—	77
> 15	—	—	21	15	27	34	26	123
Total	14	63	21	15	27	34	26	200

to each other. Most of the time, the inmates are kept under lock. They are allowed to move within the premises for a limited time span. All the activities of the inmates are closely watched. Even in the locked cells, the inmates are kept under vigilance.

Accommodation in the context of jail life means a place where the prisoner can be confined safely to serve his/her sentence under such living conditions as conducive to correctional treatment and maintenance of basic minimum standards of human dignity. In India, various prison reform committees have talked about over-crowding in jails, bad and unhygienic living conditions, and inferior quality of food. Keeping this in mind, the inmates in different jails were asked to report number of inmates in one cell. In Burail and Ludhiana jails there were less than 15 inmates who shared one cell. In Burail jail the ratio of women to men was very less and Ludhiana jail was a newer jail exclusively for women. However, in the remaining 5 jails, i.e. Jalandhar, Patiala, Amritsar, Hissar and Ambala, there was over-crowding and more than 15 persons shared the same cell. There was hardly any privacy. They had to sleep on floor on dirty beddings. Almost all the inmates of Jalandhar jail were suffering from skin ailments as their beddings had never been changed. Presence of mosquitoes, flies and mice was a normal sight.

FACILITIES FOR THE INMATES

Different studies have mentioned that women's prisons are often particularly ill-equipped and poorly financed. They have fewer medical, educational and vocational facilities than men's prisons (Dobash *et. al.*, 1986). Many prisons do not have proper arrangement of electricity. Two to three low powered bulbs hung from the ceilings in some cells make things just visible at night, but never enable reading without straining one's eyes. The sanitation inside the premises is normally not good. The prisons emit unique and extremely nauseating odour. The bad smell of tobacco, human sweat and perspiration has become a permanent feature of the prison. In most of the prisons open toilets inside the cells pump out the stinking smell of the human refuse.

TABLE 6.10
Facilities for the Inmates

Jail facilities		*Jail*						
		Burail	*Ludhiana*	*Jalandhar*	*Patiala*	*Amritsar*	*Hissar*	*Ambala*
Lighting	Electricity	14	63	21	15	27	34	26
Ventilation	Adequate	4	63	—	15	27	34	3
	Inadequate	10	—	21	—	—	—	23
Water source	Within jail	14	63	—	15	27	34	—
	Outside jail	—	—	21	—	—	—	26
Toilet	Shared with cell	14	63	—	15	27	34	—
	Shared outside jail	—	—	21	—	—	—	26

With regard to electricity, there was no difference in the responses of inmates in all the prisons. With regard to ventilation 4 cases in Burail jail found it to be adequate whereas 10 cases found ventilation inadequate. For 73 percent, ventilation was inadequate. In Ludhiana women jail, which is a newly constructed building, all the inmates reported that ventilation was adequate. In Patiala, Amritsar and Hissar jails, the inmates found ventilation quite adequate. In Ambala except 3 cases all the cases found ventilation inadequate. On the other hand, Jalandhar jail which is more than 100 years old building was in a very poor condition, where all the inmates reported inadequate and dingy conditions. With regard to water source, in all the prison except Jalandhar and Ambala jails, water source was within jail. With regard to the toilet, except in Jalandhar and

Ambala jails, toilet is shared but within the cell. Most of the prisoners were assigned the job of cleaning the toilet. It is very interesting to note that well-off, educated and those inmates whose family members were regularly visiting and providing financial support did not perform this duty. They would hire poor, uneducated prisoners with no family support, to do this job for them. The results support the findings of Dobash *et. al.*

TABLE 6.11
Quantity and Quality of Food

Food Quantity and Quality	*Jail*							*Total*
	Burail	*Ludhiana*	*Jalandhar*	*Patiala*	*Amritsar*	*Hissar*	*Ambala*	
Adequate and hygienic	6 42.9%	17 27.0%	—	6 40.0%	3 11.1%	20 58.8%	—	52 26.0%
Just palatable	4 28.6%	44 69.8%	1 4.8%	5 33.3%	16 59.3%	—	6 23.1%	76 38.0%
Unhygienic and Bad Taste	4 28.6%	2 3.2%	20 95.2%	4 26.7%	8 29.6%	14 41.2%	20 76.9%	72 36.0%
Total	14	63	21	15	27	34	26	200

Different prison reform committees have stated that food quality is not up to the mark in most of the prisons. According to Saini (2008), samples of wheat collected from five out of 19 Haryana district jails failed the test. Wheat was found to be unfit for human consumption as it was insect infested. There was a wide variation in the type of food served in the prisons under study. Quality not the quantity of the food disturbed most of the inmates. The inmates grievances centered on bad preparation of the food and consequential tastelessness and un-palatability. These drawbacks of the prison food are the natural outcome of mass cooking, outdated kitchens and utensils and indifferent attitude of the prisoners who cook food. In Jalandhar central jail, the quality of food was the worst. In Ambala, Patiala and Amritsar central jails, women had made earthen ovens and were cooking on their own. In Chandigarh and Hissar jails, inmates were satisfied with the quality and hygiene of the served food. It is interesting to note that in all the prisons there were canteens and inmates could buy anything ranging from milk, tea, jam, butter, bread, biscuits, etc. The women who could afford these items did not eat food in the jail. Either their family members provided them with raw material and they cooked on their own or a few made purchases from the canteen. Women, who were poor and had no *'mulaquat'*, served the rich inmates and did not eat the jail food. They worked for the richer inmates and thus could get 'token money' and could buy eatables from canteen. Although the quality of food in some prisons was unpalatable, researcher observed a lot of food wastage. Enormous amount of *chapattis* were found in the court yards. On enquiry, it was mentioned that they would be used as fuel for earthen ovens. The quantum of ration for prison inmates is rather too much. The poor quality of its preparation and corruption is the root cause of deteriorating food supplies to the prisoners.

HEALTH OF THE INMATES

The prison being a total institution has the responsibility of protecting and maintaining the physical and mental health of the prisoners. Female prisoners are more vulnerable to ailments like gynaecological problems, headaches, stress and emotional disturbances. Such ailments flourish in the prison as the morale of the inmates is low. As a minority group, the health needs of women are often unmet. Different research studies have highlighted the negative picture of medical facilities in the prisons. In many countries, women in prison suffer from mental health problems (including depression, phobias, anxiety, neurosis, self-harm, and suicide) at alarmingly high rates. Research indicates that women prisoners suffer mental health problems to a much higher degree than both the male prison population and the general population. Again, the reason for the very high incidence of mental illness amongst women prisoners may be related to the higher proportion of women imprisoned for drug-related crimes and higher rates of past sexual, physical and mental abuse. Mental health may further be damaged by anxiety over the safety of their children who remain unattended (Bastick, 2005). To investigate further, female prisoners were asked to comment on their general well-being, especially health.

TABLE 6.12
General Health-related Problems of the Inmates

Response	*Jail*							*Total*
	Burail	*Ludhiana*	*Jalandhar*	*Patiala*	*Amritsar*	*Hissar*	*Ambala*	
Common ailments	2 14.3%	14 22.2%	2 9.5%	3 20.0%	5 18.5%	11 32.4%	3 11.5%	40 20.0%
Infectious diseases	1 7.1%	8 12.7%	8 38.1%	2 13.3%	9 33.3%	10 29.4%	5 19.2%	43 21.5%
Gynaecological problem	4 28.6%	6 9.5%	4 19.0%	1 6.7%	2 7.4%	3 8.8%	2 7.7%	22 11.0%
Psychiatric	4 28.6%	30 47.6%	4 19.0%	6 40.0%	8 29.6%	10 29.4%	14 53.8%	76 38.0%
Nothing specific	3 21.4%	5 7.9%	3 14.3%	3 20.0%	3 11.1%	—	2 7.7%	19 9.5%
Total	14	63	21	15	27	34	26	200

The inmates were asked to state their physical and mental health. All the inmates except 19 in all prisons reported one or the other type of ailment. The most common reported problem, i.e. 38 percent was of depression, tension and stress. Maximum inmates from Ambala jail, i.e. 53.8 percent followed by 47.6 percent from Ludhiana jail reported some sort of psychiatric problem. The results coincide with the findings of Bastick. It was found that in all the prisons, general medical physician visited twice a week, but Psychiatrist or Specialists were not available to the prisoners. It was observed that medical practitioners were either missing from the prisons or wherever available, they had an authoritarian approach. The time and effort necessary to explain, to help provide insight, to gain acceptance, and to achieve confidence were absent. As is often true, when the doctor-patient relationship is imposed and not chosen, there were no element of faith and confidence. This was a major complaint by inmates who further stated that doctors regularly made disparaging comments and asked insulting questions such as, "How do you know you have a headache?" or "pain? I do not see any pain." Or "You are fond of eating medicines," or "You smell like rat". In such an environment, it is difficult to imagine how a Physician would be able to detect and treat anyone. Further, a large number, i.e. 21.5 percent of respondents reported skin infections. Maximum respondents from Jalandhar prison, i.e. 38.1 percent followed by 33.3 percent from Amritsar central jail reported skin-related ailments. Unhygienic and over-crowded living place was one of the main reasons for such infections. Of all the health problems, the gynaecological problems reported were the least.

MEDICAL FACILITIES IN THE PRISONS

TABLE 6.13
Availability and Adequacy of Medical Facilities for the Inmates

Response	*Jail*							*Total*
	Burail	*Ludhiana*	*Jalandhar*	*Patiala*	*Amritsar*	*Hissar*	*Ambala*	
Yes	12 85.7%	31 49.2%	—	7 46.7%	10 37.0%	5 14.7%	6 23.1%	71 35.5%
No	2 14.3%	32 50.8%	21 100.0%	8 53.3%	17 63.0%	29 85.3%	20 76.9%	129 64.5%
Total	14	63	21	15	27	34	26	200

The health of the prisoners depends upon the availability of medical aid. Since incarceration may have deleterious effects on the prisoners' mental health, the Model Prison Manual rightly states that "the object of medical administration is prisons in mainly to restore and maintain, physical and mental health of prisoners, and to keep up the general sanitation and hygiene of the institution to a satisfactory standard". One of the fundamental duties of prison administration is to look after the prisoners' health. However, all the prisons under study displayed a picture of shear neglect with regards to health facilities.

In all the prisons it was found that the prison administration was not doing adequate work in this regard. Inmates were asked to report whether they were satisfied with the medical facilities. More than 60 percent inmates found medical facilities inadequate. It was in case of inmates of Jalandhar central jail, where all the inmates showed dissatisfaction with regard to medical facilities. The adequate care of prisoners' health requires not merely provision for medical aid but various other facilities with regard to food, bed, air and light as well. All these conditions were missing in the case of Jalandhar central jail where females were living in very bad and inhumane conditions. Situation was relatively better in case of Burail, Ludhiana, Amritsar and Hissar jails. Conditions in case of Ambala jail were also not satisfactory. Inmates further mentioned that the time spent with each patient averaged about *'one minute'*. There was no provision of mental health services in any of the prisons under study. Allocation of healthcare personnel and equipment throughout the prisons was largely unplanned and not reflective of the actual needs. There were no registered nurses on the staff. The prisoners whose background qualified them to perform useful healthcare tasks were often given work assignment as assistants. It was found that except in Ludhiana jail there was no lady doctor available to examine the female prisoners.

SPECIAL HEALTH CARE FOR PREGNANT INMATES

Most of the prisons do not have arrangements to take care of pregnant women. All the essentials for a healthy pregnancy are missing in the prison viz. nutritious food, fresh air, exercise, extra vitamins, sanitary conditions and pre-natal care. Women in prison are denied nutritional supplements such as those sponsored by Family Welfare Program. Keeping this in mind, an attempt was made to procure information on food and healthcare of pregnant women in prisons.

Table 6.14
Special Care for Pregnant w.r.t Food and Healthcare

Response	*Jail*							*Total*
	Burail	*Ludhiana*	*Jalandhar*	*Patiala*	*Amritsar*	*Hissar*	*Ambala*	
Yes	10 71.4%	—	—	4 26.7%	12 44.4%	14 41.2%	—	40 20.0%
No	4 28.6%	63 100.0%	21 100.0%	11 73.3%	15 55.6%	20 58.8%	26 100.0%	160 80.0%
Total	14	63	21	15	27	34	26	200

The female prisoners have specific health-related problems. The issues pertaining to pregnancy, motherhood, abortion and miscarriage are specific to women prisoners. The Model Jail Manual talks about specific care for pregnant women. Keeping this in mind, women prisoners were asked to specify whether special care was being provided to them. It was found that 71.4 percent respondents in Burail jail reported that special care with regard to food was provided. Similarly, 26.7 percent cases in Patiala jail, 44.4 percent in Amritsar jail and 41.2 percent in Hissar jail mentioned that pregnant women were given milk to drink. In Ludhiana, Jalandhar and Amritsar jail no such provision was mentioned.

With regard to health, 20 percent respondents stated that special care was provided. However, 80 percent inmates reported that no special health care was provided to pregnant women. In Burail jail 71.4 percent reported that special medical care was being provided to pregnant inmates. In Patiala 26.7 percent, Amritsar 44.4 percent and Hissar 41.2 percent respondents reported that special medical facilities were provided.

RELATIONS AMONG THE INMATES

Despite heterogeneity in terms of their age, caste, social, economic and criminal background, prisoners have a feeling of belongingness to each other—a feeling generated by the

TABLE 6.15
Relations among the Inmates

Response	*Jail*							*Total*
	Burail	*Ludhiana*	*Jalandhar*	*Patiala*	*Amritsar*	*Hissar*	*Ambala*	
Congenial	4 28.6%	27 42.9%	4 19.0%	6 40.0%	7 25.9%	11 32.4%	13 50.0%	72 36.0%
Non-congenial	2 14.3%	5 7.9%	5 23.8%	—	—	5 14.7%	5 19.2%	22 11.0%
Workable	8 57.1%	31 49.2%	12 57.1%	9 60.0%	20 74.1%	18 52.9%	8 30.8%	106 53.0%
Total	14	63	21	15	27	34	26	200

'community character' of the prison milieu. Good as well as bad prisoners of the prison community reciprocate with each other and enter into a complex network of relationship. Inmates understand that they have few alternatives to alleviate their deprivations, loss of status and degradation. The inmates unite with their fellow captives to seek satisfaction of their needs. Thus, when inmates cooperate in exchanging favours that not only removes the opportunity for some to exploit others, it also enables them to accept material deprivation more easily. In addition, available goods and services are more easily distributed and shared if the inmates have a cooperative society.

In addition to exploring relationship of inmates with the staff, the relations of inmates amongst themselves were also studied. The responses of the inmates were grouped into three categories, namely, congenial, non-congenial and workable. Majority of the inmates reported 'workable' relations among themselves. All the inmates know that they had to make adjustments with the other inmates even if they do not endorse their negative behaviour pattern. Most of the inmates never wanted to make their negative feelings obvious. Therefore, they chose to respond under this category. Small group studies have shown that people have a tendency to make clique groups with the persons of similar likings and disliking. There were 72 respondents who developed congenial relations with other inmates. Majority of these respondents belonged to Ambala Jail and the least number was from Jalandhar jail. When there is a fight of basic minimal for survival, good personal relations are difficult to maintain as is obvious from Jalandhar jail. In Burail jail, 57.1 percent respondents reported that they had workable relations with other inmates. 28.6 percent reported that they had congenial relations with other prisoners. In Ludhiana women jail 42.9 percent inmates reported workable relations and only 7.9 percent reported non-congenial relations. In Jalandhar more inmates had problems as 23.8 percent reported non-congenial relations and only 19 percent reported congenial relations with other inmates. In Patiala and Amritsar central jail no inmate reported that they had non-congenial relations among themselves.

ARGUMENTS AMONG THE INMATES

Table 6.16 shows whether inmates had arguments amongst themselves. 66 percent of the respondents reported that they had arguments with other inmates. In Burail jail at Chandigarh 64.3 percent, in Ludhiana 61.9 percent, in Jalandhar 71.4 percent, in Amritsar 55.6 percent, in Hissar 70.6 percent and 73.1 percent in Ambala jail reported that they had arguments with other inmates. It was found that there were hardly any incidents of violence in women prisons. Whenever there was some outburst of violence behaviour among the women, the form of physical violence was individualistic. However, verbal aggression used to take an ugly form. Calling names, using taunting remarks, humiliating some one were the common things. Few respondents felt that the use of bad language and squabbling among inmates had a positive function as it offered an outlet for accumulated aggression in inmates due to frustrations caused by the prison environment.

TABLE 6.16
Arguments among the Inmates

Response	*Jail*							*Total*
	Burail	*Ludhiana*	*Jalandhar*	*Patiala*	*Amritsar*	*Hissar*	*Ambala*	
Yes	9 64.3%	39 61.9%	15 71.4%	11 73.3%	15 55.6%	24 70.6%	19 73.1%	132 66.0%
No	5 35.7%	24 38.1%	6 28.6%	4 26.7%	12 44.4%	10 29.4%	7 26.9%	68 34.0%
Total	14	63	21	15	27	34	26	200

ISSUES FOR ARGUMENTS AMONG THE INMATES

A close examination revealed that the causes of argument amongst inmates were trivial which as inmates admitted would not happen outside the prison. Apart from being in an environment which in itself breeds friction, conflicts were accentuated by such incidents, as for instance a shortage of commodities. Shortage of goods and services in prison viz. toiletries, confectionary, money, etc. was the cause of friction

TABLE 6.16.1
Issues of Arguments

Response	*Frequency*	*Percent*
Not Applicable	68	34.0%
Work	26	13.0%
Items	36	18.0%
Hygiene	14	7.0%
Behaviour pattern	42	21.0%
Spying for authorities	14	7.0%
Total	200	100.0%

and interest of the inmates revolving around such items were reported by 18 percent inmates. On the other hand, some of the acts such as stealing other's items led to friction among inmates. Although it is expected that common sufferings of inmates would bind them together, yet due to the condition of deprivation in prison, it appeared that the attitude of personal gain for survival was the cause of competition between the inmates at the expense of each other. Thus, it was inevitable and hardly surprising that inmates who were not affiliated with others and who did not have strong feeling of loyalty towards their fellow inmates, tended to grasp the opportunity of exploiting others, either by stealing or by engaging in commercial gains (e.g. services for goods). Prisoners enter the prison not merely as social individuals but also as persons having social ties with the outer world. Though the compulsion of the world within the walls presses them hard to unlearn the styles of their demeanor in the past, yet the habits and attitudes of the past years do not fade out. These different behaviour patterns resulted in arguments in 42 cases. Inmates also argued with one another merely for the purpose of coming closer to prison officers. For obtaining such position some inmates spied on others. If inmates criticized the officers in private and spoke ill of them in their absence, the matter was reported to the officials. There were 14 cases where inmates had argument for spying. The outstanding contributory factors to friction among inmates were boredom and particularly provocation by others. The fact that not all the inmates perceived the particular stimulus in the same way and not all of them responded to frustrating conditions by overt verbal aggression indicates that each individual handles the situation differently.

DO THE INMATES SHARE PROBLEMS AMONGST THEMSELVES?

Street (1965) observed that informal group structures grow out of primary relations among inmates in all institutions and it can be assumed to have a significant role in socializing and relating the inmates to the institution, in defining informal norms of inmate behaviour, approved set of values and beliefs. Research indicates that women's own social networks in prison are more supportive and affectionate than those formed by male prisoners. Women in prison form pseudo-families with prisoners taking different roles in relations to each other (such as mother, daughter and sister) (Giallombardo, 1966; Culbertson and Fortune, 1986).

TABLE 6.17
Share Problems with each Other

Response	*Frequency*	*Percent*
Yes	147	73.5%
No	53	26.5%
Total	200	100.0%

TABLE 6.17.1
Reactions of Inmates to the Shared Problems

Response	*Frequency*	*Percent*
Not Applicable	53	26.5%
Sympathize	55	27.5%
Share the pain	59	29.5%
Criticize authorities	3	1.5%
Make fun	9	4.5%
Guide	16	8.0%
Ignore	5	2.5%
Total	200	100.0%

It was found that women inmates in prison did not organize themselves in a cohesive and anti-institution group. However, small clique groups were noticed. Majority of the respondents shared their problems with other inmates. It was reported that when a new entrant arrives, she would meet the jail staff and all the inmates and narrate her story. Later, they preferred not to talk about their problems. Majority of the respondents shared and sympathized with each other. As there was no spatial differentiation between hardcore criminals and first timers since they stayed together, 16 respondents reported that their future course of action was guided by other inmates. The inmates with longer jail-stay guided and/or directed the fresh arrivals on their interaction with the staff and other inmates. There were 9 respondents who reported that in their weaker moments they shared their problems with other inmates. Later, they were made fun of and openly criticized. 29.5 percent respondents reported that they shared their problems with other inmates as it lessened their pain. Inmates were further probed about inmate grouping. It was found that socio-economic background, caste, region and criminogenic personality background played an important role in consolidating inmates in the prison. Another important factor that consolidated inmates groups was the similarity of habits and attitudes coupled with likeness of criminal background (for example, all the women belonging to Sansi tribe formed their clique groups in all the prisons). The results endorse the concept of pseudo-families in the women prisons as propagated by Giallombardo, Culbertson and Fortune.

DO THE INMATES GET PUNISHED IN THE JAIL?

Prisons impose careful and continuous surveillance, and are quick to punish (and sometimes to punish severely) infractions of the limiting rules. The process of institutionalization in correctional settings may surround inmates so thoroughly with external limits, immerse them so deeply in a network of rules and regulations, that majority of the inmates accept the norms. Since the rule of law is nowhere perfect, it is not surprising at all that women inmates like any other group of free men violated rules and regulations of the

Table 6.18
Punishment given to the Inmates

Response	*Jail*							*Total*
	Burail	*Ludhiana*	*Jalandhar*	*Patiala*	*Amritsar*	*Hissar*	*Ambala*	
Yes	2 14.3%	12 19.0%	10 47.6%	2 13.3%	6 22.2%	6 17.6%	5 19.2%	43 21.5%
No	12 85.7%	51 81.0%	11 52.4%	13 86.7%	21 77.8%	28 82.4%	21 80.8%	157 78.5%
Total	14	63	21	15	27	34	26	200

prison and committed offences with or without any regard for punitive consequences.

There is an assumption that inmates who do not conform to the prison rules can be punished. In any prison, certain ordinary rules of discipline are necessary so that everyday prison life may be regulated. 43 inmates who violated the code of conduct were punished. In Burail jail at Chandigarh 2 inmates, in Ludhiana jail 12 inmates, in Jalandhar jail 10 inmates, 2 inmates in Patiala jail, 6 in Amritsar jail, 6 in Hissar jail and 5 inmates mentioned that they were punished by jail authorities, while in the prison. Since women did not indulge in violent brawls and destruction of prison property as male prisoners, the severity of punishment was also mild. Findings indicate that in some cases violation of the rule was deliberate, but in the majority of the cases it was the outcome of habit or necessity such as possession of forbidden items (bidis and cigarettes), wordy duel and exchange of abuses, non-compliance of the orders of the prison officials, stealing other inmates articles, instigating some inmates who abuse or insult prison officials, etc. Leaving aside a microscopic minority, the overwhelming majority of the inmates (78.5 percent) behaved in conformity with the prison rules and regulations for the fear of punishment alone.

TYPE OF PUNISHMENT RECEIVED BY THE INMATES IN THE JAIL

What kinds of punishment were imposed upon the

TABLE 6.18.1
Type of Punishment Received by the Inmates

Response	*Frequency*	*Percent*
Not Applicable	157	78.5%
Slapped	8	4.0%
Verbally abused	26	13.0%
Threatened	9	4.5%
Total	200	100.0%

prisoners in each of the seven prisons? The 43 cases who reported that they were punished while in prison, mentioned verbal abuse, caution, warnings and threats as a type of punishment received. 8 respondents mentioned that they were slapped by women warders as a punishment. These cases experienced the act of punishment more subjectively and believed that punishment was nothing but an expression of punisher's personal vendetta. It is reported by these respondents that such punishment did not lower their prestige in the eyes of other inmates.

COMPLAINTS AGAINST THE SYSTEM

In a democratic set-up, the doctrine of the separation of power dictates that there has to be a degree of separation of functions between the three essential bodies of the state viz. the legislature, the executive, and the judiciary. For example, the judiciary adjudicates upon conflicts, between state institutions, between state and individual and between individuals, is independent of political influence in its members interpretation of the law and their judgments in a particular case. In practice, however, the separation of power has never been absolute. Similarly, the role of police is always under critical scrutiny. Police has a statutory responsibility to record crimes; they retain much discretion about whether and how to deal with the possible offences that come to their attention. Many a times, the individuals are falsely implicated by the police by submitting false evidence. The role of lawyers is also very significant as each case has to be presented before the court by the lawyer.

When legal rules and procedures are ignored or not impartially applied, injustice in the form of abuse of power or wrongful conviction can occur. Wrongful convictions can result through malpractice of police or advocates or because the trial judge is biased or corrupt. Abuse of power and other deficiencies in the criminal justice system have been reported by many researchers (Ashworth, 1998; Rozenberg, 1993).

TABLE 6.19

Complaints by the Inmates against the System

Response	*Jail*							*Total*
	Burail	*Ludhiana*	*Jalandhar*	*Patiala*	*Amritsar*	*Hissar*	*Ambala*	
Yes	11 78.6%	56 88.9%	19 90.5%	11 73.3%	21 77.8%	32 94.1%	22 84.6%	172 86.0%
No	3 21.4%	7 11.1%	2 9.5%	4 26.7%	6 22.2%	2 5.9%	4 15.4%	28 14.0%
Total	14	63	21	15	27	34	26	200

TABLE 6.19.1

Complaint against Various Authorities

Response	*Frequency*	*Percent*
Not Applicable	28	14.0%
Judiciary	39	19.5%
Lawyers	8	4.0%
Police	51	25.5%
Judiciary, Lawyers and Police	35	17.5%
Judiciary and Lawyers	12	6.0%
Lawyers and Police	21	10.5%
Judiciary and Police	6	3.0%
Total	200	100.0%

The inmates were asked to mention if they had any complaints against the prevailing criminal justice system. Overwhelmingly 86 percent reported that they had complaints against the system. 78.6 percent in Burail jail, 88.9 percent in

Ludhiana jail, 90.5 percent in Jalandhar jail, 73.3 percent in Patiala jail, 77.8 percent in Amritsar jail, 94.1 percent in Hissar jail and 84.6 percent in Ambala jail showed their grievances against prevailing system. Majority of inmates blamed Police followed by Judiciary, then lawyers for putting them into such situation. They reported that they were wrongfully convicted by falsification of evidence by the police officers; oppressive questioning and violence by police; and non-disclosure of facts by the police in front of the Magistrate. A few inmates complained against slow and cumbersome appeal procedures. They argued that court experience produces a sense of unfairness, bewilderment or pain. Such findings clearly indicate that public confidence in the police and the justice system has been eroded.

SUGGESTIONS BY INMATES FOR IMPROVING JAIL CONDITIONS

Prisoners confront a unique set of contingencies and pressures to which they are required to react and adapt in order to survive in the prison. Prisoners typically are denied their basic privacy rights and loose control over mundane aspects of their existence. They live in small, sometimes extremely bad space, often have no choice over when they get up or go to bed,

Table 6.20
Suggestions by Inmates for Improving Jail Conditions

Response	*Jail*							*Total*
	Burail	*Ludhiana*	*Jalandhar*	*Patiala*	*Amritsar*	*Hissar*	*Ambala*	
Don't know	4 28.6%	12 19.0%	2 9.5%	3 20.0%	8 29.6%	10 29.4%	4 15.4%	43 21.5%
Improve living conditions	—	4 6.3%	13 61.9%	—	8 29.6%	5 14.7%	5 19.2%	35 17.5%
Providing more facilities	7 50.0%	32 50.8%	6 28.6%	6 40.0%	7 25.9%	13 38.2%	8 30.8%	79 39.5%
Changing rules	3 21.4%	15 23.8%	—	6 40.0%	4 14.8%	6 17.6%	9 34.6%	43 21.5%
Total	14	63	21	15	27	34	26	200

when or what they may eat and so on. The degraded conditions under which they live serve to repeatedly remind them of their compromised social status and stigmatized social role as prisoners. Due to such dehumanizing conditions, inmates were asked to suggest the areas for improvement in the prevailing jail conditions.

Table 6.20 highlights the suggestions given by inmates to improve the conditions of the prison. There were 43, i.e. 21.5 percent inmates who did not give any suggestions in this regard and there were 12 inmates from Ludhiana, 10 from Hissar, 8 from Amritsar, 4 each from Burail and Ambala, 3 from Patiala and 2 from Jalandhar jails who were pessimistic in their outlook and opined that their suggestions would not yield any result because the system would not change.

The responses of remaining 157, i.e. 78.5 inmates percent were divided into three main categories viz. improvement in existing living conditions, provision of more facilities, and changes in the rules.

There were 17.5 percent respondents who talked about improving the existing living conditions like cleanliness and good hygienic food. Most of the inmates belonged to Jalandhar, Hissar and Ambala jails. A few inmates suggested improvement of the medical facilities in the prison especially providing Specialist doctors, Psychiatrists and Gynaecologists.

Of 39.5 percent inmates who suggested for provision of more facilities, more than half belonged to Burail and Ludhiana jails. They suggested that Government should provide educational facilities to women prisoners on the lines of Burail and Patiala jails where in collaboration with IGNOU, New Delhi, male inmates had educational facilities. A few inmates suggested that Government should engage women lawyers for women under-trials. There were a few inmates who suggested that there should be separate cabins for 'Mulaquat'. In all the prisons inmates were made to stand together in the prison and there was so much rush, they could hardly talk to their family members. No privacy existed. They wanted more time to meet their family members.

21.5 percent inmates, mostly from Patiala and Ambala jails, suggested that hardcore convicts should be kept in separate cells away from under-trials as they try to exploit innocent freshers.

Since there is only one women jail in Punjab, prisoners in this jail felt that they had been kept in women jail away from their family members who could not come to meet them on regular basis. They were against the idea of having women jails. According to Jail Manual, only convicts could be given work, most of the under-trials who had been languishing in jails for more than one year wanted that they should be given work so that they could remain busy. Except respondents from women jails at Ludhiana and Hissar, there were a few inmates who felt insecure as male jail staff had thorough fare to women cells which made them uncomfortable and more susceptible to physical abuse.

CONCLUSION

Women prisoners comprise a much smaller percentage of the total population than men. It is perhaps for this reason that their specific problems are more easily overlooked. When most women first enter the prison, they find that they are being forced to adapt to an often harsh and rigid institutional routine, deprived of privacy and liberty, subjected to a diminished, stigmatized status, and extremely scarce material conditions. In due course of time, transformation begins and inmates begin to adapt to their new environment.

An overwhelmingly majority of women admitted that they had congenial relations with the jail staff. Results showed that majority of inmates conducted themselves according to the rules to avoid any controversy with authorities. Some of them even discussed their problems with jail authorities. For these inmates jail authorities were a part of their large extended families. Majority of women received insufficient facilities in terms of sub-standard healthcare and unhygienic food. Except in one or two jails, women inmates were not involved in any vocational and educational programs. These deficiencies restrained these inmates to successfully reintegrate into their communities and reconnect with their families upon release. Further, the stigma assigned to incarcerated women is so strong that these female offenders are commonly considered to be 'deviant' and 'abnormal'.

The episodes of physical violence are rare in women prisons. However, they had arguments with other inmates on trivial matters as the scarcity of the facilities in the prison results in an environment of friction and conflict. On an overall, women share a common world view with other inmates. As a result they develop a feeling of closeness and proximity amongst them.

Thus the findings of the present study clearly indicate that women prisoners are faced with the formal bureaucratic structure which alienates them from their surroundings. These women experience a sense of being forced in an institution which comprises two conflicting communities of women (staff and inmates). They are not well enough equipped to cope with them whichever way they go impinge upon them. The foregoing discussion in this chapter was concerned with the life of women prisoners in the prison and the strategies they adopt to cope up with their institutional environment.

Summary and Conclusion

Gender though a fundamental, is largely an ignored issue in the field of criminal justice system. The main reason for this neglect is a small number of women incarcerated in comparison to the number of men. Further, women offenders are different to men, having different pathways to crime, different life circumstances and different habilitative or rehabilitative needs. The general lack of attention on women prisoners by both Criminology and correctional organizations is well documented. For example, Phillips and Harm (1998) stated that women had been 'in the shadow of men'. Covington (1998) stated that they were neglected and misunderstood. Lamberge (1991) noted that they have been ignored through assimilation with men. Coll *et. al.* (1998) also stated that services and ideas concerning women prisoners remained modeled on those for men.

A close examination of trends in the incarceration of women can shed more light on the larger issue of steadily rising incarceration rates. Analysis of recent prison population trends presented in this book suggests that female prison population is particularly sensitive to the factors that drive overall levels of imprisonment. It is believed that such a study will awaken the authorities to understand the needs of these women, help in managing incarcerated women, and providing appropriate resources and services to them. Such resources and services might help these women whilst imprisoned and upon release to raise their children in more positive environments, thus reducing not only their offending but also the potential for their children in becoming the next generation of offenders.

The main focus of this research has been to explore the lives of women prisoners in seven jails. There are other aspects which have been taken into consideration, such as, What were the reasons that led women to different types of crime? Whether there existed a common pattern in their background? How their children grow up in prison or live outside separated from their mothers?, and What type of relationships do they develop with the jail staff and other inmates.

All these aspects have been covered in this research through the following objectives:

- To examine the socio-economic background of the women prisoners.
- To identify the types of crimes committed by women prisoners.
- To explore the causal factors of female criminality.
- To study the consequences of imprisonment on the inmates, and their relationships with their family members.
- To examine the life of inmates in the prison and understand their relations with co-prisoners and jail staff.
- To explore the problems faced by inmates and their suggestions to improve the system.

This study was designed in such a way as to make it possible to compare female prisoners at two levels; one at the individual and other at the prison level. In this chapter an attempt has been made to recapitulate the main results that have emerged from the study, and consider its implications. A few suggestions are also proposed for future research.

SUMMARY OF THE FINDINGS

Prisons serve the same purpose for women as they do for men. They are instruments of social control. However, the imprisonment of women reflects the position of women in the society. Gender-based realities are the central determinant to explain the existence of female offenders. Women are an extremely small proportion of the overall Indian prison population, approximately 5 percent (NCRB 2007). Imprisonment rates for women are increasing rapidly, after having remained low for so many years. This increase in crime by women is mainly attributed to violent and drug-related offences. It is possible that deteriorating economic conditions are now pushing the women to the brink faster than men. As the primary caretakers of children, women may be driven by poverty to engage in more 'crimes' for survival.

The present research has focused on experiences of women in the whole justice system; the special focus has inevitably been the prisons. It is for this reason that an attempt was made to understand the lives of women inmates in 7 prisons in the state of Punjab, Haryana and Union Territory of Chandigarh.

Who are the women in prison? An attempt was made through this study to explain the background of inmates in prison. The study was conducted on 200 women prisoners. The sample included 14 female inmates from Burail jail at Chandigarh, 126 inmates from 4 jails in Punjab and 60 inmates from 2 jails in Haryana. Majority of the inmates were under-trials. This was aligned with the percentage of under-trials to the total inmates in jails in India which is 65.7 percent. Maximum under-trials were institutionalized at Patiala jail. Ludhiana and Hissar women jails had maximum number of convicts. These jails have been constructed mainly to accommodate convicts. There were 125 women inmates who had spent up to 10 years in the prison, whereas only 79 women were convicts. Such findings highlight the plight of under-trials who continue to languish in the prisons without any hearings. There were 26 inmates who had been sentenced to life imprisonment. Only two inmates were awarded capital punishment, of which one had filed an appeal in the High

Court, which was rejected. Both the inmates were involved in homicide of their family members in connivance with their male accomplices.

Findings indicate that 64.5 percent of the inmates were married and majority of them were in Amritsar Central jail. 22.5 percent of women were either widow, divorced or separated. Both married and widows, divorced or separated women had children. Maximum number of respondents, i.e. 39 percent had more than 3 children. Children were of both the sexes and ranged in the different age groups. 15 children of less than 6 years of age were accompanying their mothers and grandmothers in the prison. There were 41 children who were on their own. They did not get any help from their relatives or friends. These children were staying alone either because their mothers had been imprisoned for the homicide of their father or both the parents were imprisoned for homicide on account of land disputes. In many cases, the younger sibling was taking care of the elder one's. Lack of economic resources forced many of these children to follow the path to crime.

As mentioned earlier, most of the respondents, i.e. 64.5 percent were married before being lodged in the prison but their number decreased after incarceration. A few of them were deserted by their husbands and others were imprisoned because of homicide of their spouse. Illiteracy prevailed among the women since more than half of them were illiterates. Only 18 inmates were graduates, majority of them in Ludhiana jail; followed by Ambala jail. There were only 5 cases of highly qualified women. 2 of them were professionals, 2 post-graduates and 1 a PhD. Out of the 2 professionals one was a doctor lodged in Burail jail. Half of the inmates under study were housewives. 68 inmates who were engaged in menial work, majority of them were in Burail jail. 21 respondents were grouped under miscellaneous category including tribal women who were engaged in burglaries and thefts. Majority of the respondents were Hindus, followed by Sikhs. There was a low representation of Muslims in the sample as their population is low in the region.

For the purpose of analysis, respondents were divided into four main caste categories viz. upper, middle, backward and lower. Results show that there is over-representation of backward and lower caste women in the prisons under study. Age-wise distribution of the inmates indicates that majority of them were in the age group of 35 to 45 years. There were a few inmates in less than 18 years in age and above 55 years of age. Majority of the inmates were from rural background with nuclear households and had medium sized family. The employment status of the head of the inmate's family showed that 23 percent were unemployed, retired or disabled. Only 34.5 percent had full-time job prior to imprisonment. The distribution of total household income revealed that majority earned up to Rs. 5000 per month. Only 3.5 percent respondents earned more than Rs. 15000 per month. It is evident that those women who get caught in the system are from the marginalized sections of the society. The woman prisoner profile that emerges from this study is of a middle aged, illiterate, married woman with children, with hardly any job skills and who lives in poverty.

An attempt was made to find out the types of crime committed by women. Majority of women in the state of Punjab, Haryana and UT of Chandigarh were involved in violent crimes, followed by offences related to drugs, sex and lastly property. The results of the present study reject the findings of the various researchers who stated that a large number of women were involved in property offences. Another important finding of this study was that women who were engaged in violent offences mainly pertained to homicide of husband and/or daughter-in-law. Even when an attempt was made to explore the status of prisoners with the type of crime, it was observed that convicts were mostly involved in violent and drugs-related crimes, and under-trials in violent and sex-related offences. With regards to the marital status, results show that maximum number of widows/divorced/deserted women i.e. 53.3 percent were involved in violence. Such findings negate the results of other researchers who have indicated the involvement of presently married women in violent offences. More mothers with three or more children were involved in violent offences, and women with no child were involved in sex-related offences.

Education and occupation also determined the type of crimes committed by women inmates. Illiterate women indulged in violent and drug-related offences, whereas highly qualified women who were in higher status occupations did not engage in sex or drug-related offences but in violent crimes, mainly to settle score with their abusive spouses.

Women engaged in middle level of occupations were involved in property-related offences. Housewives and women engaged in menial types of occupations were involved in all types of crimes to supplement their income.

There was no correlation between religious background and type of crime. Both Hindu and Sikh women were involved in violent crimes. However, with regards to caste background, it was noticed that upper caste women were not involved in sex-related or miscellaneous offences. Very few women of upper caste were involved in property-related offences. Majority of them were involved in violent offences. However, women belonging to lower and backward caste were engaged in all types of crime.

More women in the age group of 18 to 35 years were involved in sex-related crimes. Very young women, i.e. below 18 years were involved in drug-related offences. Majority of inmates in the age group of 35 to 55 years were involved in violent offences. Since we have included dowry-related offences under violent type of crimes, more middle aged women were involved in these. Findings indicate that more women from rural areas were involved in violent and drug-related offences, whereas more women from urban areas were involved in sex and property-related offences. More violent crimes occurred in joint/extended families as it included dowry-related deaths. More sex-related offenders were staying alone.

Additionally, information about causes and consequences of crime was procured from the inmates. Majority i.e. 36 percent stated economic reasons for their criminal behaviour. 28.5 percent blamed their familial circumstances for indulging in crime. 14 percent inmates who suffered abusive relationships reported personal reasons for their criminal activities.

There were 21.5 percent respondents who refused to admit that they were criminals. They maintained that they were falsely implicated. With regards to the punishment, 95.5 percent inmates involved in all types of crime stated that they were wrongly punished. While some tried to find excuse in their poor economic background, others indulged in blame theory. Such responses clearly indicate that majority of the inmates had no repentance on their criminal behaviour.

Another important finding of the study was the involvement of other family members in the crime. It was found that family members of 40.5 percent inmates were also arrested for criminal activities. Majority of these were involved in violent offences, especially dowry-related.

Although the inmates did not accept that they were punished rightly, yet they felt negative consequences of confinement on their lives. 44.5 percent inmates reported concern about their family prestige. 26 percent were worried about their own self-esteem, and for 21 percent loss of social prestige was of utmost importance.

What conditions do the women face when they are imprisoned? Women are confined to a system designed, built and run by men for men. Prison authorities rationalize this because the numbers of women prisoners have relatively been low. It is for this reason that women continue to exist as non-entity in the men's prison. Even where the prisons are run by women, they are doing the work of a male supremacist prison system and society.

The prison, as originally conceived, is a place of exile from the society. People who broke the rules set by the society were to be sent out from the society, exiled for the period of time set by the court as punishment for the wrongs they have done. Once they had completed their period of exile, they were to be allowed back into the society. The high walls of a prison were built as much to keep the society out as to keep the prisoner in. Today, it is generally held that one of the objectives of the prison should be to help the prisoners to return to their communities as law abiding citizens. However, it is a difficult process. Incarceration leaves a permanent imprint on the lives of inmates. It becomes difficult for them to lead a normal life after imprisonment. There were 61.5 percent inmates who reported that they would not be able to lead a normal life after going back to the society. Rejection by the society and family would not allow them to lead a normal life. They would be stigmatized.

When inmates were asked to report their relations with their family members, 64 percent reported congenial relations.

Many of these inmates who were married reported that their children were being taken care of by their husbands, in-laws and parents. Very few, i.e. 15 percent respondents did not have congenial relations with their family members. Most of these inmates were staying alone prior to their incarceration. Majority of the inmates were visited by their family members. There were 37.5 percent inmates whose family members did not visit them. Some of them belonged to marginalized sections of the society. Poverty stricken family members could not afford to visit the inmates. Further, some of the inmates did not maintain any ties with their family members. There were a few inmates who had no one to look after their children, and it was hence difficult for these children to visit their mothers on their own.

Upon arrival at the prison, the prisoners learn to make adjustments and deal with the staff and other inmates. Approximately half of the inmates reported congenial relations with the authorities. 44.5 percent gave a diplomatic response that they had workable relations with the authorities. There were 8 cases who did not mind pointing out at their non-congenial relations with the authorities. Majority of the inmates conducted themselves according to the rules of the prison, however, 30.5 percent stated that they had arguments with the authorities as they found them discriminatory in their approach. Results indicate that 87 percent of the respondents reported that there was a constant check on their movement in the prison. All the inmates of Burail, Ludhiana, Patiala and Ambala jail reported that a female police staff was always present to check their movement. Such restrictions constantly reminded them of their loss of liberty and comforts of a free life. Once the inmates enter the prison, they try to develop intimacy with the jail staff. 60 percent of the respondents admitted that they disclosed their personal problems to the staff. However, they did not get any positive response.

Over-crowding, unhygienic living conditions were a common factor in all the prisons. Except in Ludhiana and Hissar jails which were newly constructed, conditions were far from adequate in other jails. There was a lack of adequate medical, education and vocational support for women prisoners. Lack of ventilation, poor lighting, and bad sanitation was visible in Jalandhar jail. Quality of the food was found to be very bad except in Hissar and Ludhiana jails. In some jails food was unpalatable and women were cooking for themselves, using earthen ovens.

Non-availability of a female doctor was a common complaint. No Psychiatrist paid a visit to the jails. 38 percent of the women maintained that they were suffering from some sort of psychiatric problem. Nearly half the inmates of Ambala and Ludhiana jails reported psychiatric problems. The Model jail manual reported special pre and post-natal care for pregnant women with regards to food and health facility. Since there was no pregnant female prisoner in the sample under study, most of the inmates gave their perception on the general scenario. Majority of the inmates, i.e. 80 percent reported that they did not notice any special care for pregnant women with regards to food and health. There were a few inmates who had been staying in the jail for over a decade, and during this period they explained the problems of menstruating and menopausal women.

Despite heterogeneity in terms of age, caste, socio-economic and criminal background, women prisoners develop strong bonds amongst themselves. All the inmates become a part of a large family, where they fight and argue, console and share the same world-view. There were only 11 percent inmates who reported that they had non-congenial relations with other inmates. 66 percent of the inmates reported that they had arguments with other inmates. Most of the mothers who had small children with them in the prison were involved in different conflicting situations. Issues for argument included work-related problems (13 percent), daily need items (18 percent), behaviour pattern (21 percent), spying for authorities (7 percent), and hygiene (7 percent).

The inmates spend days, weeks and years together with one another. They know almost everything about each other. 73.5 percent reported that they shared their problems with other inmates. Majority of them received sympathy and consolation. There were 9 respondents who reported that they were made fun of and blamed for their situation. Although women prisoners do not experience violent episodes as in the case of male prisoners, yet verbal abuses and small physical scuffles were a part of their daily routine. Some inmates did not mind breaking rules as they were habitual offenders. To maintain discipline and keep situation under control, the staff uses punishment like slapping, scolding, abusing, threats, etc.

Women inmates do not blame themselves for their incarceration. 86 percent complained against the system. Majority who complained were from Hissar followed by Jalandhar and then Ludhiana jails. 25.5 percent blamed the police, 19.5 percent blamed the judiciary, and 17.5 percent blamed police, judiciary and lawyers together. When inmates were asked to provide suggestions to improve the conditions in the prison, 43 inmates felt that their suggestions would carry no meaning. Therefore, they refused to comment. 39.5 percent inmates asked for more vocational and health-related facilities, and 17.5 percent asked for improvements in the living conditions with majority from Jalandhar jail. There were 21.5 percent inmates who demanded changes in the rules in terms of more liberty and freedom of movement.

IMPLICATIONS

Indian women in prison are a very specific group of individuals. They are more likely to be from poor social backgrounds, have an average of three or more children and a family network. Such women tend to be trapped in a cycle of poverty. Majority of crime committed by women relate to the unsolved social problems such as victimization and drug abuse. Women, thus, tend to come to the notice of the criminal justice system through the limitations of their lives rather than a propensity of criminal behaviour *per se.*

A theory of women and crime should be able to answer certain questions like why, for example, are women belonging to a particular social class, more involved in crime? What structural factors influence their particular patterns of crime? Female criminality should be interpreted in the context of economic, social and gender relations in the society. Therefore, a wider framework is required which can explain how gender and class interact to produce criminal patterns.

Sociologists and criminal justice experts say that women's disproportionately high rate of poverty, their increased access to areas of crime formerly dominated by males and the overall increase of violence and crime are some possible explanations for the surge. The disparity in earnings that still exists between men and women in general and for women of the marginalized sections in particular, known as the feminization of poverty, is the likely cause for that upsurge. There is a long standing association between poverty and crime. All poor people are not criminals, but poverty certainly does lead to a higher probability of crime. Drug-related offences by women have significantly increased over the recent past.

There is a positive correlation between increasing acceptance of violence in the society and the increase in violent crimes by women and men alike. We are becoming apathetic when it comes to violence. Violence is everywhere in the media and it has become an accepted way of dealing with frustration and aggression. Majority of the women in this study stated that they were not rightly punished. On the other hand their blaming the criminal justice system for their imprisonment is a testimony to the fact that there is a general acceptance for violence in the society. Thus women have started involving themselves in crimes that historically have been male dominating. Even when women commit violent offences, gender plays an important role in the crime. Research indicates, for example, that of women convicted for murder, many had killed their husbands.

As far as the women's liberation movement is concerned, it may have been of only indirect influence on female crime. Together with other changes in our 21st century society, it may have helped to break the barriers of opportunities to crime. It can not be disputed that women are becoming more aware of the changes in their opportunities and responsibilities in a consumer society. Moreover, an increase in divorce and rising unemployment has subjected them to considerable stress in coping with the duality of their roles as mothers and breadwinners.

Certain types of crime like sex and drug-related are more clearly market-oriented, i.e. the market responds rationally to demand and supply forces. Other crimes have no clear economic rationale (violent) and have only indirect relationships to economic conditions, resulting from increased stress and dysfunctions caused by poor economic situations.

Through this study it has been established that the use of a radical and feminist perspective provides a more complete understanding of women and crime.

The effects of imprisonment are more keenly felt by woman than a man, especially with regards to familial relationship. This is specifically true when she is a mother. Imprisonment causes considerable distress to both mothers and children, whether the child is brought up in the prison or is separated from the mother. On one hand, when the child is brought up in a prison, it can have damaging effect on its social and psychological development. Moreover, the child in prison is brought up in an unhealthy and unnatural environment, without the presence of father figure or other members of the family structure. This can impair the identification process and orientation of the child. On the other hand, when the child is separated from the mother due to her imprisonment, the prison breaks the mother-child bond. Either way, therefore, the imprisonment of mothers with children can foster the next generation of criminals. Apart from the damaging effects of the mother's imprisonment upon the children, woman's relationships with her spouse also get impaired.

The most damaging effect of imprisonment is labeling a class of people as criminals because they had spent time in the prison. This myth, that there is a class of people who are particularly wicked, are different from the rest, out whose selfishness is a danger, is perpetuated through the system of justice. As a consequence, women's greatest fear was that of the stigma which would get attached to them. This stigmatization further pushes them down.

While in prison, they spend 24 × 7 time on their own in a small poorly ventilated and poorly illuminated cell. Privacy within the cell is practically impossible. On visiting seven jails, poor hygienic conditions, lack of adequate medical facilities and over-crowding was a common scene. Diseases and infections associated with over-crowding, coupled with poor health and hygiene conditions in jails, are tuberculosis, Hepatitis and HIV/AIDS as additional risks for the inmates. In addition to the general medical attention required by the women, the female prison population is disproportionately affected by mental health problems, with higher levels of depression compared to both the general populations and the male prisoners. This is due to the fact that a large number of women prisoners have been victims of physical, sexual and mental abuse. The Model Prison Jail manual discusses proper medical treatment and psychotherapy for mentally disturbed patients. In practice, however, women prisons lacked these facilities and mental health problem remained largely undiagnosed and untreated.

Women in prison develop a supportive sub-culture. Although all these women do not come from similar cultural backgrounds, the sub-cultures they form in prison exhibit resourcefulness, flexibility and creativity in the social relations they develop. They develop adaptive strategies to cope with the conditions they face.

CONCLUSION

In conclusion, it can be stated that through this study, the lives of women in prison were explored against the background of the offence having been committed or alleged to have been committed. The offence is the main component of their present lives and the reason for them to be in the prison. Even though the situations and the causes of crime committed by women vary, the law only knows that it is an offence under section 302 of the Indian Penal Code and the offender must get the punishment that code sets out. Majority of the women do not have any clue where their offensive act would lead them to. Majority of the incarcerated women are illiterate and belong to the marginalized sections of the society. It has been established that women's crime tends to reflect the role that economic disadvantage plays in their criminal careers. There is a big gap between legal system and social reality. The law talks about equality between the sexes. When women commit crime, they would be punished equally like men. The social reality, on the other hand, is full of inequality. Women prisoners, thus present specific challenges for criminal justice system because they constitute a very small proportion of the prison. The profile and background of women in prison, and the reasons for which they are imprisoned are different from those of men. Existing prison facilities and programs for women inmates have all been developed initially for men, who have historically accounted for the larger proportion of the prison population. It is therefore asserted that a gender perspective must be considered while catering to the needs of women in criminal justice system, in general and prisons in particular.

RECOMMENDATIONS

The study throws out a few recommendations, mainly related to the improvements in the living conditions in the prisons.

- To ensure that the female prisoners should be supervised by female staff only.
- Female juveniles should be imprisoned separately from the adult/seasoned female inmates.
- To ensure that the under-trial prisoners should have favorable living conditions till the time their crime is proven and punishment awarded by the court of law.
- To provide proper facilities to pregnant and lactating mothers, and mothers whose children are with them in jail.
- Children living in the prisons should be protected from violence and enjoy the full extent of their rights.
- Prisoners should be provided a lady doctor on a daily basis.
- Mental health of the inmates should be routinely examined. Resources to treat such disorders should be provided.
- There is a dire need to improve the quality of food. This can be offset through reducing the quantity of food being currently provided, which is very high and leads to wastage. This action would not only reduce wastage (*refer to inmates cooking their own food on earthen chulhas with dried rotis as fuel*) but also improve the quality of food and thus the inmate's health.
- The inmates should be made to go through regular counseling sessions by behavioural experts in order to inculcate a positive outlook into the inmates towards life. This shall support and help them in becoming responsible and law abiding citizens, once they are out

of the prison.

- Provide vocational trainings to the inmates in order to keep them occupied and also help them in obtaining skills for a decent future life.

All the above mentioned suggestions also exist as basic requirements in the Model Jail Manual. However, these are actually missing in practice. It is high time that they get implemented.

SUGGESTIONS FOR FURTHER RESEARCH

Three broad areas for further research on prisons are outlined below:

- A comparative study of male and female prisoners to understand the impact of imprisonment.
- A longitudinal study of inmates once they enter the prison and later when they go back to the society.
- A study of both the prison staff and the inmates to explore how they interact with each other.

APPENDIX-1

Distribution of Crime—State-wise and in India

The below figure describes a comparative distribution of cognizable crime by women in the states of Punjab, Haryana, UT of Chandigarh.

FIG. 1
Crime by Women

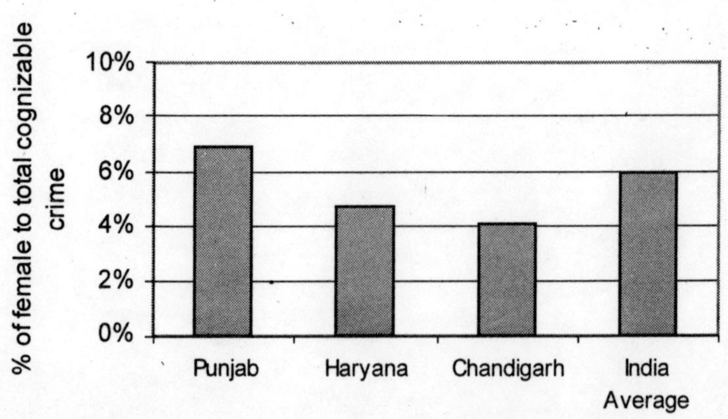

Source : NCRB, 2007.

Punjab	6.9%	Haryana	4.7%
Chandigarh	4.1%	India Average	5.9%

APPENDIX-2

Persons Arrested under IPC Crimes by Sex in States and UTs during 2007

Sl. No.	State/U.T	Total Cognizable Crimes under IFC			Percentages of Female to Total
		Male	Female	Total	
	(1)	(2)	(3)	(4)	(5)
States					
1.	Andhra Pradesh	216760	19416	236176	8.2
2.	Arunachal Pradesh	2441	37	2478	1.5
3.	Assam	58030	1372	59402	2.3
4.	Bihar	212397	7498	219895	3.4
5.	Chhattisgarh	56430	2809	60239	4.7
6.	Goa	2446	173	2619	6.6
7.	Gujarat	155838	13606	169444	8.0
8.	Haryana	67430	3316	70746	4.7
9.	Himachal Pradesh	17416	2182	19598	11.1
10.	Jammu & Kashmir	30684	2252	32936	6.8
11.	Jharkhand	44342	2147	46489	4.6
12.	Karnataka	123327	10727	134054	8.0
13.	Kerala	143682	5435	149117	3.6
14.	Madhya Pradesh	313717	15563	329280	4.7
15.	Maharashtra	264712	26601	291313	9.1
16.	Manipur	1231	75	1306	5.7
17.	Meghalaya	1517	40	1557	2.6
18.	Mizoram	1984	78	062	3.8
19.	Nagaland	760	35	795	4.4
20.	Orissa	76603	4271	80874	5.3
21.	Punjab	43781	3261	47042	6.9
22.	Rajasthan	170933	12881	183814	7.0
23.	Sikkim	593	30	623	4.8
24.	Tamil Nadu	188703	12669	201372	6.3
25.	Tripura	4135	443	4578	9.7

(Contd.)

APPENDIX-2 (Contd.)

(1)	(2)	(3)	(4)	(5)
26. Uttar Pradesh	240332	6489	246821	2.6
27. Uttarakhand	13517	956	14473	6.6
28. West Bengal	102236	7442	109678	6.8
Total States	2556977	161804	2718781	6.0
Union Territories				
29. A & N Islands	966	99	1065	9.3
30. Chandigarh	2730	116	2846	4.1
31. D & N Haveli	405	8	413	1.9
32. Daman & Diu	364	29	393	7.4
33. Delhi	47909	2835	50744	5.6
34. Lakshadweep	26	0	26	0.0
35. Pondicherry	6007	284	6291	4.5
Total (UTs)	58407	3371	61778	5.5
Total (All India)	2615384	165175	2780559	5.9

Source : NCRB 2007.

APPENDIX-3

Persons Arrested under IPC and SLL Crimes by Age Groups and Sex during 2007

Sl. No.	Crime Head	Below 18 Years		18-30 Years		30-45 Years	
		Male	Female	Male	Female	Male	Female
(1)	(2)	(3)	(4)	(5)	(6)	(7)	(8)
A. IPC CRIMES							
1.	Murder (Sec. 302, 303 IPC)	778	46	26031	1265	22560	1673
2.	Attempt to Commit Murder (Sec. 307 IPC)	625	29	27783	919	2296	1040
3.	C.H. Not Amounting Murder (Sec. 304, 308 IPC)	40	3	3003	49	2765	80
4.	Rape (Sec. 376 IPC)	815	10	14533	195	7596	254
	Custodial Rape	0	0	0	0	0	0
	Other Rape	815	10	14533	195	7596	254
5.	Kidnapping and Abduction (Sec. 363-369, 371-373 IPC)	316	31	18220	920	11345	977
	(i) Of Women and Girls	211	26	12441	757	6915	814
	(ii) Of Others	105	5	5779	163	4430	163

(Contd.)

APPENDIX-3 (Contd.)

(1)	(2)	(3)	(4)	(5)	(6)	(7)	(8)
6.	Dacoity (Sec. 395-398 IPC)	209	5	9591	104	6455	130
7.	Preparation and Assembly for Dacoity (Sec. 399-402 IPC)	129	0	8010	59	3689	14
8.	Robbery (Sec. 392-394, 397, 398 IPC)	509	7	17739	170	9186	93
9.	Burglary (Sec. 449-452, 454, 455, 457-460 IPC)	3681	63	35282	538	20472	559
10.	Theft (Sec. 379-382 IPC)	7285	213	104156	2396	58927	2123
	(i) Auto Theft	1370	3	27158	22	12823	39
	(ii) Other Theft	5915	210	76998	2374	46104	2084
11.	Riots (Sec. 143-145, 147-151, 153, 153A, 153B, 157, 158, 160 IPC)	2084	147	137549	7177	110226	7650
12.	Criminal Breach of Trust (Sec. 406-409 IPC)	20	2	6042	165	8159	274
13.	Cheating (Sec. 419, 420 IPC)	134	6	20066	737	26438	1389
14.	Counterfeiting (Sec. 231-254, 489A-489D)	12	0	1184	25	1098	34
15.	Arson (Sec. 435, 436, 438 IPC)	63	3	4905	130	4864	154
16.	Hurt (Sec. 323-333, 335-338 IPC)	4496	336	203856	12738	163122	14278
17.	Dowry Deaths (Sec. 304B IPC)	45	40	7276	1515	6251	1840
18.	Molestation (Sec. 354 IPC)	517	1	25871	321	16145	401
19.	Sexual Harassment (Sec. 509 IPC)	158	0	9359	40	3594	34

20. Cruelty by Husband and Relatives (Sec. 498A IPC)	208	164	50158	10571	45778	13838
21. Importation of Girls (Sec. 366B IPC)	0	0	52	0	28	0
22. Causing Death by Negligence (Sec. 304A IPC)	100	7	31049	91	30209	131
23. Other IPC Crimes	5983	451	434518	19920	380880	20905
24. Total Cognizable Crimes Under IPC	28207	1564	1196233	60045	962783	67871
B. SLL CRIMES						
1. Arms Act	322	0	45567	13	26514	22
2. Narcotic Drugs and Psychotropic	78	2	16818	439	13956	690
3. Gambling Act	1008	5	149738	109	143775	249
4. Excise Act	522	34	62543	2727	56758	3960
5. Prohibition Act	443	67	98303	26488	113705	44982
6. Explosive and Explosive Substances Act	8	0	2693	11	2106	24
7. Immoral Traffic (P) Act	26	34	1850	3680	1619	1865
8. Indian Railways Act	0	0	136	0	87	0
9. Registration of Foreigners Act	32	8	1450	258	1903	244
10. Protection of Civil Rights Act	0	0	158	3	148	11
(i) PCR Act for SCs	0	0	157	3	145	11
(ii) PCR Act for STs	0	0	1	0	3	0
11. Indian Passport Act	17	3	659	163	679	106

(Contd.)

APPENDIX-3 (Contd.)

(1)	(2)	(3)	(4)	(5)	(6)	(7)	(8)
12.	Essential Commodities Act	14	0	3905	29	5532	90
13.	Terrorist and Disruptive Activities Act	0	0	0	0	0	0
14.	Antiquities and Art Treasures Act	0	0	30	0	51	0
15.	Dowry Prohibition Act	34	17	3078	570	3302	779
16.	Child Marriage Restraint Act	2	0	52	4	73	19
17.	Indecent Representation of Women (P) Act	0	0	122	528	157	295
18.	Copyright Act	29	0	4179	7	3066	18
19.	Sati Prevention Act	0	0	0	0	0	0
20.	SC/ST (Prevention of Atrocities) Act	39	11	7716	205	8105	297
	(i) Prevention of Attrocities Act for SCs	9	6	716	21	754	39
	(ii) Prevention of Attrocities Act for STs	9	6	716	21	754	39
21.	Forest Act	0	0	2841	2	2930	5
22.	Other SLL Crimes	1890	111	1352904	17632	1127935	21784
23.	Total Cognizable Crimes Under SLL	4464	292	1754742	52868	1512401	75440
C.	GRAND TOTAL (A+B)	32671	1855	2950975	112913	2475184	143311

APPENDIX-3 (Contd.)

Sl. No.	Crime Head	45-60 Years		60 Years and Above		Total of Overall Age-group		Grand Total of All Persons (Cols. 13+14)
		Male	Female	Male	Female	Male	Female	
(1)	(2)	(9)	(10)	(11)	(12)	(13)	(14)	(15)
A.	IPC CRIMES							
1.	Murder (Sec. 302, 303 IPC)	9222	757	866	71	59457	3812	63268
2.	Attempt to Commit Murder (Sec. 307 IPC)	9074	416	884	51	61362	2455	63817
3.	C.H. Not Amounting Murder (Sec. 304, 308 IPC)	798	14	46	4	6652	150	6802
4.	Rape (Sec. 376 IPC)	1771	85	96	8	24811	552	25363
	Custodial Rape	0	0	0	0	0	0	0
	Other Rape	1771	85	96	8	24811	552	25363
5.	Kidnapping and Abduction (Sec. 363-369, 371-373 IPC)	3275	314	151	13	33307	2255	35562
	(i) Of Women and Girls	2123	262	97	12	21787	1871	23658
	(ii) Of Others	1152	52	54	1	11520	384	11904
6.	Dacoity (Sec. 395-398 IPC)	1462	62	94	5	17811	306	18117

(Contd.)

APPENDIX-3 (Contd.)

(1)	(2)	(9)	(10)	(11)	(12)	(13)	(14)	(15)
7.	Preparation and Assembly for Dacoity (Sec. 399-402 IPC)	667	2	14	1	12509	76	12585
8.	Robbery (Sec. 392-394, 397, 398 IPC)	2033	22	60	1	29527	293	29820
9.	Burglary (Sec. 449-452, 454, 455, 457-460 IPC)	5925	159	355	26	65715	1345	67060
10.	Theft (Sec. 379-382 IPC)	17509	552	973	48	188850	5332	194182
	(i) Auto Theft	2507	4	55	0	43913	68	43981
	(ii) Other Theft	15002	548	918	48	144937	5264	150201
11.	Riots (Sec. 143-145, 147-151, 153, 153A, 153B, 157, 158, 160 IPC)	42223	2921	4585	384	296667	18279	314946
12.	Criminal Breach of Trust (Sec. 406-409 IPC)	3436	110	241	8	17898	559	18457
13.	Cheating (Sec. 419, 420 IPC)	11842	550	1153	70	59633	2752	62385
14.	Counterfeiting (Sec. 231-254, 489A-489D)	222	4	24	0	2540	63	2603
15.	Arson (Sec. 435, 436, 438 IPC)	1611	31	134	8	11577	326	11903
16.	Hurt (Sec. 323-333, 335-338 IPC)	72170	5905	7714	602	451358	33859	485217
17.	Dowry Deaths (Sec. 304B IPC)	3277	1232	480	157	17329	4784	22113
18.	Molestation (Sec. 354 IPC)	4288	186	262	11	47083	920	48003
19.	Sexual Harassment (Sec. 509 IPC)	531	9	27	1	13669	84	13753

20. Cruelty by Husband and Relatives (Sec. 498A IPC)	20310	9258	4291	1836	120745	35667	156412
21. Importation of Girls (Sec. 366B IPC)	15	0	0	0	95	0	95
22. Causing Death by Negligence (Sec. 304A IPC)	10467	90	770	17	72595	336	72931
23. Other IPC Crimes	163288	8522	19525	1172	1004194	50970	1055164
24. Total Cognizable Crimes Under IPC	385416	31201	42745	4494	2615384	165175	2780559
B. SLL CRIMES							
1. Arms Act	6212	13	106	0	78721	48	78769
2. Narcotic Drugs and Psychotropic	4431	336	293	53	35576	1520	37096
3. Gambling Act	58145	130	7355	22	369921	515	360536
4. Excise Act	22075	1622	2421	174	144319	8517	152836
5. Prohibition Act	51512	19418	4794	1816	268757	92771	361528
6. Explosive and Explosive Substances Act	452	5	34	1	5293	41	5334
7. Immoral Traffic (P) Act	385	360	30	12	3910	5951	9861
8. Indian Railways Act	38	0	0	0	261	0	261
9. Registration of Foreigners Act	526	100	25	3	3936	613	4549
10. Protection of Civil Rights Act	63	1	4	0	373	15	388
(i) PCR Act for SCs	60	1	3	0	365	15	380
(ii) PCR Act for STs	3	0	1	0	8	0	8
11. Indian Passport Act	200	12	5	1	1560	285	1845

(Contd.)

APPENDIX-3 (Contd.)

(1)	(2)	(9)	(10)	(11)	(12)	(13)	(14)	(15)
12.	Essential Commodities Act	2018	58	125	6	11594	183	11777
13.	Terrorist and Disruptive Activities Act	0	0	0	0	0	0	0
14.	Antiquities and Art Treasures Act	12	0	1	0	94	0	94
15.	Dowry Prohibition Act	1561	538	366	76	8341	1980	10321
16.	Child Marriage Restraint Act	55	13	2	1	184	37	221
17.	Indecent Representation of Women (P) Act	39	88	0	0	318	911	1229
18.	Copyright Act	774	1	20	0	8068	26	8094
19.	Sati Prevention Act	0	0	0	0	0	0	0
20.	SC/ST (Prevention of Atrocities) Act	3674	105	299	11	19833	629	20462
	(i) Prevention of Attrocities Act for SCs	3429	92	284	11	18094	550	18644
	(ii) Prevention of Attrocities Act for STs	245	13	15	0	1739	79	1818
21.	Forest Act	984	0	33	0	6788	7	6795
22.	Other SLL Crimes	418935	11792	60655	1612	2962319	52931	3015250
23.	Total Cognizable Crimes Under SLL	572091	34592	76568	3788	3920266	166980	4087246
C.	**GRAND TOTAL (A+B)**	957507	65793	119313	8282	6535650	332155	6867805

APPENDIX-4

Number of Jails, Capacity, Population and Occupancy Rate in the Country at the End of 2006

Sl. No.	Type	Number	Capacity	Population of Inmates	Occupancy Rate
1.	Central Jail	111	117242	166740	142.2
2.	District Jail	293	92400	146353	158.4
3.	Sub-Jail	852	41187	49534	120.3
4.	Women Jail	15	2413	2830	117.3
5.	Borstal School	10	1885	923	49.0
6.	Open Jail	27	3088	2284	74.0
7.	Special Jail	20	4190	3691	88.1
8.	Others	8	1506	916	60.8
9.	Total	1336	263911	373271	141.4

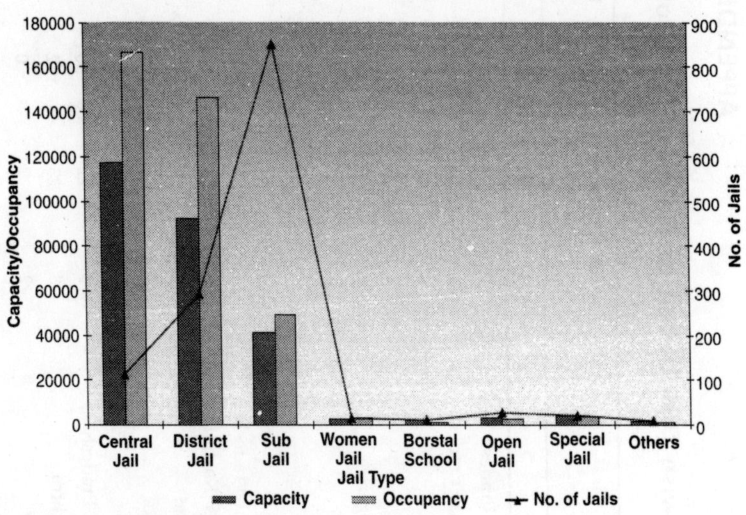

Source : NCRB 2006.

APPENDIX-5

State/UT-wise Distribution of Different Types of Jails in the Country at the End of 2006

Sl. No.	State/UT	Central Jail	District Jail	Sub-Jail	Women Jail	Borstal School	Open Jail	Special Jail	Others	Total
(1)	(2)	(3)	(4)	(5)	(6]	(7)	(8)	(9)	(10)	(11)
1.	Andhra Pradesh	7	9	120	2	1	2	0	0	141
2.	Arunachal Pradesh	—	—	—	—	—	—	—	—	—
3.	Assam	6	18	1	0	0	1	1	0	27
4.	Bihar	6	23	25	1	0	0	0	0	55
5.	Chhattisgarh	4	6	17	0	0	0	0	0	27
6.	Goa	1	0	1	0	0	0	0	3	5
7.	Gujarat	2	6	12	0	0	2	2	0	24
8.	Haryana	2	12	4	0	1	0	0	0	19
9.	Himachal Pradesh	2	2	6	0	1	1	0	0	12
10.	Jammu & Kashmir	2	8	3	0	0	0	0	0	13
11.	Jharkhand	4	19	4	0	1	0	0	0	28
12.	Karnataka	6	6	81	0	1	1	2	1	98
13.	Kerala	3	3	26	1	1	2	5	0	41
14.	Madhya Pradesh	8	22	86	0	0	0	0	0	116
15.	Maharashtra	8	23	172	1	1	3	1	1	210
16.	Manipur	2	2	0	0	0	0	0	0	4

17.	Meghalaya	0	4	0	0	0	0	0	0	4
18.	Mizoram	1	5	0	0	0	0	0	0	6
19.	Nagaland	1	3	6	0	0	0	0	0	10
20.	Orissa	0	13	52	1	0	1	2	1	70
21.	Punjab	7	5	11	1	1	1	0	0	26
22.	Rajasthan	8	25	59	2	1	10	0	0	105
23.	Sikkim	1	0	0	0	0	0	0	0	1
24.	Tamilnadu	9	6	113	2	1	1	1	1	134
25.	Tripura	1	2	7	1	0	0	0	0	11
26.	Uttar Pradesh	5	50	3	1	0	0	2	0	61
27.	Uttaranchal	0	6	2	0	0	1	0	0	9
28.	West Bengal	6	12	29	1	0	1	4	0	53
	Total (States)	102	290	840	14	10	27	20	7	1310
29.	A & N Islands	0	1	3	0	0	0	0	0	4
30.	Chandigarh	0	0	0	0	0	0	0	1	1
31.	D & N Haveli	0	0	1	0	0	0	0	0	1
32.	Daman & Diu	0	0	2	0	0	0	0	0	2
33.	Delhi	8	1	0	1	0	0	0	0	10
34.	Lakshadweep	0	0	4	0	0	0	0	0	4
35.	Pondicherry	1	1	2	0	0	0	0	0	4
Total (UTs)		9	3	12	1	0	0	0	1	26
Total (All-India)		111	293	852	15	10	27	20	8	1336

Source : NCRB 2006.

APPENDIX-6

PUNJAB STATE POLICY ON PRISONS— AIMS AND OBJECTIVES

A Jail Manual is a "digest of rules and regulations governing prisons and prisoners. The Punjab Jail Manual is stated to have been codified on the bases of the provisions of the Prisons Act and the rules framed thereunder, Transfer of Prisoners Act, Habitual Offenders Act, Punjab Good Conduct Prisoners Act and such other similar provision about a century back. The Punjab Jail Manual contains 43 chapters referring to classification of jails, establishments, general supervision security and uniforms safe custody of prisoner. Release of prisoners, classification and separation of prisoners, discipline, and daily routine, among others. The Punjab jail manual is used to manage the jails in Punjab, Haryana, J and K, H.P. and Union Territory of Chandigarh.

PUNJAB STATE POLICY ON PRISONS

Aims and Objectives

1. Punjab Jail Department shall protect society and endeavor to reform and re-assimilate offenders in the social main line by giving them appropriate correctional treatment.
2. There shall been Department of Prisons and Correctional Services, dealing with adult and young offenders—their institutional care, treatment aftercare, probation and other non-institutional service.
3. The State shall endeavor to evolve proper mechanism to ensure that no under-trial prisoner is unnecessarily detained. This object shall be achieved by speeding up trials, simplifying of bail procedures and by periodic review of cases of under-trial prisoners. Under-trial prisoners shall as far as possible, be confined in separate institutions.
4. Since it is recognized that imprisonment is not always the best way to meet the objective of punishment, the

state shall endeavor to provide in law new alternatives to imprisonment such as community service, forfeiture of property, payment of compensation to victims, public censure, in addition to the ones already existing, and shall specially ensure that the Probation of Offenders Act, 1958, is effectively implemented throughout the State.

5. Living conditions in every prisons and allied institutions meant for the custody, care, treatment and rehabilitation of offenders shall be compatible with human dignity in all aspects such as accommodation, hygiene, sanitation, food, clothing, and medical facilities. All factors responsible for vitiating the atmosphere of these institutions shall be identified and dealt with effectively.
6. In consonance with the aims and objectives of prisons in the State shall provide appropriate facilities and professional personnel for institutions shall be provided for the segregation of different categories of inmates for proper treatment.
7. The State shall endeavor to develop the fields of Criminology and Penology and promote research on the typology of crime in the context of emerging patterns of crime in the country. This will help in proper classification of offenders and in revising appropriate treatment for them.
8. A system of graded custody ranging from special security institutions to open institutions shall be proved to offer proper opportunities for the reformation of offenders according to the progress made by them.
9. Programmes for the treatment of offenders shall be individualized and shall aim at providing them with opportunities for diversified education, development of work habits and skills, change in attitude, modification of behaviour and implementation of social and moral values.
10. The state shall endeavor to develop vocational training and work programmes in prisoners for all inmates eligible to work. The aim of such training and work

programmes shall be to equip inmates with better skills and work habits for their rehabilitation.

11. Payment of fair wages and other incentives shall be associated with work programmes to encourage inmate participation in such programmes. The incentives of leave, remission and premature release to convicts shall also be utilized for improvement of their behaviour, strengthening of family ties, and their early return to society.
12. Custody being the basic functions of prisons, appropriate security arrangements shall be made in accordance with the need for graded custody in different types of institutions. The management of prisons shall be characterized by firm and positive discipline, with due regard, however, to the maintenance of human rights of prisoners. The State recognizes that a prisoner loses his right to liberty but maintains his residuary rights. It shall be the endeavor of State to protect these residuary rights of the prisoners.
13. The state shall provide free legal aid to the needy prisoners.
14. Prisons are not the places for confinement of children. Children (boys under 16 years of age and girls under 18 years of age) shall in no case be sent to prisons. All children confined in prisons at present shall be transferred forthwith to a separate institution, meant exclusively for children with facilities for their care, education, training and rehabilitation. Benefit of non-institutional facilities shall, whenever possible, be extended to such children.
15. Young offenders (between 16 to 21 years in the case of boys and 18 to 21 in the case of girls) shall not be confined in prisons meant for adult offenders. There shall be separate institutions for them where, in view of their young and impressionable age, they shall be given treatment and training suited to their special needs of rehabilitation.
16. Women offenders shall as far as possible be confined in a separate institution specially meant for them.

Wherever such arrangements are not possible they shall be kept in separate annexes of prisons with proper arrangements. The staff for these institutions and annexes shall comprise women employees only. Women prisoners shall be protected against all exploitation. Work and treatment programmes shall be devised for them in consonance with their special needs.

17. Non-criminal lunatic shall not be confined in prisons. The law shall be suitably amended for the purpose. Proper arrangements shall be made for the care and treatment of criminal lunatics.
18. Persons courting arrest during non-violent socio-political economic agitation or declared public causes shall not be confined in prisons alongwith other prisoners. Separate prisons camps with proper and adequate facilities shall be provided for such non-violent agitators.
19. Prison service shall develop as a professional career service. The State shall endeavor to develop a well-organized prisons cadre based on appropriate job requirements, sound training and proper promotional avenues. The efficient functioning of prisons depends undoubtedly upon the personal qualities, educational qualifications, professional competence and character of prisons personnel. The status, emoluments and other service conditions of prisons personnel should be commensurate with their job requirements and responsibilities. Proper training facilities for prisons personnel shall be developed at the State level.
20. The States shall endeavor to secure and encourage voluntary participation of the community in prison programmes and in non-institutional treatment of offenders on an extensive and systematic basis. Such participation is necessary in view of the objective of ultimate rehabilitation of the offenders in the community. The Government shall open avenues for such participation and shall extend financial and other assistance to voluntary organizations and individuals willing to extend help to prisoners and ex-prisoners.

21. Prisons are hither to a closed world. It is necessary to open them to some kind of positive and constructive public discernment. Selected eminent public men shall be authorized to visit prisons and give independent report on them to appropriate authorities.
22. In order to provide a forum in the community for continuous thinking on problem of prisons for promoting professional knowledge and for generating public interest in the reformation of offenders, it is necessary that a professional non-official registered body is established at the State level.
23. Probation, aftercare, rehabilitation and follow-up of offenders shall form an integral part of the foundations of the Department of Prisons and Correctional Services.
24. The development of prisons shall be planned in a systematic manner keeping in view the objectives and goals to be achieved. The progress of the implementation of such plans shall be continuously monitored and periodically evaluated.
25. The Government at the State shall endeavor to provide adequate resources for the development of prisons and other allied services.
26. Government recognizes that the process of reformation and rehabilitation of offenders is an internal part of total process of social reconstruction, and therefore, the development of prisons shall find a place in the State development plans.
27. As prisons form part of the criminal justice system the functioning of other branches of the system viz. police, the prosecution and judiciary have a bearing on the working of prisons. It is necessary to effect proper coordination among these branches. The Government shall ensure such coordination at various levels.
28. The State shall promote research in the correctional field to make prison programmes amore effective.

The Prison Act 1894 governs the organisation, functions and duties of the Prisons Department, Punjab. Punjab Jail Manual 1996 based on the Act gives details of the duties and functions of the Prison Department. The duties basically relate to the management of the prisoners both adult and young offenders as per the laid down rules and directions received from the Government from time to time. In brief, the responsibilities entails general welfare of the prisoners, their security, correction, reformation, probation and after care of the offenders. To make correctional treatment a continuous and complete process, this integrated department is called "Department of Prison and Correctional Services". The organisational structure of this department is laid down in chapter 4 of Revised Punjab Jail Manual 1996. The Principal Secretary, Department of Home Affairs and Justice, is the controlling authority of this department.

Bibliography

Abdy, A. (1992) Social Prejudicial: The Effect of Punishment on the Prisoner. Tehran: Noor.

Adler, Freda (1975) Sisters in Crime. New York: McGraw Hill..

Adwani, M.N. (1978) Perspectives on Adult Crime and Correction, New Delhi: Abhinav Publications.

Ahuja, Ram (1969) Female Offenders in India. Meerut: Meenakshi Prakashan.

———, (2006) Criminology. Jaipur: Rawat Publications.

Amnesty International (1999) http:// www.amnesty.org

Anderson, E. (1999) The Code of Street. New York: Norton Books.

Ashworth, A. (1998) The Criminal Process. Oxford: Oxford University Press.

Australian Institute of Criminology 2001, "Trends and Issues in Crime and Criminal Justice", Canberra Available on www.aic.gov.au/publications/tandi/tandi194.html

Bailey, A. and Hayes, J. (2006) "Who's in Prison?" *California Counts*, Vol. 8, No. 1, August.

Bandura, A. (1969) Causes of Delinquency. Berkeley: University of California Press.

———, (1973) Aggression: A Social Learning Analysis. Englewood Cliffs, NJ: Prentice Hall.

Bannister, S. (1989) "Another View of Political Prisoners", *Critical Criminology*, Vol. 1, No. 4.

Bartol, C.R., and Bartol, A.M. (1994) Psychology and Law: Research and Application (2nd ed.). Pacific Grove, CA: Brooks/Cole.

Bartollas, C. (1990) "The prison: Disorder personified", in M.W. Murphy and J.E. Dison, (eds.) Are Prisons Any Better? Twenty Years of Correctional Reform, Newbury Park, California: Sage Publications.

Basham, A.L. (1967) The Wonder that was India. London: Sidgnick and Jackson.

Bastick, M. (2005) "Women in Prison—A Commentary on the Standard Minimum Rules for the Treatment of Prisoners", Discussion Draft, Quarker, United Nations Office, July, pp. 56-57.

Beck, A., Gilliard, D.; Greenfeld, L.; Harlow, C.; Hester, T.; Jankowski, L.; Morton, D.; Snell, T. and Stephen, J. (1993) Survey of State Prison Inmates, 1991, Washington, DC: U.S. Department of Justice, *Bureau of Justice Statistics*, March.

Beckett, K.; Nyrop, K. and Pfingst, L. (2006) "Race, Drugs and Policing: Understanding Disparities in Drug Delivery Arrests", *Criminology*, Vol. 44, No. 1, Feb., pp. 105-37.

Bhadauria, Y.S. and Mathur, A.S. (1981) "Family Life of under-trials", *The Indian Journal of Social Work*, Vol. XLII, No. 2, July, pp. 175-80.

Bilmoria, Rani (1981) "The patterns and nature of female criminality in Andhra Pradesh" *Indian Journal of Social Work*, Vol. XLI, No. 4, pp. 393-401.

Bilmoria, Rani (1983) "Homicides by Females", *Indian Journal of Criminology*, No. 1, January.

Blumstein, A.; Farrington, D.P. and Moitra, S. (1985) "Delinquency careers: Innocents, Disasters and Persisters", *Crime and Justice*, Vol. 6, pp. 187-219.

———, (1993) "Racial Dis-proportionality of U.S. Prison Populations Revisited", *University of Colorado Law Review*, Vol. 64.

Borbora, J.; Borbora, S.V. and Baruah, R. (2008) "A Sociological Study of Women in Crime in Assam", *The Eastern Anthropologist*, Vol. 61, No. 1, Jan.-Mar., pp 105-15.

Boritch, H. (1997) Fallen Women: Female Crime and Criminal Justice in Canada. ITP Nelson. Thompson Canada Ltd.

Bourdieu, P. (1992) Invitation to Reflexive Sociology. Chicago. University of Chicago.

Bowker, L.H. (1980) Prison Victimisation, New York: Elsevier.

Bowlby, J. (1953) Child Care and Growth of Love. Baltimore: Pelican books.

Braithwaite, John (1989) Crime, Shame, and Reintegration. Melbourne: Cambridge University Press.

Brown, A. and Kirk, W. (1987) "Resource Availability for Women at Risk", Unpublished paper Presented at the American Society of Criminology, Annual meeting, Chicago, November.

Browne, A. (1987) When Battered Women Kill. New York: Free Press.

———, Miller, B. and Maguin, E. (1999) "Prevalence and Severity of Lifeline Physical and Sexual Victimization among Incarcerated Women", *International Journal of Law and Psychiatry*, Vol. 22, Nos. 3-4, pp. 301-22.

Buhler, G. (1984) The Laws of Manu. Delhi: Banarsidass. (Reprint from Oxford University's 1886-edition)

Bureau of Justice and Statistics, Prisoners 2000 Available on www.ojp.usdoj.gov/bjs/

Caddle, D. and Crisp, D. (1997) Imprisoned Women and Mothers. London: Home Office Research Study.

Carlen, P. (ed.) (1985) Criminals women in Soviet Prisons, New York: Paragon.

Chaiken, J. and Chaiken, M. (1990) "Drugs and Predatory Crime", In Tonry, M. and Wilson, J., (eds.) Drugs and Crime. Chicago: University of Chicago Press.

Chambliss, W. (1994) "Policing the Ghetto Underclass: The Politics of Law and Law Enforcement," *Social Problems*, Vol. 41, pp. 177-94.

Chapman, J.R. (1980) Economic Realities and the Female Offender. Lexington, Mass: Lexington Books.

Chatto Raj, B.N. (2000) "A Study on Children of Women Prisoners in Indian Jails", A Report Submitted to National Institute of Criminology and Forensic Sciences, Delhi.

Chernoff, W.W. and Simon, R.J. (2000) "Women and Crime, the World Over", *Gender Issues*, Vol. 18, No. 3.

Chesney-Lind, Meda (1984) "Women and Crime", A Review of the Recent Literature on the Female Offender. A Report Submitted to Youth Development and Research Center. Honolulu: University of Hawaii.

Chesney-Lind, Meda (1997) The Female Offender: Girls, Women and Crime. Thousands Oaks, CA: Sage.

Church, G.J. (1990) "The View from behind Bars", *Times*, Fall (Special Issue).

Clemmer, D. (1940) The Prison Community. New York: Holt, Rinehart and Winston.

Clinard, R.A. and Ohlin, L.E. (1960) Delinquency and Opportunity; A Theory of Delinquent Gangs. Glencoe: Free Press.

Cohen, A.K. (1966) Deviance and Control, New Jersey: Englewood Cliffs. Prentice.

Coll, C.G., Baker M.J., Fields, J.P. and Mathews, B. (1998) "The Experience of Women in Prison: Implications for Services and Prevention" in Harden, J. and Hill, M. (eds.) Breaking the Rules: Women in Prison and Feminist Therapy. New York: Harrington Park Press.

Covington Stephanie, S. (1998) "Women in Prison: Approaches in the Treatment of our most invisible population" in Harden, J. and Hill, M. (eds.) Breaking the Rules: Women in Prison and Feminist Therapy. New York: Harrington Park Press.

Crew, B.K. (1991) "Sex differences in Patriarchy: Chivalry in Patriarchy", *Justice Quarterly*, 8 (1), pp. 59-83.

Culbertson, R. and Fortune, E. (1986) "Incarcerated women: self-concept and argot roles", *Journal of Offender Counseling. Services and Rehabilitation*, 10 (3), pp. 25-49.

Daniel, A. and Kashani, J. (1983) "Women who Commit Crimes of Violence". *Psychiatric Annals*, 13 (9), pp. 697-713.

Davies, P. (1999) "Women Crime and an Informal Economy: Female Offending and Crime for Gain" *British Society of Criminology*, Vol. 2, March.

Denton, B. (1994) "Prison, Drugs and Women: Voices from Below", Report for the National Campaign Against Drug Abuse: Research into Drug Abuse Grants.

Dobash, R., Dobash, E.R., Wilson, M. and Daly, M. (1992) "The Myth of Sexual Symmetry in Martal Violence" *Social Problems*, Vol. 39. pp. 71-91.

Dobash, R., Dobash, E.R. and Gutteridge, S. (1986) The Imprisonment of Women. London: Basil Blackwell Press.

Dressel, P.L. and Barnhill, S.K. (1994) "Refraining Gerontological thought and Practice: The Case of Grandmothers with Daughters in Prison." *The Gerontologist*, 34 (5), pp. 685-91.

DUCO (2003) "A Study of Female Prisoners in South Australia", Justice Department of Crime Statistics and Research, Australia.

Ekstrand, L. (1999) Women in Prison: Issues and Challenges Confronting US Correctional Systems. Washington DC: United States General Accounting Office.

Fagan, J. (1990) "Intoxication and Aggression" In Tonry, M. and Wilson, J.Q. (ed.) Drugs and Crime. Chicago: University of Chicago Press.

Farrell, A. (1998) "Policies for Incarcerated Mothers and Their Families in Australian Corrections". *The Australian and New Zealand Journal of Criminology*, Vol. 31, No. 2.

Farrington, D.P. and Morris, A. (1983) "Sex, Sentencing and Reconviction", *British Journal of Criminology*, Vol. 23, pp. 229-48.

Fassaei, S. and Kendall, K. (2001) "Iranian Women's Pathways to Imprisonment", *Women Studies International Forum*, Vol. 24, No. 6, pp. 701-10

Flood-Page, C., Campbell, S., Harrington, V. and Miller, J. (2000) "Youth Crime: Findings from the 1998/1999 Youth Life Styles Survey." Home Office. Research Study 209, London: The Home Office.

Foucault, M. (1977) Discipline and Punish: The Birth of the Prison. Harmondsworth: Penguin.

Free, M. (2002) "Race and Pre-sentencing Decisions in the United States: A Summary and Critique of the Research", *Criminal Justice Review*, Vol. 27, No. 2.

Fuller, L.G. (1993) "Visitors to Women's Prison in California: An Exploratory Study." *Federal Probations*, 57 (4), pp. 41-47.

Gabel, S. (1992) "Children of Incarcerated and Criminal Parents: Adjustment, Behaviour and Prognosis." *Bulletin of the American Academy of Psychiatry and the Law*, 20 (1), pp. 33-45.

Gabel, S. and Schindledecker, R. (1993) "Characteristics of Children whose Parents have been Incarcerated", *Hospital and Community Psychiatry*, 44 (7), pp. 656-60.

Garg, R. (2006) "Increasing Tendency among Women in Committing Crimes". Unpublished Ph.D. Thesis submitted to Chaudhary Charan Singh University.

Ghosh, S. (1993) Open Prisons and the Inmates, New Delhi: Mittal Publications.

Giallombardo, R. (1966) Society of Women: A Study of a Women's Prison. New York: John Wiley and Sons, Inc.

Gibbons, T.C.N. (1971) "Female Offender", *British Journal of Hospital Medicine,* September, pp. 279-86.

Gibbons, D.C. (1965) Changing the Law Breaker: The Treatment of Delinquent and Criminals. New Jersey: Englewood Cliffs.

Gibbons, D.C. and Garity, D.L. (1963) "Some Suggestions for the Development of Etiological and Treatment Theory in Criminology", *Social Forces,* Vol. 38, October, pp. 51-58.

Goffman, E. (1961) Asylum: Essays on the Social Situation of Mental Patients and Other Inmates. New York: Doubleday.

Gottfredson, M. and Hirschi, T. (1990) A General Theory of Crime, Stanford, CA: Stanford University Press.

Greenfeld, L. and Snell, T. (1999) "Women Offenders", BJS Special Report, NCJ 175688.

Griffith, P. (1971) To Guard my People: The History of the Indian Police, Bombay: Allied Publishers.

Gursanky, D., Harvey, J., McGrath, B. and O' Brien, B. (1998) "Who's Minding the Kids? Developing Coordinated Services for Children whose Mothers are Imprisoned", Australia: Social Policy Research Group.

Hagan, J. and Dinovitzer, R. (1999) "Collateral Consequences of Imprisonment for Children, Communities, and Prisoners" in M. Tonry and J. Petersilia (eds.) Prisons, Crime and Justice, Chicago: University of Chicago Press.

Hagan, John (1993) "The Social Embeddedness of Crime and Unemployment", *Criminology,* 31, pp. 465-92.

Hampton, B. (1993) Prisons and Women. Sydney: University of New South Wales Press.

Harrison, K. (1997) "Parental Training for Incarcerated Fathers: Effects on Attitudes, Self-esteem and Children's Perception", *The Journal of Social Psychology,* 137(5), pp. 588-93.

Hart, K. (2000) "The Assessment of Female Offenders", Paper Presented at the Women in Corrections; Staff and Clients Conference convened by the Australian Institute of Criminology in Adelaide, 31 Oct. 1-Nov., 2000.

Harvey, W.B. (1986) "Homicide among Young Black Adults: Life in the Subculture of Exasperation." in Darnell Hawkins, (ed.) Homicide among Black Americans, Lanham, MD: University Press of America.

Hawkins, G. (1976) The Prison: Policy and Practice, Chicago: University of Chicago Press.

Hawkins, Darnell, F. (ed.) (1986) Homicide among Black Americans, Lanham, MD: University Press of America.

Healy, K.; Foley, D. and Walsh, K. (1999) Parents in Prison and their Families, Queensland, Australia: Catholic Prison Ministry.

Heidensohn, F. (1991) "Women as Perpetrators and Victims of Crime: A Sociological Perspective", *British Journal of Psychiatry*, May (10), 50-54.

———, (1997) Women and Crime. New York: Penguin Books.

Hirschi, Travis (1969) Causes of Delinquency: Berkeley: University of California Press.

Hockings, B., Young, M., Falconer, A. and O'Rourke, P. (2002) Queensland Women Prisoner's Health Survey. Brisbane: Queensland Department of Corrective Services.

Holzer, H. (1996) What Employers want: Job Prospects for Less Educated Workers. New York: Sage.

Homans, G.C. (1969) "The Sociological Relevance of Behaviorism" in Burgess Robert and Don Bushell (eds.) Behavioral Sociology. New York: Columbia University Press.

Howell, A.P. (1936) "Notes on Jails and Jail Discipline in India", Cited in Datir, R.N. (1978) Prison as a Social System. Bombay, Popular Prakashan.

Huling, T. (1991) Breaking the Silence. Albany, New York: Correctional Association of New York.

International Centre for Prison Studies (2006) Available on http://nicic.gov/Library/018662.

Jensen, F.G. and Jones, S. (1976) "Perspectives on Inmate Culture and Study of Women in Prison", *Social Forces*, Vol. 54, pp. 590-603.

Johnson, R. (1986) "Family Structure and Delinquency: General Patterns and Gender Differences", *Criminology*, Vol. 24, pp. 65-84.

Johnson, P.C. (2003) Inner Lives: Voices of African American Women in Prison. New York: New York University.

Jois, R.M. (1990) Legal and Constitution History of India. Vols. 1 and 2. Bombay: N.M. Tripathy Ltd.

Jones, S. (1998) Criminology. London: Butterworths.

Keaveny, M.E. and Zauszniewski, J.A. (1999) "Life Events and Psychological well-being in Women Sentenced to Prison", Issues in Mental Health and Nursing, 20 (1), pp. 73-89.

Kim, B., Gerber, J. and Kim, Y. (2007) "Characteristics of Incarcerated Women in South Korea who Killed their Spouses: A Feminist and Age-graded Theory of Informal Social Control Analysis." *The South West Journal of Criminal Justice,* Vol. 4, No. 1.

Kingi, A. (1993) "The Impact of Incarceration on African American Families: Implications for Practice", Families in Society: *The Journal of Contemporary Human Services*, 74, pp. 145-53.

Kingi, V.M. (1996) "Mothers in prison". *Journal of the New Zealand Association of Probation Officers*, Sept., pp. 12-14.

Klein, S.R. and Bahr, S.J. (1996) "An Evaluation of a Family Centered Cognitive Skills Program for Prison Inmates", *International Journal of Offender Therapy and Comparative Criminology*, 40 (4), pp. 334-46.

Korbin, J. (1989) (ed.) Child Abuse and Neglect Cross Cultural Perspectives. Los Angeles: University of California.

Kuckreja, N.S. (1986) "A Socio-Demographic Study of Women Prisoners", Unpublished Ph.D. thesis Submitted to Poona University.

Kurshan, N. (1996) "Behind the Walls" In E. RosenBatt (ed.) Criminal Injustice: Confronting the Crises, Boston: South End Press.

Lamberge Danielle (1991) "Women's Criminality, Criminal Women, Criminalised Women? Questions in and for a Feminist Perspective", *The Journal of Human Justice.* Vol. 2.

Leclair, D. (1990) "The Incarcerated Female Offender or Victim?" Boston: Massachusetts. Division of Correction, Research Division.

LeFlore, L., and Holston, M.A. (1989) "Perceived Importance of Parenting Behaviors as Reported by Inmate Mothers: An Exploratory Study". *Journal of Offender Counseling, Services and Rehabilitation*, 14(1), pp. 5-21.

Legislative Council Staff, (2001) available on www.legis.wisconsin.gov/lc/committees/study/2000/DEVD/files/alt_presentation.pdf

Leonard, E. D. (2002) Convicted Survivors: The Imprisonment of Battered Women who Kill. New York: State University of New York Press.

Lindesmith, A.R. and Dunhan, H.W. (1941) "Some Principles of Criminal Typology", *Social Forces*, Vol. 19, March, pp. 307-14.

Lloyd, A. (1995) Doubly Deviant Doubly Damned: Society's Treatment of Violent Women. London: Penguin.

Lowenstein, A. (1986) "Temporary Single Parenthood: The Case of Prisoners' Families", *Family Relations*, 35 (1), pp. 79-85.

Mackenzie, D.L., Robinson, J.W. and Campbell, C.S. (1989) "Long-term Incarceration of Female Offenders", *Criminal Justice and Behavior*, Vol. 16, No. 2, pp. 223-28.

Maher, B.A. (1966) Principles of Psychopathology: An Experimental Approach. New York: McGraw Hill.

Mann, C. (1988) "Getting even? Women who Kill in Domestic Encounters", *Justice Quarterly*, 5 (1), pp. 33-53.

Mathews, R. (1999) Doing Time: An Introduction to the Sociology of Imprisonment. Basingstoke: Macmillan.

McClellan, D.S., Farabee, K. and Crouch, B.M. (1997) "Early Victimization, Drug use and Criminality", *Criminal Justice and Behavior*. 24 (4), pp. 455-76.

McCord, W. and McCord, J. (1964) The Psychopath. Princeton: Van Nostrand.

Mishra, B.N. (1985) "Juvenile Delinquency: A Case Study in Orissa", Unpublished M.Phil. Dissertation Presented at Utkal University, Orissa.

Mishra, S. and Gautam (1982) "Female Criminality: Causes and Consequences", Readings in Criminology. Souvenir. Calcutta.

Morash, M., Bynum, T.S. and Koons, B.A. (1998) "Women Offenders: Programming needs and Promising Approaches", U.S. Deptt. of Justice, National Institute of Justice.

Morris, A. and Wilkinson, C. (1995) "Responding to Female Prisoner's Needs", *The Prison Journal*, 75(3), pp. 295-305.

Moyer, I. (1985) The Changing Roles of Women in the Criminal Justice System. Prospect Heights, IL: Waveland Press Inc.

Naffine, N. (1996) Feminism and Criminology. Philadelphia: Temple University Press.

Nagla, B.K. (1982) "Women and Crime: A Sociological Analysis of Women Criminality in India", *Indian Journal of Social Work*, Vol. XLIII, October 3, pp. 273-82.

———, (1991) Women Crime and Law. Jaipur: Rawat Publications.

Nettler, G. (1984) Explaining the Crime. New York: McGraw Hill

O' Keefe, M.O. (1997) "Post Traumatic Stress Disorder among Incarcerated Battered Women: A Comparison of Battered Women who Killed their Abusers and those Incarcerated for Other Offences", *Journal of Family Violence*, 12 (1), pp. 1-19.

Ogle, R.S., Maier-Katkin, D. and Bernard, T.J. (1995) "A Theory of Homicidal Behavior among Women", *Criminology*, 33, pp. 173-94.

Pandey, S.P. (2004) "Children of Women prisoners in Jail: A Study in Uttar Pradesh", Study Conducted by Pandit Govind Ballabh Pant Institute of Studies in Rural Development, Lucknow.

Paramaguru, Pon (1984) "Women and Crime", *Indian Journal of Criminology*, Vol. 12, No. 2, July, pp. 98-101.

Parker, R.N. (1989) "Poverty, Subculture of Violence and Types of Homicide", *Social Forces*, June, Vol. 67, pp. 983-1007.

Parsad, S.K. (1982) "A Study of Women Murderers in Tamil Nadu", Readings in Criminology, Souvenir, Indian Society of Criminology.

Pennix, P.R. (1999) "An Analysis of Mothers in the Federal Prison System", *Corrections Compendium*, 24 (12), pp. 4-6.

Petersellia, J. (2000) "When Prisoners Return to the Community: Political, Economic and Social". Sentencing and Corrections: Issues for the 21st Century, Nov., No. 9, U.S. Department of Justice.

Phillips Susan, D. and Harm Nancy, J. (1998) "Women Prisoners: A Contextual Framework" in Harden, Judy and Hill, Marcia (eds.) Breaking the Rules: Women in Prison and Feminist Therapy. New York: Harrington Park Press.

Pillai, A. (1983) Criminal Law. Bombay: N.M. Tripathi.

Plugge, E., Douglas, N. and Fitzpatrick, R. (2006) The Health of Women in Prison. Department of Public Health, University of Oxford.

Pollack, Otto (1950) The Criminality of Women, Philadelphia: University of Pennsylvania Press.

Pollock, Byrne, J.M. (1990) Women, Prison and Crime, Belmont, California: Brooks/Cole Publishing Co.

Prasad, S.K. (1982) "A Study of Women Murderers in Tamil Nadu", Readings in Criminology, Souvenir, Indian Society of Criminology.

Ragib, A. (1987) "Pengangguram Merupokan Factor Itama Mengebabkan Penign Kalam, Jenayah Harta di negeri Pahang." Diploma sains Kepolisian Project Paper, University, Kebangssan, Malaysia cited by Sidhu, Amar Singh (2005), "The rise of Crime in Malaysia." *Journal of the Kuala Lumpur Royal Malaysian Political College*, No. 4.

Rao, Venugopal (1991) Criminal Justice. Delhi: Konark Publishers.

Reiss, A. and Roth, J. (1993) Understanding and Preventing Violence. Washington D.C.: National Academy Press.

Rocawich, L. (1987) "Lock them up", The Progressive, August.

Rozenberg, J. (1993) "Miscarriages of justice" in E. Stockdale and S. Cacale (eds), Criminal Justice Under Stress. London: Blackstone.

Rubin, N. (1987) "Women Behind Bars", McCall's, Aug., 1987 cited in www.prisonactivist.org/archive/women/women-and-imprisonment.html

Sabri, B.M. (2002) "Penggauron daer Jenayah : SatrecKajjan keatas banduran dipenjaru sg Bulluh. "Diploma sains sissantm Project Paper. University, Kebangssan, Malaysia cited by Sidhu, Amar Singh (2005), The Rise of Crime in Malaysia, *Journal of the Kuala Lumpur Royal Malaysian Police College*, No. 4.

Saini, M. (2008) "Five Jail wheat Samples Failed Test", News Report in *The Times of India*, July 17, 2008.

Sampson, R.J. (1987) "Urban Black Violence: The Effect of Male Joblessness and Family Disruption", *American Journal of Sociology*, Vol. 93. pp. 348-82.

Sanger, S.P (1967) Crime and Punishment in Mughal India. New Delhi.

Saxena, R. (1994) Women and Crime in India: A Study in Socio-cultural Dynamics. New Delhi: Inter India Publications.

Schreiber, T. and Poggie, S. (1988) "Women in Prison; Does Anyone out Here Hear?" *Resist Newsletter*, No. 206, May.

Shakur, A. (1978) "Women in Prison", The Black Scholar, Vol. 9, No. 1, April, p. 9.

Shaw, M., Rodgers, K., Blanchette, J., Hattem, T., Seto Thomas, L. and Tamarack, L. (1991) Paying the Price, Federally Sentenced Women in Context, User Report No. 1991-5, Ottawa: Solicitor General Canada.

Sheridan, M.J. (1996) "Comparison of the Life Experiences and Personal Functioning of Men and Women in Prison", *Families in Society*, 77 (7), pp. 423-34.

Simon, R.J. (1975) Women and Crime. Lexington. Mass: D.C. Heath and Co.

Singh, M.K. (1981) "Women and Crime Phenomena", *Indian Journal of Social Work*, Vol. XIII, No. 3, October.

Sokoloff, N.J. (2005) "Women Prisoners at the Dawn of the 21st Century", *Women and Criminal Justice*, Vol. 16, No. 1/2, pp. 127-38.

Steffensmeier, D. and Schwartz, J. (2003) "Trends in Female Crime: Is Crime Still a Man's World?" In B.R. Price and N.J. Sokoloff (eds.) The Criminal Justice System and Women Offenders, Prisoners, Victims and Workers, New York: McGraw Hill.

Stoller, N. (2000) "Improving Access to Healthcare for California's Women Prisoners". A Working paper presented for the California Program on Access to Care, California, Oct.-2000, cited in www.ucop.edu/cprc/

Street, D. (1965) The Inmate Group in Custodial and Treatment Settings", *American Sociological Review*, Vol. 30, No. 1, pp. 40-55.

Taft, D.R. (1950) Criminology. New York: McMillan.

Taxman, F., Byrne, J.M. and Pattavina, A. (2005) "Racial Disparity and the Legitimacy of the Criminal Justice System: Exploring Consequences for Deterrence", *Journal of Healthcare for Poor and Underserved*, Vol. 16, No. 4, Suppl. B, November, pp. 57-77.

Thapar, R. (1990) A History of India, Volume I, London: Penguin.

The Times of India, (2008) "Quiet Killers on the Prowl", June 01.

The Tribune (2007) "From behind bars", Monday, July 02, Chandigarh.

Toch, H. (1979) 'The Psychology of Imprisonment' in H. Toch (ed.) Psychology of Crime and Justice, New York: Holt, Rinehart and Winston.

Tonry, M. (1997) "Ethnicity, Crime and Immigration", *Crime and Justice*, 21, pp. 1-30.

Trevethan, S. (2000) "An Examination of Female Inmates in Canada: Characteristics and Treatment". Paper Presented at the Women in Corrections: Staff and Clients Conference Convened by the Australian Institute of Criminology, in Adelaide, 31 Oct.-1 Nov.

Trickett, A., Osborn, D.R., Seymour, J. and Pease, K. (1992) "What is different about High Crime Areas?" *British Journal of Criminology*, Vol. 32, No. 1, pp. 81-89.

WA Department of Justice (2002) Profile of Women in Prison: A Report for the Western Australian Department of Justice, Community and Juvenile Justice Division, Perth: Department of Justice.

Wacquant, L. (2002) "From Slavery to Mass Incarceration", *New Left Review*, Vol. 13, January-Feb.

Walmesley, R. (2007) World Prison Population: International Centre for Prison Studies Available at www.prison studies.org

White, H. and Gorman, D.M. (2000) "Dynamics of the Drug-Crime Relationship" in Lafree, G. (ed.) Criminal Justice 2000: Vol. 1: The Nature of Crime: Continuity and Change, NCJ 182408, National Institute of Justice, USA, pp. 151-218.

Willis, K. and Rushforth, C. (2003) "The Female Criminal: An Overview of Women's Drug use and Offending Behaviour", Trends and Issues in Crime and Criminal Justice. No. 264, Canberra: Australian Institute of Criminology.

Wolfgang, M. and Ferracuti, F. (1967) The Sub-culture of Violence. London: Tavistock.

Woodrow, J. (1992) "Mothers inside Children Outside" in R. Shaw (ed.) Prisoner's Children—What are the Issues? London: Routledge Press.

Yochelson, S. and Samenow, S. (1976) The Criminal Personality. Vol. 1, Northvale, NJ: Aronson.

Young, D.S. and Smith, J. (2000) "When Moms are Incarcerated: The Needs of Children, Mothers and Care givers", Families in Society, *The Journal of Contemporary Human Services*, 81 (2), pp. 130-47.

Index